Religion, Identity and Nationhood

Religion, Identity and Nationhood

The Sikh Militant Movement

Paramjit S. Judge

RAWAT PUBLICATIONS

Jaipur • New Delhi • Bangalore • Mumbai

ISBN 81-7033-949-9

Published by
Prem Rawat for **Rawat Publications**
Satyam Apts., Sector 3, Jawahar Nagar, Jaipur 302 004 (India)
Phone: 0141 265 1748 / 7006 Fax: 0141 265 1748
E-mail: info@rawatbooks.com
Website: www.rawatbooks.com

New Delhi Office
4858/24, Ansari Road, Daryaganj, New Delhi 110 002
Phone: 011-23263290

Also at Bangalore and Mumbai

Typeset by Rawat Computers, Jaipur
Printed at Chaman Enterprises, New Delhi

Contents

Preface

The Sikh militant movement that spanned one-and-a-half decades raised a lot of issues, many of which questioned the character of Indian state and the alleged greatness of the Indian tradition. Punjab never witnessed such a magnitude of violence and killings in the post-independent period. Punjabis were reminded of the riots of 1947 in which the people who died and got displaced or uprooted numbered in millions. In the 1980s, the Sikhs living in villages began to discuss albeit quietly the possibility of the formation of Khalistan. The main thrust of this work is that there is a reason to think on the issue of how the facts are presented and what kind of events and facts are selected for presentation. Still the more important issue was how a particular narrative becomes a part of people's perceptions. The study of Sikh militant movement from this perspective entails second level analysis in the sense that what Bhindranwala and the militant leaders after his death said and did was that they articulated the already existing narratives available in popular Sikh tradition in which the valour and martyrdom of the Sikhs are glorified. In other words, there was no rupture in the construction of the tradition. The fact that such a tradition could be used for political purposes showed the strength with which it had existed as a collective representation. This work is an attempt to understand how the militant narrative constructed religion, identity and nationhood by subverting the Sikh community.

There are two sources of the idea of working on the narratives of the Khalistan movement. While working on the terrorist movement with my colleagues, Prof. Harish K. Puri and Jagrup S. Sekhon, both from Guru Nanak Dev University, we took into consideration these narratives. However, owing to the focused nature of our empirical work and limitations of time, these could not be examined extensively. Secondly, during my visit to Punjabi University, Patiala, Dr. Harvinder Bhatti, a close friend and fellow activist of yester years narrated the content of one clarification that had appeared in one of the newspapers. That particular clarification I could not trace, but it set the ball rolling. I remain indebted to them.

For writing this book my employer Guru Nanak Dev University, Amritsar, granted me sabbatical leave, which enabled me to write it without the teaching load. In the process of data collection, many friends and colleagues helped me. Varinder Walia, special correspondent of *The Tribune* helped me in many ways. I am also grateful to the staff of the *Ajit* at Jalandhar for their kind assistance and their willingness to give information. However, most of my work was done in the library of Guru Nanak Dev University, Amritsar. I am thankful to the library staff for their help and cooperation. My special thanks are due to Malkit Singh, who gave me the interview that was quite insightful with regard to the understanding of how village and religion coexisted in Jarnail Singh Bhindranwala. My special thanks are also due to my dear friends who are always there to help and encourage me in my moments of doubt. I, therefore, take this opportunity to acknowledge them. They are, Satya Pal Gautam, S. S. Sekhon, Maninder S. Hundal and Navdeep Singh Tung.

The presence of my wife Gurpreet and son Neil has remained reassuring and their love and attention remained my source of strength. I dedicate this work to them.

Paramjit S. Judge

Introduction

The story of Punjab crisis is well-known and considerable literature has been published in various forms. The writers on Punjab crisis belong to various shades of intelligentsia, such as academicians, journalists, bureaucrats, police officers, army generals and politicians. Among the academicians, prominent economists, political scientists, sociologists and psychologists have made seminal contributions to the understanding of the crisis that plagued Punjab from 1978 to 1993. In a way, what happened in Punjab during this period drew the attention of all the socially concerned people. In spite of all this, there have been serious gaps in the studies of this crisis. To call it a crisis is to express it pejoratively as well as normatively. We, therefore, find that the period of 'crisis' is known by various expressions like the Sikh militant movement, the Khalistan movement, terrorist movement and so on. A militant movement that sustained for one-and-a-half decades requires analysis from various perspectives. Still the literature is insufficient, incomplete and limited. The present work has limited but crucial objective, that is, to map the ideological articulations of the Sikh militant movement that emerged in the form of narratives.

Writers identify and agree on five essential features of social and political movements.[1] The first feature is that a movement is always a collective endeavour. In other words, it always involves the participation of a large number of people. These people do not come together randomly, as we see in the case of crowds; rather they share certain common social, economic, cultural or religious characteristics. The second feature of a movement is its organisation. The level of organisation may vary from highly centralised to loosely coordinated acts. The third feature of a movement is its durability. It sustains over a period of time, but one cannot predict its age. It may continue for some months to decades. The fourth feature of a movement is its orientation towards change. Movements vary from being revivalist to revolutionary. Whatever may be the case, movements always involve change. We thus can understand movement as a collective and organised endeavour that is oriented towards changing the existing state of affairs in/of the society and it sustains for some period of time. However, such a definition is incomplete without taking into account the fifth and the final feature of a movement, that is, ideology and interest. In view of the fact that it is an organised effort to bring about change, it is logically necessary to assume that this orientation cannot be thought without ideology.

The significance of ideology in the modern times has increased for many reasons. According to Lukacs (1971), the question of ideology is related with consciousness and it is a consequence of the capitalist development. Capitalism destroyed spatio-temporal boundaries between the states as well as freed the wage labour. It has now become possible to consciously plan a movement for change. The views of Blumer (1957) are similar to this, but his perspective is different. It is clear that the ideological articulation of the movement by its leaders influences, shapes and sets its objective(s). The economic deprivation can be articulated in class terms, but it could also be articulated by using ethnic, religious, regional or cultural contexts. In the latter case, however, the deprived must be homogeneous in terms of one of the contexts. Thus, ideology also influences the nature and content of a movement.

Social movement, in the light of the above features, should be understood as a process of achieving something other than what existed in society. Touraine (1985: 749) rightly points out, "The notion of social movement, like most notions in the social sciences, does not describe part of 'reality' but is an element of a specific mode of constructing social reality".[2] Touraine maintains that social movement as social conflict entails an opposition between movement and the institution. Still, in another essay, Touraine (1988) analysed the emergence of new social movements in the 1960s.[3] While referring to the terrorist movements, he points out, "The recent terrorist movements, like the anarchist actions of the nineteenth century, occur at the moment when a certain type of society, and the social movements that pertain to it, are dying out" (ibid.: 129). The implications of what Touraine has stated are important for the understanding of social movements in terms of social conflict and interacting actors. First of all, social movements are aimed at construction of social reality which means that these are aimed at achieving something new with regard to the society. A movement, as a process of construction of social reality, assumes the centrality of the ideology that entails and implicates the individuals to participate in the action. It thus becomes important to examine the way the ideology is articulated. In the case of the communist and anarchist movements, the understanding of the process of articulation of ideology has been historically known though each society was having its own peculiarities. For example, the methods adopted by the Chinese communists were different from those of Russia. Despite all this difference, the ideology and its articulation was quite discernible.

The articulation of ideology is simultaneously a process of its reconstruction. The parties supporting the same ideology may not necessarily articulate it in the same and common manner. There is always a tendency to contextually situate ideology in the specific time and space dimensions. To continue with the examples of Russia and China, the two communist countries articulated Marxism in different ways with regard to the revolutionary struggle. The movements based on religious ideologies also show the similar character. Though the legitimacy to the movement is derived from the articulation of the religious ideology, yet its content may entail the construction and reinterpretation of the religion. The Sikh militant movement that spanned for one-and-a-half decades from 1978 to 1993 could also be understood as such a movement. It was a violent movement and used terrorist methods to realise its aim of achieving the independent state of Khalistan, and as they alleged, for the Sikhs.

In its lifetime of fifteen years, the Sikh militant movement made an assertive effort to define the Sikh religion, identity and nationhood. The entire movement experienced two stages of this construction that took place through narratives. In the first phase, Jarnail Singh Bhindranwala, who led the militant movement, constructed religion and religious identity through his speeches and also in the form of his activities in which he baptised (*amrit chhakauna*) a large number of young Sikhs. In the second phase that began in 1984 after the death of Bhindranwala in the Operation Blue Star, the militant leaders left nothing to ambiguity so far as the objective of their struggle was concerned. They made it clear in a meeting of the Sarbat Khalsa in 1986 that their aim was to achieve an independent state of Khalistan for which they had to wage the armed struggle. Simultaneously, they made an effort to construct the Sikh community by disciplining it. In other words, they enforced religious ethic, as they understood it. In the process of articulation of the Sikh ideology, the coercive power of the militants played an important role, which could be seen from the responses of the Sikh masses in the form of clarifications with regard to their alleged violations of the ethic.

The theoretical framework of the present study is constructed from the model of the structure of narrative as expounded in a work of Lyotard (1986). The primary and important function of narrative is to send a message, which either betrays or clearly presents the position of its creator. In a situation where the creator is a person representing a movement, such a message emanates and draws rationale from its ideology and practice. To make it clear we may use the framework provided by Lyotard to understand the structure of narrative. Before we proceed to specify the components of narrative, it is worthwhile to quote him (1986: 30) at length thus:

> Narration is no longer an involuntary lapse in the legitimation process. The explicit appeal to narrative in the problematic of knowledge is concomitant with the liberation of the bourgeois classes from the traditional authorities. Narrative knowledge makes a resurgence in the West as a way of solving the problem of legitimating the new authorities. It is natural in a narrative problematic for such a question to solicit the name of a *hero* as its response. Who has the right to decide for society? Who is the subject whose prescriptions are norms for those they obligate?

Though Lyotard's above statement has Western context, yet its relevance, at the general level, is quite evident. The questions he has raised form the essential basis of the present work. It would become clear if we precisely describe what Lyotard identifies as sender, referent and addressee as the components of narrative:

(a) Sender: The creator of referent (message)
(b) Referent: The content of the narrative
(c) Addressee: The recipient of the referent

The sender has to observe rules while sending the referent to the addressee, which could be a potential sender. In other words, without observing rules (scientific rules, norms, traditions), the referent is devoid of legitimation. However, the nature of the referent may vary according to the conditions – both objective and subjective – of the movement. The narrative may be denotative, the purpose of which is to designate a particular action or occurrence in the light of ideology or tradition. In a militant movement, it involves designating somebody as traitor or hero. The narrative could be prescriptive or proscriptive, i.e., requesting or ordering the addressee to do what the sender regarded as desirable or undesirable. Finally, the addressee may become the sender to clarify his position. Such narratives though emerge from the power relations but a degree of observation of rules derived from tradition and ideology remain present in the interaction between the sender (power holder) and the addressee who has to become sender in order to clarify his/her position. It thus becomes clear that in a movement the narratives could be treated as discourse involved in the construction of social reality. Since all social movements are aimed at social construction, the discourse specifies the nature of social construction.

Lyotard's formulation has a specific context of the status of knowledge in the post-modern societies. Knowledge has been understood in the sense Plato defined *epistme* in relation to *doxa*. In the present study, the relevance of this theoretical model may be located in the nature of the source material that has been used, which conforms to the structure of narrative. The complexity in the analysis has increased due to the fact that in this narrative power and violence constitute the essential elements. If we take the classification offered by Guha (1983) of evidences as forms of discourse, then it may be pointed out that the source material constitutes the primary discourse in a limited sense, as only the construction of religion, identity and nationhood on the part of the militants has been taken into consideration. Guha has identified discourse at three levels in which the official documents regarding the event of insurgency constitute the primary discourse. In this study, the events are in the backdrop of the construction of religion, identity and nationhood. When Jarnail Singh Bhindranwala was delivering his speeches from the platform by sharing it with the leaders of the Shiromani Akali Dal, he was addressing the audience that included *jathas* that were going for voluntary arrests in the Dharam Yudh Morcha. Similarly, the warnings and tributes that appeared as messages of the militants were in tandem with the uninterrupted incidences of terrorist violence in and outside Punjab. In this respect, what Bhindranwala was speaking to the Sikh masses and what the militants were sending constitute the primary discourse.

Coupled with the theoretical framework of narrative as a discourse is the phenomenological approach of Schutz that has been used to highlight the existence of the inter-subjective world in a multi-religious society. In this work, this inter-subjective world has been christened as eclectic space, which consists of traditions, local history and its consciousness, cultural practices, and in the case of the multi-religious societies, it is an interactive experience of other religion(s) in the structure of everyday life despite the existence of differences, hierarchies and exclusion. It is largely due to the existence of eclectic space that communities differ despite the common religion. Eclectic space performs many functions, the foremost of which is the development of inter-cultural understanding. Inter-cultural understanding in this respect is not a consciously learned behaviour, but it is an emergent property of the inter-subjective world.

The significance of ideology in social and political movements has been emphasised time and again by the social scientists. Can we say that Sikhism became the ideology of the Khalistan movement? What were the principles of Sikhism that could be identified as the basis of the launching and continuity of the movement? To answer all these questions, there was a need to explore what was written and stated by the militants on the question of Khalistan, future society, polity and economy. Interestingly, the militants did not write much to make a conclusive analysis of the Khalistan movement as a result of which the major sources of understanding the ideological articulation were the speeches of Jarnail Singh Bhindranwala and the press statements of the militants. Thus, the present work is aimed at tracing the mode of the presentation of the collective self of the Sikh community in terms of religion, identity and nationhood from two sources. The first source is that of the speeches of Jarnail Singh Bhindranwala who emerged as the undisputed leader of the militant movement till 1984. Bhindranwala remained the guiding spirit of the movement even after his death. In 1982, he permanently moved to the Golden Temple complex at Amritsar where he died in the Operation Blue Star, in 1984. During two years of his stay in the Golden Temple he addressed many public gatherings. Most of his speeches were recorded by his followers and sold in the market. At present, fourteen such audio-cassettes are available and are exclusively sold by the Damdami Taksal. I transcribed all the audio-cassettes. It has been found that the Punjabi newspapers and magazines published some of his interviews, but a few of these I have come across are edited in terms of the presentation of Bhindranwala's ideas. Two such interviews have been mentioned in this work.

The second source is comprised of thc 'messages' sent by the militants as well as people from different walks of life. These messages, in the forms of 'warnings', 'tributes' and 'clarifications', predominantly appeared in the Punjabi newspaper, *Ajit*, during the movement.[4] One of the major reasons for selecting this paper was its large circulation among all the newspapers of Punjabi. The current circulation of the paper is 2,50,000.[5] It was also informed to the author that an average of eight persons read one copy of the newspaper. Moreover, in the earlier stages of the movement, the militants chose this newspaper for their objectives. Later on, the militants changed their orientation towards the *Punjabi Tribune.* Thus, the *Punjabi Tribune* was also examined to look into the commonality of the messages with the *Ajit*. Whatever the militants sent to the newspapers was published after they first threatened the journalists and then the editors. A journalist in an interview informed that the militants went to the extent of saying that they would cut as many parts of their bodies as many words they removed from their press statements. It goes without saying that some of the scribes also fell victim to the militants' bullets. Jaspal Singh of Rayya in Amritsar district, who collected a large number of messages of the militants that were published in the *Ajit*, was shot dead, because, as alleged by the militants, he was selling a particular group of newspapers.

On the basis of the above facts, there is a reasonable ground to accept the authenticity of these messages. However, entry of certain vested interests of the motivated individuals cannot be ignored. All those messages that appeared in the newspapers could be classified into four headings, namely, warnings, claims, tributes and clarifications. From the end of 1988 to that of 1990 the frequency and volume of these messages kept on escalating. In the beginning of 1991, when O.P. Malhotra, the then Governor of Punjab, imposed censorship on newspapers, these messages began to decline but at no stage these disappeared. The messages continued to appear till the first half of 1993 in a noticeable manner. If we have to describe the years 1990 and 1991 in terms of these messages, we may say that the terrorists converted the newspapers into mailboxes. In a way, the narratives in which the militants were the senders of the messages betrayed certain unique features of the movement itself. One could make out the organisations, their working and relationship within and between them. One of the necessary conditions to send the message was its appearance in the newspapers. The newspapers became the intermediate between the people and the militants and any rupture in that could stop the flow of the message anytime. This is what in the beginning of 1991, O.P. Malhotra, the then Governor of Punjab, did by imposing censorship on newspapers. The structure of these narratives was as follows:

1. So far as warnings, responsibilities and tributes are concerned, the sender was one or the other militant group. However, clarifications moved (i) from militants to government, (ii) from people, particularly those who were warned, to militants, and (iii) from a militant or a militant

group to the other group. The most important among these clarifications were those that were sent by the people in general and our discussion in Chapter 8 would largely be based on such clarifications.

2. Referent involved diversity and would be our major focus of analysis. In the case of warnings, there was a tremendous range in the number of issues raised by the militants. The same was the case with the clarifications. Only the tributes were confined to one issue.
3. Addressees who were warned also hailed from the diverse walks of life. In case of clarifications, anybody could be the sender.

Certain features were specific to each of the messages, which have been covered in the relevant chapters. The most important messages appeared under the title 'warnings', as these evoked response of the people to clarify their stands with regard to particular issues. It is important to know the quantitative dimensions of these messages, particularly warnings and clarifications. The number of warnings issued each year starting from 1986 has been shown in the following table:

Year	*Number of Warnings*
1986	5
1987	23
1988	40
1989	33
1990	305
1991	14
1992	30
Total	450

It may further be pointed out that warnings appeared even in claims and the news about the formation of new organisations. In the present analysis only about 20 per cent of those warnings have been analysed, which appeared under the heading "*Chitawani*" or "*Tarhna*".

The discussion in the eighth chapter is based on the analysis of 332 clarifications that appeared from 1986 to 1992. In the second half of 1990, there was a dramatic escalation of killings by the militants and as the year approached towards end, there was a sudden spurt in the number of clarifications appearing in the newspapers and 50 clarifications were published.[6] In 1991, the largest number (215) of clarifications appeared and in the next year these began to decline and virtually stopped after September 4. Even then, 61 clarifications appeared in the *Ajit* in 1992. The following table provides the year-wise number of clarifications:

Year	*Number*
1986	2
1988	2
1989	2
1990	50
1991	215
1992	61
Total	332

The third type of messages appeared in the form of tributes (*shardhajalian*) to those militants who had been killed mainly in encounters (fake or real) with the police. The number of advertisements that appeared everyday in the later phase of the movement was numerous to the extent of twenty. The frequency of tributes kept on rising as we move towards the end of 1990. According to one journalist, there were fifty tributes appeared on one day in 1990 in the *Ajit*. The author did not try to enumerate these advertisements. The major reason for this was the similarity that these tributes had with each other in terms of the wording of the advertisements. Only two kinds of wording were used to pay tributes. Whereas one of them would begin with "in the struggle started by Bhindranwala", the other was worded "in the present struggle".[7] However, the overwhelming appearance of these tributes could be observed while going through the newspaper.

A clarification with regard to certain words and expressions may be given here. In the existing literature, the word 'Bhindranwale' is used, but throughout this book 'Bhindranwala' has been used instead. Similarly, while mentioning Jarnail Singh Bhindranwala, the prefix of 'Sant' has not been used. The reason is simple but profound. He did not resemble the notion of Sant as exemplified by this tradition. Moreover, his spheres of activities that have been examined belong to polity and religious fundamentalism.

The first chapter of the book provides a sociological profile of the Sikhs as a religious community. The main reason for starting the discussion from this profile is to situate the speech contents of Bhindranwala in context of his existential and social background to have some insights into his mass appeal. It may also help in making a sense of the messages of the militants. This chapter specifically takes into cognisance the social divisions among the Sikhs. The second chapter looks into the process of emergence of communal politics in Punjab by covering three important aspects, namely, political dynamics of Punjab, background history of the making of the legend of Bhindranwala, i.e., the history of Damdami Taksal, life story of Bhindranwala and the delineation of the events leading to his emergence in politics.

In the third chapter, the issue of the construction of Sikh identity, starting from the Singh Sabha movement to its fundamentalist assertion, has been investigated. The articulation of the Sikh identity by Bhindranwala forms the core of this chapter.[8] The fourth chapter is again largely based on the speeches of Bhindranwala with regard to whether the Sikhs are a separate nation. The issue has its background in the construction of religious nationalism during colonial period that led to the formation of Pakistan in 1947. The fifth chapter is organically linked with the third and fourth chapters in the sense that in the constructions of identity and nationhood the Sikh militant movement also defined the other that could be excluded from these. In the process, the movement defined what is Hinduism and what are the features of the Hindus? The militant movement also tried to draw its legitimacy from the constructed tradition of militancy and martyrdom in Sikhism. In the sixth chapter, an attempt has been made to make sense of the articulation of this tradition in the speeches of Bhindranwala as well as the messages of the militants later on. The hermeneutics of these messages have been deciphered in the context of the Sikh history and the historical evolution of the Sikh traditions.

In the seventh and eighth chapters, the interaction between the militants and the Sikh masses, as mediated by the coercive power of the former, has been analysed. This interaction took place through the, and in the form of, messages that appeared largely in the Punjabi newspapers under the headings 'warnings' and 'clarifications'. The concluding chapter traces the process of subverting the Sikh community that was accelerated by Bhindranwala and intensified by the militant leaders. The argument that has been offered is that in a multi-religious societies like ours an attempt to valorise the community may give rise to temporary mobilisation, but the eclectic space that differentiates the society from community never disappears.

Notes

1. A considerable literature exists on the concept of social movement. Instead of making a review of each and every view, it is beneficial to give a kind of analytical summary of these views. However, even then, some of them may be mentioned here. These are: Smelser (1962), Cameron (1967), Heberele (1968) and Rao (1978). Cameron (1967: 11) is of the view that "a social movement occurs when a fairly large number of people band together in order to alter or supplement

some portion of the existing culture or social order". Though most of the definitions tend to agree with what Cameron has stated, yet there is a basic difference in how social movement could be located in theoretical perspective. For instance, functionalists regard social movements as episodic in character that tend to threaten the maintenance of the system.

2. Melucci (1985) also regards social movements as social constructions. He (ibid.: 795) writes, "I define analytically a social movement as a form of collective action (a) based on solidarity, (b) carrying on conflict, (c) breaking the limits of a system in which action occurs". In this understanding of a social movement the actor is posited in the centre stage of social construction.
3. It is interesting to note that in recent times a lot of concepts are used that lack time-space universality. For example, post-modern, post-capitalist, post-industrial, new social movements, etc. All these concepts have something temporary ingrained in them.
4. Some of the messages also appeared in the *Punjabi Tribune*, but for a short period.
5. The figure is based on the information provided by the office of the *Ajit* to the author.
6. All those clarifications that came from the common people and appeared in the *Ajit* as well as the *Punjabi Tribune* were paid advertisements.
7. The difference in the wording of the tributes had a lot to do with inter-organisational dynamics and the way the militants located Jarnail Singh Bhindranwala in the struggle for Khalistan. The Babbar Khalsa International never accepted Bhindranwala as the guiding spirit of the movement.
8. This chapter is the revised version of an already published article under the title "Politics of Sikh Identity and its Fundamentalist Assertion" in *Economic and Political Weekly*, 39 (32), August 7, 2004.

1

Mapping the Sikh Community

In the contemporary sociological literature, the studies of religious communities are limited due to the emerging trend of analysing ethnicity. The usage of the concept of ethnicity with regard to the Sikhs has remained one of the paradigms of analysis (e.g., Gupta 1997; Purewal 2000). Popular expressions such as 'Sikh ethnic community' and 'Sikh ethno-nationalism' have been put to use, but such expressions are more frequently and emphatically used by the Sikh diaspora writers. The Sikh militant movement, generally viewed as a struggle for Khalistan, has drawn the attention of many and ways of distinguishing the Sikhs as a distinct homogenous community, demarcated from Punjabi Hindus and Indians in general, have multiplied.[1] The shift of certain Western countries from 'the melting pot' ideology to multiculturalism has also paved the way for treating Sikhs as a distinct cultural and ethnic community where religion has been the chief basis of demarcating them from others hailing from India. Such a trend necessitates a sociological analysis of the Sikh community.

What is the sociological profile of Sikhs? Generally, the religious communities cannot be easily studied, because they are large, widely spread and socially diverse. Once it is clear that religion and religious community are separable, it becomes obvious that the examination and analysis of religious community would focus on the social, cultural and economic trajectories that characterise it within the given time and space contexts instead of assessing and evaluating the degree of 'deviation', which it may carry from the established religious discourse. Muslims of India, Turkey and Albania are very distinct communities from each other. In the case of the Sikhs, the situation is somewhat different, as the size of the Sikh community in comparison to Muslims and Christians is small. Its geographical spread is largely limited to Punjab (India) and the presence of the Sikhs elsewhere is mainly due to migration, which implies that there is an underlying commonality among the Sikhs. It however does not mean that the Sikh community is devoid of diversity. There is a lot of diversity in the Sikh community, as is evident from the formation of sects and subsequent formation of communities within the large context of Sikhism. For example, Kukas or Namdharis constitute a distinct community within the fold of Sikh religion.[2] Despite their limited spatial spread and small size, the Sikhs constitute a heterogeneous, plural and diverse community, but not to the extent we find in Islam, Christianity or Hinduism.

The discussion on the profile of the Sikh community has been divided into five parts. Whereas the first part traces the socio-historical background of the emergence of the Sikh community, the second takes stock of its social structure. The third part examines the cultural trajectories of the Sikh community and the fourth focuses on its economic life. Both the parts have a broader canvas of the social and economic milieus of Punjab within which an attempt has been made to locate the Sikh community. The fifth part succinctly deals with the Sikh diaspora.

I
SOCIO-HISTORICAL BACKGROUND

The Sikh movement was a part of the larger and composite Bhakti tradition in the medieval India. The great religious teacher, Guru Nanak Dev, initiated it in the 16th century. He institutionalised his teachings by nominating his successor, which initiated the process and tradition of transference of charisma. In 1604, Guru Arjun Dev, the fifth guru, compiled the works of Guru Nanak Dev and his four successors and the writings of other saints as the Adi-Granth, which became the sacred scripture of the Sikhs. A turning point marked the period of the sixth guru Hargobind, symbolised by his donning of two swords – one of the continuing spiritual authority and the other of temporal power. However, it is the tenth guru of the Sikhs, Guru Gobind Singh, who brought fundamental changes in the Sikh belief system and practices. He founded 'Khalsa Panth' – a body of followers directly linked to the guru. Baptism ceremony obliged the followers to keep unshaven hair, wear arms and use the epithet of 'Singh' in their names. This clearly distinguished them from others who did not accept the new order – the 'Singh' from the other 'Sikh'. A militant ideology articulated and legitimised armed struggle against oppression when all the alternative means were exhausted. During his lifetime, he organised his Khalsa followers into an army, which waged battles against the rulers. Another significant contribution made by Guru Gobind Singh was that he abolished personal guruship before his death in 1708. Hereafter, guruship would be in the Panth – the Sangat (congregation) and the Granth (the sacred book). The differences between 'Singh' and 'Sikh' remained, but without any construction of the discourse of identity.

The geographical space of the Sikh movement was the undivided Punjab. Being located on the north-west frontier of the Indian sub-continent Punjab has experienced numerous invasions, which took definite shape with the rise of Islam in the Middle East. The spread of Islam and arrival of new rulers with different culture and civilisation made an everlasting impact on Punjab. A large number of people in Punjab embraced Islam, which was largely a consequence of the impact of Sufi movement. Muslims came to constitute a preponderant majority of the population in the province, the Sikhs constituting about 7 per cent of the population during the 18th century.

After Guru Gobind Singh, the rise of 'Singhs' to power was a part of the political process marked by three factors. One was the decisive decline of the Moghul empire and power by the middle of the 18th century. This gave chance to other powers to emerge, i.e., the Marathas and the British. Second was Sikhs' determined confrontation with invaders such as Nadir Shah and Ahmed Shah Abdali. The third battle of Panipat in 1761, which ended the expansionist designs of Marathas being the third factor.

Given the absence of an effective central authority, the Sikhs established their domination in Punjab by forming confederates, generally called *missals*. Later on, beginning with his rule in 1799, Maharaja Ranjit Singh unified most of the confederated area through force, annexed other areas and established his empire. Bulk of the ruling class, consisted of the 'Singhs', majority of whom were Jats, and patronage was extended to Sikhs of other affiliations. The gulf between the nobility and common peasantry was wide. Chroniclers recorded sharing of religious faith alongside class and caste distinctions in social relations. After Ranjit Singh's death in 1839, the Sikh power waned within a decade and the British annexed his state in 1849.

The interaction between the British and the Sikhs can be divided into three phases. In the first phase, the decline of the former ruling class was accompanied by the British effort to win over a major section of the Sikhs by preferential recruitment to the army recognising them by anthropological expression, such as martial race. In other words, the first phase spanning from 1849 to 1906 was the period of the Sikh support to the British empire. It was also the period of the beginning of religious reform movements, such as the Arya Samaj and the Singh Sabha, the latter emphasising Sikhs' distinct identity and boundary demarcation from Hindus. The Arya Samaj further contributed to this sharpening of the demarcation through the Shudhi movement, the purpose of which was to reconvert to Hinduism those who had earlier converted to Islam and even Sikhism. In fact, the attempt of the Arya Samaj to include Sikhs as the potential reconvertees to Hinduism vindicated the views of Kahn Singh Nabha (1973) that Sikhs were not Hindus. The second phase is the shorter period between 1906 and 1919, when the Sikhs began to move towards opposition to the British rule. The agitation of the farmers in 1906 in the canal colonies began the process and the Ghadar movement initiated by the Punjabis living in North America was the culmination of this process. During the last phase of communal electorates between 1920 and 1947, the Sikhs became differentiated as a political category. Participation in the democratic and militant struggle for freedom was accompanied by communitarian politics more as a reaction to the Muslim League's two nations theory and demand for a Muslim majority state of Pakistan. As the demand for Pakistan was accepted and India was partitioned, the plausibility of the realisation of a separate sovereign state based on a common religion became a fact. In the subsequent years, the political vested interests were to articulate Khalistan for the Sikhs. Though the demand for Khalistan never became the part of agenda of the Sikh leadership, yet at certain levels it was always lurking in their minds in one form or the other at the time of India getting independence.

II
SOCIAL FORMATIONS

In the sociological analysis of the Indian society, caste system figures most predominantly. A prominent notion is that caste system was found only among the Hindus. However, it has now become an accepted view that despite the egalitarian ideologies, caste differentiation existed and is still continuing to exist among Muslims, Sikhs and Christians. There is a serious flaw in this accepted and prevalent view of the presence of caste system among the non-Hindus. It is generally understood that the caste hierarchies among the non-Hindus are congruent with those of the Hindus. This is not the case. All the three religions are based on the equality among the faithful, in the sense that in each religious community all are equal. This being the minimum commonality among the three religions, it may be expected that no hierarchy on the basis of birth and the practice of endogamy would be in existence among them. When empirically it is found that there is a prevalence of caste nomenclature among them, we reach via short route to conclude that caste system exists among the non-Hindu religious communities. It leads one to logically conclude that caste is the essence of Indian civilisation. However, as Srinivas (1966) has rightly pointed out, even among the Hindus caste system has never been an unchanging and rigid hierarchical order. For him 'varna' system was rigid, but it was a broad division giving opportunities to changes in the caste status through collective endeavour. One common thing among the non-Hindus is that we find limited presence of the Brahmins. The Kshatryias and Vaishyas are also in small numbers. It is mainly the Shudras and ex-untouchable castes, which have historically converted to Islam, Christianity and Sikhism in large numbers than the upper castes.

After the conversion to egalitarian religions, various hitherto lower castes experienced changes in their existential conditions. Conversely, some castes might have converted to other religions after perceiving some change in the living conditions of those who had embraced the new religion earlier, as is the case of Jats' conversion to Sikhism that has been explicated by Habib (1976). The Jats had already attained economic prosperity and by converting to Sikhism they were able to improve their social status. The first to establish their hegemony in the Sikh community also enforced the social differentiation based on the caste nomenclature, which, as a result of constant practice of social exclusion, came very close to the Hindu caste hierarchy (Judge 2002). However, the incumbents in the positions of higher castes were radically different from those of Hindus. In other words, the caste hierarchy among the Sikhs, as it emerged over a period of time, was distinct from the Hindu caste order with Brahmins at the top. There were also some changes in the caste nomenclature after their conversion to other religions. For example, a Hindu Chuhra or Bhangi was called Balmiki, and if he were a Muslim, he would be called Mussali, whereas the Sikh would be known as Mazabi. The tenth guru of the Sikhs also called them Rangretas. In order to discourage any discrimination against them and also to reward them for their services, the Guru had said, *"Regrete, Guru ke bete"* (Rangretas are sons of the Guru) (Singh 1985). Similarly, a Sikh Chamar was called Ramdasia. Still another nomenclatural change could be witnessed in the case of the carpenter and Kalal castes, which were, after their becoming Sikhs, known as Ramgarhias and Ahluwalias respectively. Interestingly, over a period of time, the Hindu Kalals also became Ahluwalias – a process that is not well studied by the ethnographers.

Bingley wrote his book on the Sikhs in 1880s. In a way, he is one of the pioneers to distinguish various castes among the Sikhs, but at the same time keeping the idea that Sikhism had an egalitarian ideology. According to him, various castes among the Sikhs were: Jats, Brahmins, Rajputs, Khatris, Aroras, Labanas, Mahtons, Kambohs, Sansis, Ramgarhias, Chhimbas, Jhiwars, Ramdasias, and Mazabis or Rangretas (Bingley 1985). He also added the Deccani Sikhs who had converted to Sikhism owing to the visits of gurus to South India, particularly Nanded. Bingley (ibid.: 47) makes an interesting comment on the Brahmin Sikhs thus:

> The renunciation of caste which formed the fundamental principle of Guru Govind Singh's teaching, was naturally inimical to the ideas of the Brahmans, whose intelligence taught them that they had little to gain from Sikhism. Brahman Sikhs are consequently few, and the number enlisted is not large. Though individually often excellent soldiers, their enlistment is not generally desirable, as their influence over Sikhs of lower castes is apt to detrimental to discipline, and to destroy the *raison d'etre* of Sikhism.

Bingley's purposive analysis of the Brahmin Sikhs in the context of whether they should be recruited in the army shows the way the British tended to construct the social structure of the Indian society. Assuming that caste affiliation forms the essence of Indian social structure within which the patternisation of social interaction had occurred, the British officials constructed each religious community as divided on the basis of caste from within. Such an enumeration of the religious communities tended to give an underlying unity to the society, which was independent of religions. In such a situation, Sikhism felt most threatened, as it perceived itself closer to Hinduism. This threat was that of total submergence. As Sikhism had constructed its mythology against Muslim rule in India, it also felt distanced from Islam. Being a small religious community, the Sikhs sought to construct Sikh identity distinct from the then existing religious communities. Interestingly, among the various caste associations formed in Punjab, one was that of Mahaton Sikhs, who sought to be recognised as a martial race so as to get recruited in the army. The fact that the recruitment policy of the British involved differential treatment to different castes among the Sikhs, the formation of such associations was inevitable. Bingley approached the Sikh castes for the purpose of recruitment to the army.

The Singh Sabha movement began in 1881 and immediately after that an alternative interpretation of the Sikh community began to appear. Since the primary purpose of the movement was to reform the community from within by emphasising single form of Sikh identity, the Sikh intelligentsia geared itself in providing new interpretations to the historical events. The primary orientation was to construct a new tradition of Sikhism so as to demarcate its boundaries from Hinduism. At this juncture, the castes, which had lower status as Hindus, but enjoyed higher status as Sikhs began to argue that there were no caste inequalities among the Sikhs. Not only that the Singh Sabha movement became the fountainhead of the creation of new mythology as well as alternative interpretation of the Sikh history. It is in this backdrop that Kahn Singh Nabha wrote his polemical work *Hum Hindu Nahin* (We are not Hindus) in 1898. In this book, he seeks to establish that there is no caste inequality among the Sikhs.

Nabha is very clear to the limited purpose of his work. He (1973:1) states it clearly thus: "After reading this book the readers must be able to understand that the Sikhism is a distinct religion from Hinduism and other religions. However, it should not happen that you begin to oppose Hindus or abuse Hinduism." As a typical polemical work, it covers fifteen areas with sweeping observations by relying heavily on Sikh religious hymns. What draws attention of a sociologist is that he gives second preference to the issue of caste and varna. It is this issue that forms the basis of what he thinks is the real distinction between the Sikhs and the Hindus.

In the section on varna and caste, Nabha addresses the issue to the Hindus. It implies that the book was meant for both the Sikhs and the Hindus. He seems to be telling the Hindus that their religious texts give pre-eminent position to the Brahmins. Here he quotes from *Manusmriti.* Normatively, the position of the Brahmins signifies injustice to the people of the God. The second criticism he labels against the caste system is the ascriptive character of the caste status. Caste is determined by birth, he avers. Nabha (ibid.) concedes that there are status groups among the Sikhs, namely, *gyani* (scholar), *granthi* (priest), *sipahi* (soldier), *zamindar* (landowner), *vipari* (trader), and *langri* (cook). However, these positions are not determined by birth and may change. For example, a scholar may clean the shoes of the devotees. The third and the most important issue, according to Nabha, is the practice of untouchability among the Hindus. The Guru has merged the four varnas and castes and created the Sikh religion.

Kahn Singh Nabha tried to refute what was obvious and visible among the Sikhs, that is, the presence of castes and the practice of caste-based discrimination. There is no denying the fact that caste hierarchy among the Sikhs was qualitatively distinct from that of the Hindus (Judge 2002). The issue of the nature of caste hierarchy requires elucidation and clarification. In the anthropological and sociological literature, caste has been understood broadly from three perspectives. The first is the indological perspective, which defines caste in the light of the ancient Hindu scripts. It takes cognisance of certain texts such as *Manusmriti, Dharamashastra*, etc. to define and understand the caste. The second provides a definition from structural functional perspective according to which caste system is regarded as a system of stratification. Thirdly, caste has been understood as a system of unequal distribution of power sustained by the Hindu religious ideology of Dharma-Karma. Ghurye (1969) identified five features of the caste system, which combine all the three perspectives. According to him (ibid.: 2), "The outstanding features of the Hindu society when it was ruled by the social philosophy of caste, unaffected by the modern ideas of rights and duties may be discerned to be six". These are segmental division of society, hierarchy, restriction on feeding and social intercourse, civil and religious disabilities and privileges of the different sections, lack of unrestricted choice of occupation, and restrictions on marriage.

The most notable dimension of Ghurye's explication of caste in the form of six features is that he clearly states that it is the essential feature of the Hindu society. If that is the case, then it should be made clear that in the case of non-Hindu 'religious societies' there would be different features of inequalities marked by the ascribed status. Obviously, the criteria that define the Hindu society are guided by the religious ideology, which is expected to be absent among the non-Hindus. Among the Sikhs, for example, the ideology of *karma* was replaced by the principle of equality among men. As it echoed through the verse in the *Guru Granth Sahib* – the sacred book of the Sikhs: "*Manas ki jat sabhe ek hi pechanvo*" (All are humans, and they have same identity). It was not only the emphasis on equality, but also the discontinuity of the defining principle of caste hierarchy that distinguished Sikhism from the Hinduism. The defining principle of caste hierarchy from ideal typical perspective was the binary opposition between manual and non-manual labour. When the first guru started cultivation at Kartarpur after his *udasis*, it was a radical shift in practice towards the caste equality, as the cultivators had been identified as Shudras in the light of the ideology of caste (Judge 2002).

Could Sikhism eradicate caste inequality and discrimination? It is difficult to answer this question. McLeod (1975:82) has referred to the contemporary writings and is of the view that "caste distinctions were...obliterated within the eighteenth-century Panth". He (ibid. 84) further writes: "...Entry to the Panth was open to all and within it caste was certainly discounted. It was, however, by no means obliterated. It survived in terms of commensality and marriage patterns, demonstrating in both that degree of tenacity which has proved so puzzling to successive generations of foreigners." In order to show the tenacity of caste, McLeod also alludes to the fact that none of the Sikh Gurus married out of their caste.[3] He (ibid.: 93-94) provides a kind of hierarchy of castes among the Sikhs on the basis of the census of 1881 thus:

> .... This leaves us with two agrarian castes (Jat and Kamboh); two mercantile castes (Khatri and Arora); four artisan castes (Tarkhan, Lohar, Nai, and Chhimba); and two outcaste groups (Chamar and Chuhra). To these we should add one smaller caste

> with a particularly interesting history within the modern Panth. This is the Kalal or distiller *zat*, the Sikh members of which style themselves Ahluwalias. These eleven remain the principal constituents of the Panth.

The identification of various castes by Bingley as well as McLeod clearly indicates that the caste hierarchy among the Sikhs was different from that of the Hindus. The castes occupying the higher position among the Sikhs would have been the Shudra castes according to the principles of the Hindu caste system. The caste hierarchies among the Hindus and the Sikhs became competitive in the sense that the castes that acquired higher caste status after converting to Sikhism belonged to the Shudra castes as Hindus. After acquiring the upper caste position in the Sikh fold these castes perpetuated and enforced the caste inequality within the community. In other words, the hierarchy of castes among the Sikhs was no more based on the distinction between the manual and non-manual work as a result of which the new upper castes developed vested interests in creating distances from Hinduism.

Much of the confusion on treating the caste stratification among the non-Hindu communities has been created in sociology and social anthropology due to indiscriminate application of the concept of dominant caste as provided by Srinivas (1987). Srinivas (1966) has convincingly argued that caste is dynamic and varna is fixed. In other words, caste positions are constantly changing, whereas varnas remain unchanged. The idea of the dominant caste has emerged from this notion of dynamic character of caste. Thus, we find that if a caste belongs to a lower varna but occupies a position of political and/or economic domination, then it may safely be called a dominant caste without disturbing the fixed varna positions. What has happened in most of the studies on caste stratification among the non-Hindu communities is that instead of characterising the caste hierarchy in terms of the way the religious change has transformed it, the upper castes are understood as the dominant caste. The underlying assumption is that caste hierarchies are unchanging. In reality, there is a religious basis of hierarchy, as Max Weber (1948) rightly highlighted the absence of the Brahmin and his paramount position in the caste system among the non-Hindu religious communities.

If we examine the caste background of the priests (known as *Bhai* in Punjabi) among the Sikhs, then we may find that most of them belong to the middle castes like Bhatra, Chhimba and others, and sometimes to the dalit castes like Ramdasia and Julaha. This is both an indication and consequence of the lower status of the priests among the Sikhs. However, distinct from the gurdwara priests are the heads of various *deras*, who carry a tremendous influence and power within the Sikh community. One simple evidence of this aspect is that two presidents of Shiromani Akali Dal in recent years were drawn from the Sant Samaj, namely, Sant Fateh Singh and Sant Harchand Singh Longowal. The Sant Samaj has mainly remained confined to the religious sphere of Sikhism, whereas the gurdwara priests are part of the social structure of the rural and urban life.

III
CULTURAL TRAJECTORIES

The survival of local cultures in the face of the gigantic invasion of the homogenising forces of modernisation of Western capitalism has given enough reasons to the sociologists to think of culture as relatively autonomous, resistant to change and source of individual and collective identity. Since religion is the basis of core values of a community, there is also a tendency to interpret culture in terms of religious framework. In fact, culture is much larger than the religious values and practices. In a society where we have centuries' old existence of two or three religious communities, equating culture with religion alone is fatalistic. In the case of Punjab where three major religious communities existed till 1947, it is not possible to provide a cultural profile of the Sikhs without contextualising it within the larger framework of the society in Punjab. At the same time, Sikhism has influenced Punjabi culture in a significant way as Islam did earlier.

However, it should be reminded that Sikhism did not change everything. For example, the system of mate selection among the Sikhs is not uniform though the Shiromani Gurdwara Prabhandak Committee (SGPC) has prepared a document known as *Anand Karaj* the purpose of which is to clearly set rules for regulating the institution of marriage. Most of the Jats still practise *gotra* exogamy of both mother and father, whereas the Aroras, irrespective of their religion, practise preferential cross-cousin marriage. Jyoti (1983) has shown that though caste has no basis in Sikh marriage, yet caste endogamy is practiced. Such continuity in practises is attributed to the persistence of caste system, but in a way it has lot to do with traditions. In comparison with the Western tradition of love marriage that follows the institution of dating, there is largely a practice of arranged marriage with a powerful custom of preferential mate selection in India. One may find the prevalence of the tradition of love marriage among many tribal communities in India. Thus, the institution of marriage in India is private, informal and exclusive affair in which the autonomy of the family is paramount. In such a situation even the legal enactments cannot effectively intervene till the members of the family come out of it and appeal to the state for help, as it generally happens in the case of exceptionally small number of love marriages in which the families have strong objections. Among the Muslims of Punjab the rules of mate selection were influenced by the religion and have remained so. In fact, the conduct of marriage ceremony is largely shaped by the religious norms. One may say that religion and culture are not coterminous, but, at the same time, the two are entwined together influencing each other. Geertz (1973: 123) treats religion as a cultural system as for him its importance "lies in its capacity to serve, for an individual or for a group, as a source of general, yet distinctive, conceptions of the world, the self, and the relations between them, on the one hand – its model *of* aspect – and of rooted, no less distinctive 'mental dispositions' – its model *for* aspect – on the other". It is from these conceptions, which mediate between the self and community and in certain situations the 'others' that religion and culture tend to converge powerfully to provide a distinct identity to a community in multi-religious society.

In the delineation of the cultural profile of the Sikhs, an attempt would be made to look into only one important dimension. It is the overwhelming presence, influence and domination of the Jat syndrome within the Sikh community and its cultural manifestations. The Jats of Punjab, whether Muslims, Hindus or Sikhs, distinguish themselves by making a subtle variation in the pronunciation from their counterparts in other parts of the country as they call themselves *Jatt* though in terms of the *gotra* nomenclatures they come close to their counterparts in Haryana and other parts of the country.[4] Whatever might be the commonalties and differences between Punjabi *Jatts* and non-Punjabi *Jats*, their domination in Sikhism is beyond any doubt. According to the 1931 census, they were 60 per cent of the total population of the Sikhs. The conversion of the Jats to Sikhism took place at the time of the fifth guru of the Sikhs. Banerjee (1962: 35) informs that at the time of the sixth guru the most preponderant among the Sikhs were the Jats. He also points out that the Sikh gurus made certain adaptations to accommodate the Jats as "the permission to take animal diet that was given by Guru Hargobind might very well have been a necessary and inevitable concession to the traditional habits of the Jats..."

Banerjee (ibid.) has made an attempt to characterise the Jats of Punjab on the basis of various sources. One of the main features of the Jats that emerges powerfully is their tribal character in both solidarity and feuds. An example of this solidarity and feud among many is refusal to intermarry. Banerjee (ibid.: 38) gives the following story that may be regarded as a representative of this dimension thus:

> The Dhillons would intermarry with all *gots* except with the Bals. The story is that a family bard or mirasi from a Dhillon village was refused help, when in difficulties in the Bal country, and in revenge cursed the Bal clan. Mirasis were in those days more of a power than they are now, and the Dhillon clan took the feud, which survives to this day in the refusal to intermarry.

Banerjee has cited this story from Amritsar Gazetteer, 1914, which indicates that it might have been a part of the general consciousness of the time. Pettigrew (1978), later on, did her empirical study of the political system of the Sikh Jats in which she has authoritatively highlighted the solidarity and feud as part of their culture. In other words, there is a reasonable basis to argue that the conversion to Sikhism has not completely eliminated the tribal features of the Jats. It is also now well-known that the structure of solidarity and feud is not confined to the village, rather it extends beyond the village to form a large network of unity and contestation. There is a notable difference between the Sikh Jats and their Hindu counterparts in Haryana. There is a complete absence of Khap Panchayats among the Sikh Jats, whereas in Haryana, as pointed out by Sangwan (1997), the Khap Panchayats combine a large number of villages belonging to one *gotra* of the Jats, and these Khaps actively intervene in formal politics.[5]

The identity of the Jats with Sikhism is well established, but is rarely recognised in Sikh scholarship, as it decentres the dominant discourse of social equality in theory and practice of Sikhism. It is in sociological and social anthropological writings on the Sikh community that one finds the comments on the pre-eminent position of the Jats. Pettigrew (1978:41) makes the following observation on the relationship between the Jats and Sikh faith thus: "The Jats considered themselves to be 'born Sikhs' and did not think other Sikhs deserved the title of sirdar. Each Jat felt tremendous pride that it was *his* section of the community that had built up the military organization, which led to the establishment of Sikh rule in the Punjab. He felt that prestige lay with the Jats because of this..." The important issue related to the relationship between the Jats and Sikhism is what Kaur (1986) points out as the dialectics of local and regional construction of identities. At the village level, the Jat is dominant and secure in his Sikh identity, whereas at the regional level he has to interact with the non-Jat Sikhs. She (ibid.: 238) writes: "Non-Jat Sikhs, who are not in a dominant position, and who have to differentiate themselves from Hindus of the same caste (for example, Khatris and Ramgarhiyas), have to display the overt symbols of their religion."

It may be reminded that as a caste, the Jats, irrespective of their religion, are peasant proprietors and their presence in the Punjabi folk culture is overwhelming. The Jat is an important character in the poetry, love stories and other folk songs in which the valour, bravery and sometimes the romance are depicted. Two most popular epics, namely, Heer-Ranjha and Mirza-Sahiban are the love stories of Jat couples. The following couplet presents Heer in the context of her caste:

> *"Jhang Sialan the Jatti, Badnami jehne khatti,*
> *Nahin Yaar Valon Hatti, Preet dekho Heer di."*[6]

> (The Jatti of Jhang who earned ill repute, but did not betray her lover; see the love of Heer for Ranjha.)

Similarly, the other love epic Mirza-Sahiban, which is written by Peelu, who was a Jat by caste, contains numerous references to the Jat caste. The following couplet is one of such references:

> *"Hujre Shah Mukim de ik Jatti araz kare,*
> *Main bakara devan pir de je sir da kant mare."*[7]

> (The Jatti prays to Hujre Shah Makeem that if her betrothed dies, then she would offer a goat as thanksgiving to the pir.)

The mention of the Jat woman in the earlier texts is an indication of how such references were acceptable to a caste group, which was numerically preponderant and dominant in a state that was based on agrarian economy. Baneerjee (1962) has pointed out that the Jats were also regarded as plunderers. The Jat identity within the framework of Sikhism has not diminished. Gurharpal Singh (2000: 85-86) informs us that the Jats constitute 80 per cent of the total population of the Sikhs, in spite of which "the overall impression is still of caste homogeneity rather than division". Such a comment defies even the common sense understanding that in an agrarian economy a caste group that owns land and constitute 80 per cent of religious community shall not maintain, articulate and manifest its domination over others.[8] We further encounter a religion-based stratification model created by Gurharpal Singh according to which the following occupy the position in the descending order in the hierarchy: Amritdharis (baptised Sikh carrying the five symbols), Keshdharis (unbaptised but supporting unshorn hair), Mona-Sikhs (the clean shaven), and Sahajdharis. At empirical level it is virtually impossible to have such status groups in Punjab.[9]

In the contemporary Punjab, particularly after one-and-a-half decades of fundamentalism, the emphasis on the distinct Jat identity has not waned in Sikh community. One of the popular songs in Punjab these days was sung by late Surjit Singh Bindrakhia and it is written by Shamsher Singh Sandhu. Some of the lines are given below:

> *"Tun hain jatt di Pasand, Jatt ne viahouni aan.*
> *Bahman di nahin eh tan jatt di hai yarri,*
> *Jatt nun hai yaari, jaan ton bhi piari."*[10]

> (You are the choice of Jat; Jat will marry you. It is not Brahmin's love; it is Jat's love. For Jat love is dearer than death.)

In fact, the Punjabi folk songs are full of references to Jat. What is interesting to note is that the Jat community has not objected to even the mention of Jatti (the Jat woman) in songs. Such a powerful assertion of caste identity in modern India that too in the case of the egalitarian Sikh religion is an expression of many dimensions of the complex social and cultural dynamics of the community. What we find is that the regional and caste cultures have dialectically interacted with the religious cultural system and the result is the coexistence of the two, which provides a composite character to the community in spite of many attempts at homogenising the Sikh identity.

IV
ECONOMIC PROFILE

The social scientists have highlighted the association between the caste and the occupation in the context of Indian society. The hereditary character of the occupations in India has remained the order of the day for most of the people till recently. The sociology of economic life of the communities is thus possible to ascertain and examine in spite of the fact that the class system has emerged in modern India fracturing the hereditary character of the occupations. The emergence of new occupations in the modern development process is also being perceived as the source of social mobility for the low castes. One may rather examine the historically existing congruence between caste and occupation in such a situation and then investigate the deviations, alterations and ruptures that have occurred due to the development process. Besides mapping the change in the Sikh community in terms of caste and occupation, sociological perspective also examines religion with regard to its role in changing the economic orientations of its members. Durkheim (1976) views religion in terms of its functions, which, according to him, are performed to uphold the society. In other words, religion functions to provide stability, order and equilibrium to the society. The position of Marx (1975: 175-76) is somewhat different, but stating that religion is the opium of the masses also amounts to emphasising it as a factor in maintaining the social order. The fact that religion can uphold and maintain the given social order it also becomes an important variable that can influence our social life.

What is significant about religion as a factor is that at the time of its emergence it may become a force of social change for the community. After the community life gets routinised, it becomes the basis of social stability.

Weber's (1976) theory of the Protestant ethic and the spirit of capitalism may be examined from this perspective. Weber has shown the relationship of the capitalist economic orientation and activity with the Protestant ethic. The implications of such a thesis is that religion is a factor in economic life, for it shapes and reorients people's perspective towards the way they take up work, whether for survival or accumulation of wealth. The Arya Samaj is generally regarded as a kind of movement in the context of Punjab, which had economic implications. Similarly, we also find that some of the scholars think that the Sikh movement had a lot of commonalities with the Protestantism. Marenco (1976) opines that the only fundamental difference between Sikhism and Protestantism is that the former sees religion and politics inseparable, whereas the latter emerged from the struggle for separating the two.

Marenco (ibid.: 311) has worked out the changes that occurred among various classes and castes of the Sikhs under the British rule in the light of two indicators, namely, corporate caste mobility and individual social mobility.[11] She has found that the Jats benefited most from the changes under the British rule, which is evident from the fact that out of the total fifteen changes introduced by the British, the Jats experienced corporate social mobility in eleven cases, whereas the artisan and menial castes experienced it in two each.[12] The Sikh trading castes experienced only the individual social mobility. The notable aspect of economic changes of the castes among the Sikhs between 1911 and 1921 are to be found in the case of professional occupations, such as legal, medical, and teaching (ibid.: 240). In contrast to the Khatri and Arora Sikhs, the number of Jats among these professions increased more than two times. The Tarkhan and Saini Sikhs also showed tremendous increase though their number was smaller than the Jats, Khatris and Aroras.

The findings of the study of Marenco give us an idea of the economic heterogeneity among the Sikhs that largely corresponded with the caste hierarchy. It was primarily in the context of individual social mobility that we find that members of different castes moved out of their traditional occupations. It may however be inferred that the British were primarily concerned with the collection of maximum revenue from land as a result of which they brought improvements in agriculture and established 'canal colonies', which largely benefited the landowning classes and castes. The recruitment to army was linked with the notions of an independent peasant as well as martial race, which prompted the British to give preference to the Jat Sikhs. A consequence of this policy of the British rule in Punjab was the reinforcement of position of dominance of the Jats within the Sikh community. There was still another important aspect of the British policy in the first decade of its rule that may be mentioned here in the words of Domin (1974:28-29) thus:

> The comparatively moderate land revenue assessment in Punjab ... reflected the influence of the industrial interest, which passed also for a speedy and large-scale project of irrigation systems to extend cultivation and enhance the agricultural output. This economic want coincided with the political goal of having the disbanded Khalsa soldiers settled down as fast as possible in the countryside. ... The first result was the Bari Doab Canal devised to water especially the area of Majha populated thickly by the Sikhs.

The British continued to support the landowning cultivating caste throughout the first half century of their rule. The twin objectives of having the maximum land revenue by providing impetus to the agricultural growth as well as recruitment of the soldiers from amongst this class with a preference for the Jat Sikh shaped the British policy. In spite of all this, Punjab faced perpetual agrarian crises, one of which was the increasing indebtedness and alienation of land of the cultivating classes. The Land Alienation Act, 1901 was precisely aimed at preventing the alienation of land to the urban money-lenders. Barrier (1979) informs that the Act failed to prevent indebtedness among the peasantry in Punjab. It was left to Sir Chhotu Ram and the Unionist Party to free peasantry by writing off all debts of the peasantry to the moneylenders. The Act further consolidated the position of the Jats in terms of the control of the land, as all the non-cultivating tribes and castes lost the right to purchase agricultural land. In the absence of industrialisation, the landownership was one of the major avenues of social mobility and some of the upwardly mobile castes might have lost the opportunity to exploit this avenue. One may refer to the Ramgarhias or Tarkhan Sikhs in this regard. In spite of all these developments, the agrarian agitation began in 1906 in the 'canal colonies', which were supposedly inhabited by those people who could be regarded as the backbone of the British rule in Punjab.[13]

It is clear from the discussion that the British rule in Punjab reinforced and consolidated the power of the owner cultivators, who predominantly belonged to the Jat caste. The British policy towards the development of agriculture entailed twin objectives, namely, the maximisation of revenue and resettling the soldiers after their service in the army. As the Jats were numerically predominant among both the owner cultivators and the soldiers, the British policy could be understood in terms of its support to the consolidation of the dominant position of the Jat landowners who at the turn of the century began to dominate in the Singh Sabha movement. They were overwhelmingly numerous in the Gurdwara reform movement that began later on. The political participation of the Jats could be understood in terms of the revolution of the rising expectations. The economic prosperity raised their expectations. However, their perception of what they had achieved was far below their expectations. It is important to remember that starting from the agrarian agitation of the farmers in 1906 Punjab experienced the Ghadar Party movement, the Babbar Akali movement and the Gurdwara reform movement within the first three decades of the 20th century in which a majority of the participants belonged to the Jat caste.

If we examine the economic heterogeneity among the Sikhs in the post-colonial phase, we find that there is hardly any change from the colonial period except for the rising proportion of the people joining the newly emerged occupations in the public sector. The Khatris and Aroras are traders and businessmen. The Jats are predominantly owner cultivators. It is generally said that the Jats of Punjab form the backbone of the Green Revolution – a phenomenon of high agricultural growth rate. Besides Jats, there are other castes that are operating small landholdings. These are Sainis, Kambohs, Labanas and Mahatons. Ramgarhias are artisans by caste occupation and they have moved to industry and they are regarded as the most mobile among the Sikhs (Saberwal 1990; Judge and Bal 1996). Still there are a large number of Ramgarhia families living in villages, as Bal (1995), in her empirical study of some villages in Amritsar and Gurdaspur districts, shows that 52.94 per cent of the Ramgarhias are engaged in traditional occupation under the *jajmani* system, whereas 30.59 per cent of them have shifted to the market-oriented activities and the rest combine the both. The third important caste among the Sikhs is that of the Mazabi – about 20 per cent among the Sikhs – who are landless agricultural labourers.[14] Over a period of time, the development process brought a lot of occupational changes among the Sikh castes, but it is the Green Revolution that has radically altered the economic structure of Punjab.

What is known as the development of capitalism in agriculture, the Green Revolution is responsible for dramatically reducing poverty in Punjab.[15] The trade and agro-industry have developed as a result. The class formation among the Sikhs living in rural areas has occurred. The Jats have benefited directly, but over a period of time, the sub-division in the landholdings, owing to the tradition and law of inheritance as well as indebtedness, has marginalised a large chunk of the Jat peasantry. In the economic development of the post-colonial period, the Indian state has played a decisive role in bringing out the Green Revolution. Sims (1988) has shown that after the Indo-Pak war in 1965, the Indian government took a decisive step towards self-sufficiency in foodgrain production and it looked for a region(s) that could do it in the shortest possible time. Punjab, with its already available infrastructure and the farmers' experience of irrigation, was the natural choice.[16] Since a lot of research has been conducted on the effects of the Green Revolution, there is no need to do the review of literature. What is relevant here is to see how the Sikhs could be linked and related to this economic transformation. In this regard, two observations may be made. First, the Green Revolution brought prosperity for the farmers. The farmers of Punjab are largely owner cultivators and mostly belong to the Jat, Saini, Kamboh, Labana and Mahaton castes and among whom the Jats are the most numerous. The Jats, Kambohs and Sainis are both Hindus and Sikhs.[17] An overwhelming majority of the Jats in Punjab is Sikh. In other words, the Green Revolution further made the Jats economically more powerful and after the Green Revolution the joint farming declined in both Punjab and Haryana. It was regarded as a result of the breaking of joint holdings, because the small farms became economically viable. It was a short-term change as in the next generation the small farms got marginalised because of sub-division of landholdings due to inheritance.

The second important dimension of the Green Revolution was that since it was primarily a consequence of technological breakthrough in the area of inventing hybrid seeds, it had its inherent weaknesses, flaws and gaps. The entire bio-technological development took place in the West, particularly in the United States of America, and it was confined to the local agricultural needs. The revolution created a monoculture of wheat and paddy in which irrigation was primary (Shiva 1989). This resulted in the intensive use of water in agriculture. Not only this, it also put water on the political agenda of the political parties. The farmers of Punjab, among whom the Sikhs are numerically preponderant, became amenable to the exploitation of political vested interests. Gurr (1970) has shown how the perception of relative deprivation among the people creates political instability and violence. Gill (1994) and Gill and Singhal (1985) have argued that social and economic contradictions of the capitalist development in Punjab agriculture have a lot to do with the emergence of Punjab crisis. Purewal (2000: 73) makes it clear that Green Revolution created a class of Kulaks who became an important agent in creating the crisis thus: "Sikhism has become an ideological weapon of the Kulaks to build a 'common' bond among the Sikhs of all classes and to bring them under their command." We are hardly aware of whether this could be empirically verified, but there is no denying the fact that classes among the landowning castes emerged as a result of forces unleashed by the Green Revolution. It is important to note that the Green Revolution affected hitherto relatively stagnant villages of Punjab and it stirred both the imagination and expectation of the landowners. Among them were the numerically preponderant and politically dominant Jat Sikhs. The emergence of militant movement was a consequence of a complex parallelogram of forces in which the agrarian development played an important role. One of the major discourses that became popular and caught common people's perceptions was the overlapping of various categories, such as urban Hindu trader and rural Sikh farmer. The former was explained as the exploiter, whereas the latter was the exploited. The economic conflict between the two transformed into communal divide. Such explanation might have worked but it was too simplistic to be accepted.

V
SIKH DIASPORA

The international migration of the Sikhs is an important aspect of their profile. The proportion of the Sikhs among the Punjabis is so high that the one could replace the other for expression. Neither the Punjabi culture nor the Sikh religious values show anything that could encourage and facilitate the migration of the Sikhs from their native place except for pilgrimage. The *udasis* of the first guru of the Sikhs, Guru Nanak Dev, had a qualitatively distinct character, as it was the path of the gurus, saints and *fakirs*. For the landlocked Punjab, the profane ways of migration were through the recruitment to the army and for the purposes of trade. In the pre-British Punjab, these two avenues were limited and confined, but it is plausible to make a conjecture that for reasons of trade the business class might have been moving from one to another country. The international migration of the Sikhs in fact was the migration of the ex-soldiers who belonged to the peasantry. A majority of the peasantry was drawn from the Jat caste and thus the Sikh pioneers largely belonged to this caste. In the pre-colonial period, the number of Sikh migrants in different parts of the world was between one to one-and-a-half lakh. Interestingly, they were spread all over the world including South America. In the post-colonial period, the migration of the Sikhs has dramatically increased and now they are mainly concentrated in the English-speaking world and their number exceeds one million. Tracing the history of how the Sikhs abroad constructed India, we come across the story of their journey from the militant nationalism to their support to the separatist movement for Khalistan. At no point of time, however, all the Sikhs got involved with any of the movements, e.g., a considerable number among them in the USA and Canada remained indifferent to the Ghadar Party and its activities in the first and second decades of the 20th century. Similarly, a majority remained indifferent to the idea of

Khalistan. The pioneer Sikhs, who went to the North America in the beginning of the 20th century, formed the Ghadar Party. When the First World War broke out in 1914, most of the Ghadarites returned to India to wage armed struggle for independence of their country. The lofty objective of the Ghadar Party could not be achieved, because they found an altogether different situation in Punjab where the Sikhs in particular were more interested in joining the army. The drive to the recruitment to the army was a kind of movement in which the nationalist leaders, including Mahatma Gandhi, were participating. The diaspora Sikhs failed, and were arrested and punished, but in the process they enriched the legendary tradition of martyrdom.

There are two important features of the pioneer Sikhs in North America that must be kept in mind in the study of Sikh diaspora. One, an overwhelming number among them belonged to the Jat caste and most of them hailed from the Doaba region of Punjab, particularly the Hoshiarpur and Jalandhar districts.[18] Two, they organised their community life by keeping the gurdwara at the centre due to which it did not remain confined to performing religious functions. Gurdwaras became part and symbol of social and cultural unity of the Punjabis comprised by Sikhs, Hindus and Muslims. Hans (2002) is of the view that the gurdwaras continued to perform this function till 1984.

The response of the overseas Punjabis in general and the Sikhs in particular to various occurrences, events and movements in Punjab could be observed as an uninterrupted and unbroken chain of excitement, affiliation and support on ideological basis. One of the major events in the post-independent period was the emergence of the Naxalite movement in India, which also struck its roots in Punjab. The police oppression against the Naxalites led to the emigration of some of them to Canada. The Punjabis responded to this movement by forming the Ghadar Party of India (Marxist-Leninist) under the leadership of Hardayal Bains.

Later on, some Punjabis also organised the Indian People's Association of North America (IPANA) (Judge 1992). The Indian Workers' Association in England remained one of the oldest organisations, which has always responded to the events in Punjab. However, these organisations did not confine themselves to the Sikhs because of their ideology. These tended to have broader orientations in spite of the fact that a majority among them have been Sikhs. There is a need to make a distinction between individuals belonging to different religions pursuing a common goal and members of one religious community articulating the religious needs, orientations and interests specific to the religion.

As pointed out earlier, gurdwaras became the central place for the diaspora Sikhs so far as their religious and cultural needs were concerned. This continued to be so till this day. It is interesting to note that the ascendance of gurdwaras, particularly in England, has a lot to do with the politics of recognition. Helweg (1990: 50) makes it clear when he comments: "The gurdwara did not come by this position of prominence accidentally. It had to compete for leadership with organisations like the Indian Worker's Association. Ultimately, the gurdwara gained recognition as the representative institution by the British host society. ... The host society recognised it as primary institution representing the immigrant community."

In England and Canada, the caste divisions manifest themselves in the form of religious institutions. As a community, the Sikhs are replica of their counterparts in India. There are separate gurdwaras of each caste among the Sikhs in Punjab though none is prevented from entering anyone on the basis of caste. Therefore, in those cities of Canada and England where the Sikhs constitute a large number, the caste-wise pattern of gurdwaras can be discerned. The prominent castes that have consciously gone for their own places of worship are Ramgarhias and dalits (Judge 2000). Various communitarian practices and institutions that the Sikhs have evolved are again the replica of what is the case with the religious community in

India. Caste endogamy is practised and sometimes enforced in the community. This also implies that the Western institutional practices like dating are discouraged. There is a continuous effort to enforce the practice of arranged marriage the negative effects of which could be observed in the form of prevalence of violence against women among them.

In the present scenario, it is becoming more and more difficult to ignore the Sikh diaspora in any study of social and political dynamics of Punjab. The Indian state has played an important role by emphasising the crucial importance of NRIs (Non-Resident Indians) in the development of the country. In a conference of the NRIs organised by the Government of India in New Delhi in January 2003, the then Prime Minister of India announced the provision of dual citizenship for certain categories of Indians living abroad. Interestingly, the Sikhs have been consistently demanding for this provision since long (Judge 2002). The invitation to NRIs to invest in India has been accompanied by liberal policies to accommodate their interests. In spite of the fact that still a majority of the Sikhs belong to the working class, a considerable number of them have become successful entrepreneurs. On top of this, we find that Sikhs abroad have also emerged as political elites in England and Canada. The premiere of British Columbia was a Sikh when the New Democratic Party was in power. There are other examples of Sikhs being elected to public positions in England too.

There is a reasonable basis to argue that some among the Sikh diaspora were the initiators and articulators of the demand for a separate Sikh state of Khalistan. Two names prominently figure in this regard. The first is that of Jagjit Singh Chauhan, who published the advertisement of Khalistan in *New York Times* in 1971. The second notable Sikh is Ganga Singh Dhillon who was also active in late 1970s articulating the demand for Khalistan.[19]

To conclude, it may be stated that in mapping the Sikh community one has to take into consideration the trajectory of caste with its economic dimension. The Jats, both as a caste group and as a class of predominantly owner cultivators, occupy the central place in the social and cultural landscape of the community. Since the caste division, differentiation and hierarchy have continued to exist and persist, the analysis of the community highlights the gap in ideology and practice of Sikhism, which for social anthropologists may not look unusual.

Notes

1. Such attempts have influenced and shaped the way the Sikhs are portrayed and presented visually in paintings, movies, books, etc. Most of the books on the Sikhs carry the photograph of the Khalsa on the cover pages. Recently, on the cover pages of the book by Basran and Bolaria (2003) and Singh and Barrier (2004), a Nihang Sikh attired in his traditional dress has been shown. The latent function of this portrayal is that it gives an impression to others as if this is the only identity of the Sikhs that distinguishes them from the Hindus.
2. The Kukas are an endogamous group and strictly observe puritan ideology expounded by its founder Baba Ram Singh.
3. Such an argument, however, does not invalidate the fact that the Sikh gurus opposed caste-based inequality. Recently, changes could be witnessed in certain respects. In a religious function held recently in a village in Hoshiarpur district, the author observed that the priest was Julaha, the cook was Ad-dharmi and those cooking chapatis belonged to the Bazigar caste. All these castes are the scheduled castes.
4. It may be interesting to note that Singh (2002) uses the expression Jatt, implicit in which is the view that the Sikh Jats constitute a distinct, exclusive and privileged caste group.
5. Khap Panchayats, which could be the feature of the Jats, were not merely the caste panchayats. In fact, these were *gotra*-based panchayats. In Haryana, these panchayats are actively engaged and intervening in the social life of the community.
6. This couplet is part of the folk representation of the love of Heer and Ranjha.

7. The author of these lines is believed to be Peelu – a medieval poet who wrote the epic of love of Mirza-Sahiban for the first time.
8. We are hardly aware of the source of this information regarding the proportion of the Jats among the Sikhs. The figure is unbelievable exaggeration of the demographic size of the Jats within the Sikh community.
9. This model stands in contradiction to the overwhelming proportion of the Jats Singh has informed of. Among the Jat Sikhs of Punjab there is tremendous digression from the ideal typical Khalsa identity. Even then, they enjoy a dominant position and do not carry any sense of marginality. Gurharpal Singh has shown a total lack of understanding of social and cultural trajectories in the case of the Sikh dynamics.
10. The Brahmins objected to the negative construction of the image of their caste, but it hardly made any effect. It is still one of the most popular songs in Punjabi.
11. Marenco makes a distinction between corporate and individual forms of social mobility. The caste group that has experienced corporate mobility is the one that benefited the most from change. On the other hand, the individual mobility has not largely affected the status of the caste.
12. The four areas of change that the British introduced, according to Marenco, in which the Jats did not experience corporate social mobility were: increase of money in circulation and a true money economy, growth of towns and cities, building of factories, and emergence of a government official group in government service positions. It is clear from the above that there was a reinforcement of the position of the Jats in the rural areas. It created conditions for both the change and continuity in the case of the Jats. They prospered but remained peasants as a result of which they persisted in their traditional way of life.
13. In the princely states of Punjab, there was biswedari system of revenue collection. This system was quite similar to that of the zamindari system of permanent settlement areas. It also implies that the exploitation of the peasantry was considerable in these areas. We also find peasant movement, particularly, the Praja Mandal Movement and the Red Communist Party Movement, in the areas of the princely states.
14. There are other castes among the Sikhs who belong to the lowest rungs of the caste hierarchy. The Sansi, Ramdasia, and Bazigars are

involved in different economic activities, but most of them are still engaged in low status occupations.

15. Various studies have shown a decline in poverty levels in Punjab (e.g., Shergill and Singh 1995). However, the influx of migrant labour from Uttar Pradesh and Bihar in urban areas has prevented its disappearance.
16. Here farmers' experience implies those farmers who had been operating land in the Canal Colonies before 1947. After partition they moved to the Indian Punjab.
17. The Kambohs are widely spread in Punjab, next only to the Jats. The Kambohs of Amritsar and Jalandhar districts are largely Sikhs, whereas those belonging to Sunam in the Sangrur district are mostly Hindus.
18. After the formation of new districts of Punjab, we may now add Nawanshahar district, which has been carved out of Jalandhar and Hoshiarpur districts.
19. Ganga Singh Dhillon remained quite active in the late 1970s.

2

Emergence of Communal Politics

The Shiromani Akali Dal (henceforth Akali Dal) has always maintained that religion cannot be separated from politics. Essentially a party representing the Sikhs, the Akali Dal invariably raised issues that concerned the Sikh religious interests in normal times. During the election times the Akali Dal combined economic issues with those of the religious to appeal to all sections of the people of Punjab. The Akali Dal also controls the Shiromani Gurdwara Parbandhak Committee (SGPC) and plays the role of regulating religious affairs of the community. In the previous chapter, Marenco's comment was referred in which she brought out the fundamental difference between Sikhism and Protestantism with regard to their position on the relationship between religion and politics. The Akali Dal claims to be the party that represents the Sikhs' interests, but it is not the only party in India claiming to be representing a religious community. The Bhartiya Janata Party (BJP) derives support through the articulation and politicisation of communal identities by taking up 'Hindutva' as its guiding ideology. The Akali Dal is also a regional party like the Telugu Desam, the DMK, National Conference, etc.

Representing a religious community as well as a region provides a peculiar dynamics to the functioning of the Akali Dal. Though it has been consistently competing with the Congress Party in the elections, yet the Akali Dal also has a long history of collaboration with the Congress. Mahatma Gandhi's support to the Akali struggle for the control over the Sikh gurdwaras and shrines in the earlier 1920s is a notable example of this association between the two. Since independence the Akalis have pursued the politics that has pushed the party towards confrontation with the central government run by the Congress Party in the 1970s.

In this chapter, an attempt has been made to examine how the dual role of the Akali Dal contributed to the emergence of communal politics, particularly the rise of Jarnail Singh Bhindranwala. The discussion has been broadly divided into three parts, namely, the political dynamics of Punjab, history of the Damdami Taksal, and various features of the militant movement. In a nutshell, this chapter is primarily aimed at explicating, describing and analysing the emergence of communal politics, which formed the backdrop of the militant movement. However, the discussion subsumes various issues raised and investigated in the previous chapter. The first part largely substantiates the conclusion of the first chapter in the sense that the dynamics of political system is structured into the constantly contested relations of dominance and subjection in social and cultural life of Punjab. The second part on the Damdami Taksal may seem little out of place for those who are not familiar with the Akalis' political behaviour. It may be stated clearly that the objective of discussing the history of the Taksal is to locate Bhindranwala within the Sikh community from wherein he emerged as the militant leader. The second part is further divided into two sections. In the first section, the focus is on the general description of the Damdami Taksal, whereas the second section takes stock of the profile of Jarnail Singh Bhindranwala. Obviously, the third part of the chapter describes the events that characterise the situation best described by the experts as 'Punjab crisis'. The discussion in this part is aimed at tracing various events starting from the beginning of the movement to its final suppression in 1993.

I
POLITICAL DYNAMICS

The political dynamics of Punjab, like any other region, is complex and is not devoid of certain uniqueness of its own. Let us look at what makes Punjab political process a distinct and unique in its own right. Punjab is one of the few states, which are not having Hindu majority, but it is the only state with the Sikh majority. Before independence, the Muslims constituted the majority community. Immediately after partition, the Hindus constituted majority. The reorganisation of the state in 1966 on the basis of language created the Punjabi Suba with the Sikh majority. It is generally taken for granted that the Akali agitation for Punjabi Suba was primarily aimed at having a Sikh majority state (Nayar 1966). However, the Akali Dal has so far failed to perpetuate its formal political domination uninterruptedly, as the Congress continues to challenge and replace it regularly.

The issue of language has remained volatile even today as it overlaps the communal identities. Tandon (1963: 66-67) has written on the language of Punjabis in the pre-independence period. It is adequate to quote him at length thus:

> Our language, Punjabi, has no script and hardly, until lately, any except religious literature. For centuries the Muslims had used Persian which the Sikhs continued as their court language. The Sikhs had evolved the Gurmukhi script for writing Punjabi by modifying the Sanskrit alphabet, but this they did to avoid the sacrilege of recording their holy book, the Granth Sahib, in Persian script, the script of the Muslims against whom they had revolted.[1] Persian however continued to flourish as the language of culture and communication. Educated Punjabis were

> therefore bilingual, speaking Punjabi and reading and writing Persian.
>
> The British brought Urdu with them from the United Provinces and Delhi, and supplanted Persian. At the same time, they brought English....
>
> Hindi, in the Devanagri script, arrived later and was confined at the beginning to the Brahmins and to our women, the latter through the influence of Arya Samaj.

Tandon has succinctly and lucidly described the real situation in Punjab during the early British rule. The fact that Punjabi had no script of its own had serious political ramifications for the relations between the Hindus and the Sikhs after independence. The Punjabi was written in the Persian or Shahmukhi script, but the emergence of the Singh Sabha movement contributed to the popularisation of the Gurmukhi script. In fact, the Gurmukhi script was also popularised in the 19th century by the Hindu *parchariks* (preachers) who wrote various discourses by using this script. What is notable is that the language of these discourses was essentially classical Braj.[2] In fact, the Sikh religious literature in the 19th century was largely in Braj; two of the examples of which are *Dasam Granth* (most of it is in Braj) and Bhai Santokh Singh's *Suraj Parkash*. The Arya Samaj movement simultaneously popularised not only Hindi but also Devanagri script. All this began in the late 19th century but gained momentum in the next century. The impact of the Singh Sabha movement can be seen in the form of another movement of writing the literature in Gurmukhi script though the most popular form of writing Punjabi continued to be the Persian. Thus, we find a complex situation in which a majority of the people of Punjab, including Hindus, Sikhs and Muslims, speaking Punjabi and writing in Persian script. The Sikh leadership was making all-out efforts to popularise the Gurmukhi script among the Sikhs, whereas the Arya Samaj was popularising Hindi in Devanagri script among the Hindus.

The independence of the country was accompanied by the partition in which the states that were affected most included Punjab and Bengal. Communal riots broke out in Punjab as a result of which the Hindus and Sikhs from the Western Punjab and the Muslims from the East Punjab were forced to take refuge on the other sides of the newly created international border. The complex situation prevailing in Punjab with regard to the language began to have its ramifications in the form of polarisation of the Hindus and the Sikhs. It seems ironical that there was no conflict between the Hindus and the Sikhs with regard to the swift and radical elimination of the Urdu language and the Persian script from the school curriculum of the state with an exception of Malerkotla region.[3] We have no record of controversy on these issues whether the Punjabi should be written in the Persian script or not. However, once the Persian script disappeared, the important issue that came to the fore was the identification of the script for the Punjabi language. Since the Urdu language and the Persian script were identified with the Muslims, the communalisation of the script and language in the post-colonial Punjab also became a part of the process, which had begun in the 19th century.

Though the politics of language had its roots in the history of the separation of spoken language from the language of culture and sometimes communication, yet the rise of vernacular languages in India was a part of the process of emerging nationalism, and collective and regional identity. The first step that the government had undertaken in the post-colonial India was the reorganisation of the states on linguistic basis. In Punjab, the politics of language and its overlapping with the religious identities might have dissuaded or discouraged the Union Government of India from the reorganisation of Punjab. The communal divide between the Sikhs and the Hindus is dominantly based on the language controversy though the economic division between the Sikh cultivators and the Hindu traders has been added to this divide as another factor. In the census of 1951, the political mobilisation took place in order to determine what was the mother tongue of *Punjabi-speaking* Punjabis. "The Hindus recorded their mother language as Hindi" is the common phrase used by the Sikh leadership. Interestingly, a considerable proportion of the dalits of Punjab also recorded Hindi as their mother tongue. Nayar (1966) attributes this act of the dalits to their exploitation in the hands of the Sikh farmers in the rural areas. The association between the religion and the recording of the mother tongue may be regarded as one of the important factors in the postponement of the reorganisation of the state for a while. However, the entire issue left bitterness between the two communities, which frequently came to the fore in various ways. The vernacular press, particularly the newspapers from Jalandhar, played an important role in communalising the issue of language in Punjab. In terms of the imposition of the Gurmukhi script, the Sikh leadership aimed at establishing its hegemony, whereas the politicisation of this matter led to some kind of rejection of their mother tongue by the Punjabi-speaking Hindus. Not everyone played and participated in the politics of language, but it has become a part of the life of the Punjabis in many ways and in the religiously charged political situation, the Hindus are made responsible for this betrayal.

The politicisation of language did not prevent the formation of Punjabi Suba, but only delayed it. Even before the formation of Punjabi Suba (about which a lot has been written) the understanding of the domination of various social and religious groups may reveal the structure of political dynamics of Punjab. Nayar (1966: 121-22) has provided some data on the social background of the Sikh leaders thus:

> ... Both Congress Sikhs and Akalis are overwhelmingly of rural origin (over 75%), though Congress Sikhs are more so. Only a small number were born in a town or city....
>
> As far as caste composition is concerned, both groups show the predominance of the same caste groups. Among both Congress

Sikhs and Akalis, the Jats are the predominant caste group (over 50%) though more so for the Congress Sikhs (70%) then for the Akalis (54%)...

The political domination of Jats in the region prior to the formation of Punjabi Suba was obvious. It might also be true for the Haryana region, as it later on emerged that the Hindu Jats began to monopolise the state politics. An examination of the social background of the leaders of the communist parties may provide certain interesting information. Most of them belong to the Jat caste. Even in the case of the Naxalites, the same was true (Judge 1992). The caste background of the leaders of the political parties in Punjab had tremendous consequences for the political dynamics of the state after the formation of the Punjabi Suba. The articulation of various demands on the part of the Akalis was largely Jat-centric.

It was pointed out in the beginning that the main objective of the struggle for Punjabi Suba was to have a Sikh majority state and it was opposed by the Hindus. The Indian government was aware of this situation, as it can be interpreted from the writings of Puri (1983 and 1989) and Narang (2000). It also implies that when the Government of India took the decision to form the Punjabi Suba, it did so with the clear understanding that it was creating a Sikh majority state. Narang (ibid.: 305-6) observes that the Indo-Pak war and subsequent decision of Sant Fateh Singh to postpone his agitation and self-immolation created the conditions for the formation of Punjabi Suba. "During the war, the role of Punjabis in general and Sikh population in particular was highly appreciated. In view of all these developments, within two days of the cease-fire, the central government appointed a three-men cabinet committee consisting of Y.B. Chavan, Indira Gandhi and Mahavir Tyagi, to examine afresh the demand for Punjabi Suba."

The Punjabi Suba created a Sikh majority state leaving out certain Punjabi-speaking areas and from then onwards another era of the emergence of new issues began. Before we go into those issues, it would be worthwhile to first focus on the political consequences of the formation of the Punjabi Suba. Immediately after the formation of the Punjabi Suba, the Akalis came to power in the state in the elections that were held in 1967. They remained in power only for a short period, as there was a split in the Akali Dal and Lachhman Singh Gill, with the support of the Congress, ousted the then Chief Minister, Gurnam Singh. Since the Jats dominated in the political dynamics among the Sikhs, the implication was that they were also competing with each other for power and irrespective of the political party affiliation, the political competition among them manifested in the inter-party interaction and politics. Pettigrew (1978) has shown how the Kairon-Rarewala conflict entailed struggle for domination in the period prior to the formation of the Punjabi Suba. It also involved the future politics of Punjab where the Jat elite competed with each other through various political parties. As a result, Punjab experienced alternative rule of two parties and the Akalis continued to compete with the Congress for formal power. Since the Akali Dal, along with its basic orientation and manifestation, was essentially a party with a base among the Sikhs, it got trapped into the process of articulation of the Sikh interests with aggressive posture so as to sustain and enlarge its appeal among the Sikhs. In the process, the Akali Dal reached a point of no return and ultimately shared the platform with the extremist Sikh leader, Jarnail Singh Bhindranwala, in 1982. However, on the way to its association with the extremists, the Akali Dal continued to exhibit and indulge in its aggressive posture with a short interlude immediately after the emergency in 1977 when it was a partner in the Janata Party government.

Two aspects of the period following the formation of Punjabi Suba require some explication. The first is that Chandigarh was turned into an apple of discord between Punjab and the newly formed Haryana. Till this date, no decision has been made regarding the status of Chandigarh, which the Akali Dal has invariably used to mobilise the Sikhs. Darshan Singh Pheruman, who went on fast unto death and died, symbolises the struggle of the Sikhs for Chandigarh. The reason for not taking decision on the transfer of the city has always remained an intriguing issue. One can only make a conjecture that the elite of the city exercise strong influence in the Centre and they do not wish to go to any of the states. This lack of conviction of the Indian government is a readymade weapon in the hands of the Akalis. However, the issue of Chandigarh only evokes emotional response when it is combined with some other issue(s).

Secondly, one of the most emotive and contentious issues has continued to be the sharing of river water between Punjab and Haryana. The Green Revolution phenomenon, which has become indispensable for understanding various dimensions of the polity, economy and society of Punjab and Haryana, was and continues to be based on intensive irrigation besides the extensive use of chemical fertilisers and pesticides, and hybrid varieties of seeds. Over a period of time, the Punjabi farmer has shifted to the wheat-paddy monoculture involving intensive irrigation giving rise to the politics of water in the region. Water has become the most valuable resource and the presence of a large number of peasant proprietors in both Haryana and Punjab makes it the decisive issue with regard to the electoral politics. The politicians are therefore keeping the issue of water alive without any serious effort at resolving it. Haryana, being the successor state, has certain riparian rights over the resources of Punjab and these issues could have been handled amicably. However, this did not happen and the Akalis who could not keep their party in uninterrupted rule exploited these issues, but they also did it by twisting the economic issue to an instance and illustration of discrimination against the Sikhs. There emerged some readymade and set slogans that have come to stay and form an integral part of the mobilisation strategy (in some cases, these may be rationalisations) of the Akali Dal. These are as follows: *"Panth khatre wich hai"* (The Panth is in danger); "*Sikhan nal dhakka ho riha hai*" (There is discrimination against the Sikhs).

Such slogans, coupled with the demands for higher prices for the procurement of wheat and paddy, and river water for Punjab, have given rise to the continuous articulation of the issue of centre-state relations and state autonomy. More powers to the state may be regarded as one of the fundamental issues. The Akali Dal is not the only one demanding for state autonomy, but it is the only party that is based on religion in the secular context. The Akalis' demand for state autonomy may be perceived as communal demand and this is exactly what has happened. Dhami (1977: 161) wrote that owing to the outdated ideology of the Akali Dal, "its support base is mainly confined to the local rural Sikh peasantry, the result is that they develop a different type of attitude which for want of a better phrase may be termed regional chauvinism". The Anandpur Sahib Resolution, prepared by the Akalis, became one of the most controversial documents in the post-independence period and everybody tried to interpret it in his own way. The interpretations varied from characterising it as a separatist to defending it as a document that raises demand for more powers to the state. There is no denying the fact that it was prepared at the time when the Akalis were out of power and the religious flavour in its wording created doubt among others.

A way of understanding and interpreting the orientations of the Akali Dal in the Punjab politics is to find out certain basic contradictions that seemed specific to the state before the rise of the BJP following the Ram Janma Bhoomi issue in the beginning of the last decade of the 20th century. The foremost among these contradictions was that in a secular country, the Akali Dal was based on the ideology of Sikhism or so it proclaimed. It invariably articulated the issues and problems being faced by the Sikh community. In a Sikh majority state, the religious card did not help the Akalis to remain in power without any threat. It began to raise issues, like centre-state relations, more autonomy to the states that concerned with all the states of the countries. As the posture becomes more radical, the situation develops volatility that requires somebody to take it to the extreme. Marx (1973: 152) once wrote: "A nation and a woman are not forgiven for the unguarded hour in which the first available adventurer is able to violate them." He, however, forgot to add religious community. Jarnail Singh Bhindranwala emerged as the first available adventurer and the Akalis had already prepared a situation for him to make the best use of it in the name of religion and community without bothering whether the two were same or different. Who was Jarnail Singh Bhindranwala? What does Bhindranwala mean? Can we say, as some seem to claim, that Bhindranwala was largely responsible for the emergence of the crisis in Punjab? In order to give the answer, an attempt has been made to trace the background of the Damdami Taksal and the personal background of Jarnail Singh Bhindranwala in the next part.

II
DAMDAMI TAKSAL AND BHINDRANWALA

The word 'Damdami' seems to be derived from the Punjabi word *dam* which means breath and it is historically connected with the few days of rest that the tenth guru of the Sikhs, Guru Gobind Singh, took after leaving Anandpur Sahib at Talwandi Sabo where the Gurdwara Damdama Sahib is presently located. The literal meaning of Taksal is mint and metaphorically, it would imply that the place from where the real Sikh emerges. In other words, a Taksal is a seminary where a man is trained right from his childhood into proper recitation of Gurbani and *kirtan* (singing hymns). The story how the idea of having a seminary is related to Guru Gobind Singh is found in the history of Damdami Taksal (1994). The story is woven around an incident that occurred when a Sikh, while reciting Gurbani pronounced some words wrongly, which led the tenth guru to intervene and explain to him that how the meanings could undergo a change if the words were pronounced wrongly. Since the Guru had advised the Sikh in the presence of others, one of the Panj Piaras, Bhai Daya Singh, approached the Guru to guide the congregation in this respect. However, the Guru could not find time for it though he promised to do so. When the Guru left Anandpur Sahib and reached and stayed at Talwandi Sabo, the Singhs reminded him of his promise. He told them to go to Dheer Mall at Kartarpur Sahib to get the Granth that had been prepared by the fifth guru so that the *bani* of the ninth guru could also be included in it.[4] Baba Deep Singh met Dhir Mall and requested him to hand over the Granth. Dhir Mall challenged that if the tenth guru represented the charisma of the first guru, as was the case of the fifth guru, then he could himself prepare the Granth.

It is in such circumstances that Guru Gobind Singh dictated the entire Gurbani to Bhai Mani Singh and he also undertook the task of interpreting it. Two of his devout Sikhs, namely, Bhai Mani Singh and Baba Deep Singh, were involved in the writing of the Granth. The dictation and simultaneous interpretation of the Gurbani took nine months and nine days. According to the story as narrated in the official history of the Damdami Taksal, the tenth guru nominated the *Guru Granth Sahib* as his successor when he was at Nanded. When Baba Deep Singh returned to Punjab, he started his Taksal at Damdama Sahib, whereas Bhai Mani Singh went to Amritsar. After the martyrdom of Baba Deep Singh, we find that there is a line of successors and Jarnail Singh Bhindranwala was fourteenth in this line. It may be noted that till the tenth head of the Taksal, that is, up to Baba Bishen Singh Muralewale, there was no suffix called 'Bhindranwala'. The suffix 'Bhindranwala' began with Baba Sunder Singh who belonged to the village Bhinder Kalan in Ferozpur district. Korpal (2001: 16) writes about Sant Sunder Singh Bhindranwala in an interesting manner thus:

> He had spread the fame of the Taksal as far as Rameshwarm in the south, Brahamputra in the east, Kashmir, Himachal and Nepal and other hill territories in the north. He also instructed his followers to wear arms along with attaining their knowledge

of Gurmat. He, who baptized thousands of Sikhs in a day, through his inspiring discourses for 28 days, so significantly contributed to liberating a Gurdwara in Mukatsar that the Damdami Taksal began to be called Bhindranwale Taksal thenceforth.

Sant Sunder Singh died in 1930 and it is obvious that he was a witness to the changes in not only the Sikhism but also the relations among various religious communities. The influence of Tat Khalsa on his emphasis on five 'Ks' to carve out a distinct Sikh tradition could not be ignored. Also, the establishment of new nomenclature, that is, Bhindranwala, seems to suggest that before Sunder Singh there could be certain contentions and contestations among the followers or between the followers and the relatives of the deceased heads of the Taksal. However, there could be another dimension. It has been found that most of the heads of the Taksal were very active and mobile in spreading the "true interpretation of the Gurbani". They were able to establish many gurdwaras at different places. Sant Sunder Singh Bhindranwala, in comparison to other heads of such centres of learning, proved to be more charismatic as a result of which the others got marginalised and their influence remained confined and localised. Sant Gurbachan Singh Bhindranwala, the twelfth in the succession of heads of the Taksal, died in 1969 at Mehta in Amritsar district. Sant Kartar Singh succeeded him and things changed in a qualitative manner, as the Sant became more aggressive in his sermons and turned the religion to the political space thus competing with various other such godmen for influence. The example of Kartar Singh Bhindranwala substantiates the general view that the political orientation of a religious leader creates an ideology emphasising more and more Puritanism in the religious practice, as such an emphasis is politically functional.

Sant Kartar Singh Bhindranwala shifted his headquarters from the village Bhinder Kalan to Mehta where his predecessor had died. The reasons for shifting had something to do with the internal conflict in the Taksal after the death of Baba Gurbachan Singh. In spite of his credentials, the Akali leaders "Sant Chanan Singh, Sant Fateh Singh, Justice Gurnam Singh and Gurcharan Singh Tohra conspired to make his rival Mohan Singh the *Taksal* head" (Kaur 1990: 52). However, unlike the earlier heads of Taksal, he maintained the suffix 'Bhindranwala'. Immediately, after becoming the self-styled chief of the Taksal, Kartar Singh carried on his activities quite aggressively and in the process came into conflict with the Nirankaris. According to Sant Kartar Singh, the Nirankari sect was bogus, as it believed in the living guru. He also became critical of the gurus of the Nirankari sect for imitating the Sikh gurus. Kaur (ibid.: 53-54) points out:

> In fact, the Damdami Taksal had been fighting a war of sorts with the Nirankaris since the time of Sant Gurbachan Singh. Contrary to the general belief that it was the *Taksal* heads who launched the offensive, provocation had actually come from Niranjan Singh, a top ranking Nirankari. He had tried to set up Nirankari Bhawan at various places in Punjab which at times put the *Taksal* in direct confrontation with the Nirankaris. For instance, he deliberately invited the Nirankari head Baba Gurbachan Singh to set up a Nirankari Bhawan at the historic city of Hargobindpur, where the *kar seva* was being carried out by then *Taksal* head Sant Gurbachan Singh. This led to minor clashes.

Before Sant Kartar Singh Bhindranwala could start a crusade against the Nirankari sect towards the end of his life, the political scenario began to change rapidly. Indira Gandhi had imposed emergency and was ruling over the country as a dictator. During this period, the Akali Dal was the only political party, which continued to protest against Mrs. Gandhi by sending *jathas* - group of volunteers - to court arrest. All other political parties except the Communist Party of India (CPI) were in disarray as most of the leaders had either gone underground or arrested.[5] The history of Damdami Taksal (1994) records an event during the emergency in which Sant Kartar Singh had to interact with Mrs. Gandhi on December 7, 1975 on the occasion of the celebrations of the third centenary of martyrdom of the ninth guru of the Sikhs, Guru Tegh Bahadur, at Ram Leela Ground, New Delhi. When Mrs. Gandhi reached the spot, everybody stood up to welcome her, but Sant Kartar Singh kept on sitting and later on, he rebuked all Sikhs for this act by pointing out that in the presence of the *Guru Granth Sahib* no Sikh should have stood up. After this, as the Damdami Taksal (1994) alleges, Mrs. Gandhi talked about the martyrdom of Guru Tegh Bahadur. The Sant again told her that because of the ninth guru it could become possible for her to become the Prime Minister. What we can discern from the official history of the Taksal is that had there been no Guru Tegh Bahadur, the history of India would have been different and Aurangzeb might have succeeded in converting all Hindus to Islam. Such a belief still persists among the Sikhs.[6] From this, as alleged by Damdami Taksal (ibid.), began the hostility of Mrs. Indira Gandhi towards the Sant.

However, the dynamism of Sant Kartar Singh could be noticed during the period of emergency.[7] When most of the Akali leaders were in prison, he organised 37 processions. In the process, he came in conflict with the administration of Gurdaspur district and at that time, the Deputy Commissioner of this district, Niranjan Singh, was a Nirankari. Sant Kartar Singh was regarded as a man of learning and in his whirlwind tour of Punjab, he baptised a large number of Sikhs. It was during such a journey that he met with an accident in August 1977 and died. With him ended an era of the Damdami Taksal during which Sikh orthodoxy was aggressively interpreted, preached and spread through the Khalsa principles. The successor of Sant Kartar Singh Bhindranwala was Jarnail Singh Bhindranwala with a different background from his predecessor. Since he emerged as the main actor in the subsequent period in Punjab politics and religion eclipsing, for a short period, everybody else and marginalising the dominant players in the politics of the state, there is a need to know a little bit more about him. The Damdami Taksal (ibid.) describes him as the heartthrob of the Sikh youth and some people regard him as the greatest Sikh of the 20th century.[8] The role of individual in history has always been a debatable and contentious issue. One may argue that in the absence of Hitler there would have been no World War II. The writing and notion of counter-history is grounded in the argument that one has to make sense of the course of history in the absence of certain events. In this way, we can know and identify the crucial significance of certain events that have occurred in history. Jarnail Singh Bhindranwala occupies such a place where we can raise a question whether it is possible to think of Punjab problem and Sikh militant movement in his absence. It is difficult to give a satisfactory answer, but there is a reasonable basis to argue that he was the main catalyst who triggered forces of destruction and violence.

Jarnail Singh belonged to the Jat caste and his *gotra* was Brar. He belonged to the twin villages called Rode Lande in the then Faridkot district. The village Rode belongs to the Barar *gotra*, whereas the *gotra* of the Lande village's Jats is Sarao.[9] The people of Sarao claim their village to be the original village, while Rode came to exist as *nanaka dheri* village.[10] The people of Lande generally regarded their neighbours as aggressive and quarrelsome. It may be reminded that these are typical inter-village stereotypes that have also been pointed out by Pettigrew (1978) in a somewhat different manner. Jarnail Singh was born in 1947 and "he was the second son from the second wife" (Kaur 1990) of Joginder Singh. The people of the village do not have a reasonably good knowledge about him, as Joginder Singh began to live on his small farm. It is now known that Joginder Singh was in association with the Damdami Taksal and Sant Gurbachan Singh, the then head of the Taksal, chose Jarnail Singh as his special pupil. Most of the scholars, who have written on the life of Jarnail Singh Bhindranwala, have missed an important dimension of the social life of Punjab of which he was a typical instance. In the Sikh religious tradition, the respect of and veneration for the saints is a highly prescribed behaviour. There is a large number of *maths* or *deras* of the Sikh saints and most of these *deras* preach religious orthodoxy with a few exceptions. These saints are now identified with a collective name called Sant Samaj. The Damdami Taksal falls in this category of religious practices within Sikhism. These *deras* also have an important function for the society, as they provide employment to a large number of persons. For example, the Damdami Taksal trains young people in the recitation of the Gurbani and after completing their training they become *pathis* or *granthis*. Many families, such as of Joginder Singh, give one of their sons to *dera* largely due to hard conditions of their life. Obviously, Jarnail Singh was one such case. It now seems clear that the devotion and intensity of Jarnail Singh might have made him a special follower of the Sant. The arrival of Jarnail Singh on the seen as the fourteenth head of the Damdami Taksal changed the direction of the events, as he intensified his criticism of the Nirankaris that subsequently led to the clash between the two. Since it is generally believed that the Punjab crisis began with the clash, our discussion of various features of the militant movement in Punjab would start from it in the next section.

III
SALIENT FEATURES OF THE MILITANT MOVEMENT[11]

The preceding discussion covered two important dimensions of the first phase of the Sikh militant movement that may be identified in terms of various occurrences and events as the background conditions of its emergence. Following the positivist tradition, there is a strong tendency in sociology to give causal explanation of a social movement. Contrary to such a perspective, an attempt shall be made to describe the events that occurred and contributed to the growth and escalation of the militant movement. Both covert as well as overt developments took place in the 1970s that led to the mobilisation of Sikh identity and autonomy. Various incidents that contributed considerably to the making of the Punjab crisis were independent from each other. Only the combined effect of these incidents and the emergence of Jarnail Singh Bhindranwala created a pattern as if all processes were interlinked. At the manifest level, the issue of Khalistan was raised by Jagjit Singh Chauhan when he got published a half-page advertisement in the *New York Times* on October 12, 1971. Chauhan had no connection with the Bhindranwala phenomenon, which started seven years after the advertisement. Similarly, the passing of the Anandpur Sahib Resolution in 1973 by the Akali Dal was a strategic document on the autonomy of states for electoral gains. Bhindranwala picked up the Anandpur Sahib Resolution as the demand charter of the Sikhs. The significant rise of the Sikh diaspora till the mid-1970s contributed to the development of the idea of the independent Sikh State. Some of the prominent Sikhs abroad raised the issue of Khalistan. The Congress Party, too, had its share in this process when Giani Zail Singh virtually sponsored the formation of the Dal Khalsa, which articulated the glory and autonomy of the Sikhs. The Congress and the Akali Dal – the two major political parties – competed with each other on capturing the votes of the Sikhs. In the process, both tried to revive Sikhism in their own ways showing holier-than-thou behaviour.

All these developments combined in a strange way when the violent clash at Amritsar between the adherents of Nirankari sect and the followers of Jarnail Singh Bhindranwala, the head of the Damdami Taksal, took place on 13 April 1978. This resulted in the killing of 13 followers of Bhindranwala and three Nirankaris. This incident tended to provide both legitimacy and excuse for armed attacks on the Nirankaris including the murder of its chief, Baba Gurbachan Singh, in 1980. Besides the above, other events of this period are: the Akali Dal

Conference at Ludhiana, the elections of the Shiromani Gurdwara Prabandhak Committee (SGPC) in which Jarnail Singh Bhindranwala was marginalised, the murder of the editor of *Punjab Kesari*, Lala Jagat Narain, the arrest and release of Bhindranwala, dismissal of the Akali Dal-led government in the state, the formation of Congress government with Darbara Singh as the Chief Minister following fresh elections and the organisation of killing squads by Bhindranwala.

It is important to mention here that the most significant event that occurred and which decisively influenced the course of events was the arrest of Amrik Singh and Thara Singh of Damdami Taksal in July 1982 when they came to Amritsar for fighting the case of the arrested driver, who was an employee of the Taksal. Jarnail Singh Bhindranwala rushed to Amritsar when he heard of their arrest and thereon he initiated the process of sending the *jathas* (band of followers) for arrests. It may be opined that the process that was initiated by Bhindranwala might not have sustained for long had the Akali Dal not supported it out of panic. At that time, the Akali Dal (Longowal) was organising the *morcha* (campaign) at Kapoori in which other parties were also participating. When the news reached Sant Longowal about the action of Bhindranwala, he and other Akali leaders rushed to Amritsar. It seems in retrospect that since there was nobody in authority present in the Golden Temple to prevent Bhindranwala from sending the *jathas* to give voluntary arrest to protest against the arrest of his two close aides, there was a fear that he might control the affairs of the Sikhs. After Longowal met Bhindranwala and discussed the matter with him, the Akali Dal withdrew from the *morcha* at Kapoori and started the Dharam Yudh Morcha. It proved to be the turning point in the emergence of militant movement in Punjab. It also implied that Jarnail Singh Bhindranwala had moved away from the Congress and joined hands with the Akali Dal. The period between August 1982 and June 1984 became eventful in which Bhindranwala emerged as the powerful Sikh leader having a strong base among the youth. He was able to marginalise the other Akali leaders. He delivered many speeches during this period and in most of the cases he shared the podium with the leaders of the Akali Dal – the prominent among them were Sant Harchand Singh Longowal, Jagdev Singh Talwandi and Sukhjinder Singh. The Congress Party, ruling at the Centre, made the things difficult for a possible solution when in November 1983, the Darbara Singh-led government was dismissed following an incident in which a few Hindu bus passengers were killed and the President's rule was imposed. Since Bhindranwala was highly critical of Darbara Singh (he used to call him Zacharia Khan – an 18th century governor of Punjab, who was widely hated by the Sikhs), the idea might have occurred to the Prime Minister and others in the Union Government to remove him for a possible solution. Anticipating the police action, the militants inside the Golden Temple started preparing themselves to confront the forces. Extensive fortification of the entire Golden Temple Complex under the direction of Gen. Shabeg Singh was done. It was Jarnail Singh Bhindranwala who virtually ruled over Punjab through his campaign of terrorist violence.

The next phase began with 'Operation Blue Star' in June 1984 when the Indian Army was ordered to attack and enter into the Golden Temple Complex for the purpose of flushing out militants. The fierce battle that raged inside resulted in significant loss of life and extensive destruction of the Akal Takhat. Bhindranwala and his close aides were killed.[12] However, the strike on the most sacred place of the Sikhs led to a widespread feeling of hurt and anger. There was a revolt in the Sikh Regiment of the Indian Army too. The post-Operation Blue Star happenings further alienated the Sikhs from the Indian state. On October 31, Prime Minister, Indira Gandhi, was assassinated by her Sikh bodyguards and in retaliation thousands of innocent Sikhs were killed in riots that followed in Delhi, Kanpur and many other places. By the end of 1984, when Rajiv Gandhi was elected as the Prime Minister, the situation seemed to have reached the extreme level of hostility of the Sikh community towards the Indian government. Following the anti-Sikh riots, the militants started reorganising and in the beginning of 1985, they began their activities.

In the beginning of the fourth phase, the dialogue between Sant Harchand Singh Longowal and the Prime Minister began and culminated into the Rajiv-Longowal Accord in July 1985. Soon after, Sant Longowal was shot dead by the militants. The restoration of the democratic process raised hopes of a possible solution to the Punjab problem. However, the Barnala-led government faced the crisis when the factional fight led to the split in the Akali Dal. The accord, which was signed between the Prime Minister and Sant Longowal, was never implemented reinforcing the belief that the Indian government was not interested in solving the problem. The militants succeeded in organising themselves by the beginning of 1985 and in the initial period, they made attempts at creating the riot situations between the Sikhs and the Hindus in the cities of Punjab. There were tensions in many cities, but with the exception of Batala, all such tensions were short-lived. Even in Batala, the tension between the Hindus and the Sikhs did not remain permanent. The militants tried to forcibly close down the tobacco and liquor shops, but were unsuccessful.

The militant violence continued to escalate much more seriously, particularly after the formation of the Panthic Committee and declaration of the armed struggle for Khalistan in 1986. In the beginning, there were only two organisations, namely, the Khalistan Commando Force (KCF) and Babbar Khalsa International. The KCF was associated with the Panthic Committee, whereas the Babbar Khalsa was an independent organisation as it sprang from the Akhand Kirtani Jatha, which aimed at the elimination of the Nirankaris. During the crucial phase of conflict between Bhindranwala and Longowal, the Babbar Khalsa had supported the latter. As the members of the Panthic Committee began to drift away from each other, the KCF also started to split. The entire process led to a mushroom growth of militant organisations and rising number of new recruits. The militants began to rely on terrorist methods for its struggle. In the 'Operation Black Thunder' in 1988, the police encircled the Golden Temple and militants were forced to surrender. Sarab Jit Singh (2002: 150), who was the Deputy Commissioner of Amritsar district at that time, pointed out: "After Operation Blue Star, terrorist violence remained suppressed for several months, but in the case of Operation Black Thunder it spurted in the wake of the surrender of the first batch of militants and continued to increase." The escalation of violence after the Operation Black Thunder had no parallel in the earlier phase of the movement and it remained so till the first half of 1992.

Still another feature of the fourth phase was the social reform programme announced by the Panthic Committee led by Dr. Sohan Singh in 1987. The militants codified what they expected from the Sikhs. In the process of charting out their social reform programme, they also articulated the meaning of the Sikh. The important feature of this definition was identification of desirable and undesirable behaviour at the individual, social and formal institutional levels. The militants made it clear that the Sikhs who did not follow their code of conduct could be punished. Though the code of conduct was aimed at reforming the Sikh community, yet it had tremendous repercussions for the Sikh identity as well as the creation of the moral community. The detailed discussion of this issue would be made in the next chapter.

An important and interesting dimension of the social reform programme was the use of print media by the militants to reach the masses. This attempt created a new discourse of militancy in Punjab that took shape in the form of 'warnings and responsibilities'. As we would see,[13] these warnings in particular began with some specific issues, but within a couple of years, these started expanding their scope to virtually cover every aspect of the life of the Sikh community.

In the fifth phase, we find a series of initiatives undertaken at the national level by three successive Prime Ministers, two of whom were from the non-Congress political parties. When V.P. Singh took over as the Prime Minister in 1989, he appealed to the militants to join the mainstream. However, the appeal of V.P. Singh backfired in the sense that there was a sharp rise in the activities of the militants.[14] What happened was an important and interesting socio-cultural phenomenon noticed generally in such situations. Perceiving the statement of the Prime Minister to be an indication of some kind of accord along the lines of Assam, it was thought that the militants might then become political leaders participating in elections. This encouraged a large number of youth to join the militants and, at the same time, the police became temporarily passive. Militant activities shot up dramatically during this period and the police was thoroughly demoralised. After the dissolution of the Barnala-led government, the state remained under the Governor's rule till 1992. A significant point that needs mention here is related with the period when Chandra Shekhar succeeded V.P. Singh after the withdrawal of the support by the BJP following the *rath yatra* of L.K. Advani. Chandra Shekhar, the successor of V.P. Singh as the Prime Minister, pursued the line of conciliation towards the militants through middlemen and direct negotiations. There is, however, a reasonable basis to suggest that during the period when he was the Prime Minister, the proportion of the militants among the killed began rising (Puri, Judge and Sekhon 1999). When P.V. Narsimha Rao became the Prime Minister in 1991, he decided to hold elections in Punjab in February 1992.

The final phase began when Beant Singh became the Chief Minister in 1992 following an election that saw an effective boycott led by various Akali Dals and militant groups. Immediately after Beant Singh took over as the Chief Minister, he initiated the process of the suppression of the militant movement by giving extraordinary powers to the police. Within the first year of his rule, the back of militancy was effectively broken. The process that was initiated during the period when Chandra Shekhar was the Prime Minister saw its culmination in 1992-93. When on March 1, 1993 the people of Punjab woke up to read and hear the news of Gurbachan Singh Manochahal's death, it was clear that the movement had decisively failed. The usual call for bandh that had become a recurring phenomenon in Punjab did not find any support or compliance of the people. The life had become normal. Barring a few incidents, the terrorist activities progressively declined to the extent of extinction by the end of 1993. In 1995, a suicide bomber, perhaps the most dramatic action after 1993, killed Beant Singh.

The period of one-and-a-half decades of the movement was more complex than the description of various phases may tend to suggest. The social life of Punjab, particularly the disturbed areas, changed to adapt to the reign of terror in which the two players, namely, the militants and police, remained the dominant competitors. The stories of atrocities of the militants as well as the police were widely known in the state. The most important change that occurred in the rural areas of Punjab was that everything would come to a standstill after the sunset. Though Gupta (1997) calls it the construction of the space by the Sikh community where there is a tendency to overemphasise the given reality, but he did not stay in Punjab that too in the villages for the sufficient period to validate such an observation. The government did its best to help the militants in creating terror. For example, the buses would stop plying after a particular time. In the cities the cinema houses were directed not to run the night shows resulting in the virtual end of nightlife. Since there were no Vidhan Sabha elections held for long time in the state, the centralisation percolated to other bodies of the civil society. In the universities and colleges there were no elections held for student councils for years. Militancy also proved to be functional for the government to suppress democratic process to bring them under bureaucratic control. During the last years of the militancy, the hero of Punjab was

K.P.S. Gill – the police chief whom the media also called as super cop. He along with his other colleague police officers was the most visible actor in the governance of the state. The bureaucracy administered the state in its usual invisible manner, but in the absence of democratic process, the development of the culture of administration without accountability became the norm.

Linked with the absence of the elected government of the people of Punjab were the police excesses and atrocities on the common people as well as the militants. It may however be clarified that even after the democratic process began in 1992 the government continued to depend upon the police for the suppression of the militant movement. The unpopularity of the militants among the Sikh masses was the major factor in ending the militancy though many other factors contributed towards its failure. The study of Puri, Judge and Sekhon (1999) revealed that among the migrants from the villages of Amritsar and Gurdaspur districts, the proportion of the Sikhs was considerably high. It is difficult to pinpoint certain crucial factors that were responsible for its failure, because most of the exercise seems to be a process of logical construction that has occurred, and to use Hume's argument, is the effort of the mind in constructing the causal connection between the two variables. In the analysis of the failure of the movement, the social and demographic characteristics of the population of the state might have played a significant role. The Sikhs constitute about 60 per cent of the population of the state and they are divided on the bases of caste, political ideology and economic status. Religion is the single uniting factor among the Sikhs, which might have proved insufficient to create the kind of cohesiveness in the community that is invariably the requirement of such movements.

The militant movement was no doubt aimed at achieving the separate state of Khalistan. It used terrorist methods to achieve its objective. Two issues that require emphasis have been the migration of the people from the villages and the disappearance of the individuals without any trace. In the first case, it is important to mention that among the migrants from the villages the Sikhs constituted a considerable proportion, which indicates that the Sikh militant movement affected both the religious groups in the villages. Most of the Sikh migrants were either related to the police personnel or they wanted to escape from extortions. However, the police was also an important factor in pushing the people to the cities from the villages. In a study conducted by Bal and Judge (2001), it was found that the migration of the Hindu traders from the villages created a vacuum that was later on filled by the Jat businessmen. The transformation in the caste background of the traders has, however, remained least noticed phenomenon in Punjab. Something that has drawn the attention of the entire nation is the disappearance of people in Punjab during the period of militancy. The gravity of the situation was only realised when Jaswant Singh Khalra – an Akali and pro-militant human rights activist – was picked up and subsequently killed by the Punjab police and it came to the public notice that as a human rights activist he was investigating the large-scale disappearance of the people. It has now become known that police cremated a large number of unidentified bodies in Amritsar and probably elsewhere too. The issue has been taken up by the human rights organisations and it shows the ugly side of the state measures to curb militancy in Punjab.

The trajectory of the Khalistan/militant movement followed the path of terrorism and its roots could be located in the way the Sikh identity has been politicised to control the religious affairs of the community. The political behaviour of the Akali Dal and those who aspire to dislodge them from the support base that it has been enjoying may be situated in the forefront of the emergence of the militant discourse. The obsessive emphasis on the singular Sikh tradition on the part of the Akali Dal as well as the other religious sects within Sikhism tried to minimise the basis of the eclectic space among different religious communities. The eclectic space that had emerged due to the co-existence of the different communities was undermined as it was done in 1947.

Notes

1. This observation is difficult to substantiate in the light of the fact that the second guru of the Sikh, Guru Angad Dev, developed Gurmukhi from the already available business script called *lande* (Pashaura Singh 2004).
2. Such handwritten texts are still available from the families who bothered to preserve these things. Author traced one such text from a family connected with 19th century aristocracy. It is written in Gurmukhi and it is *Ram Katha*. Interestingly, the language of the text is Braj.
3. The Muslims, falling under the princely state of Malerkotla, were rather protected by the Sikhs in 1947. The story goes back to the times of the tenth guru. When the Governor of Sarhind ordered that the younger two sons of the guru be buried alive, the only one to oppose it was the Nawab of Malerkotla.
4. Dhir Mall (1627-1677) was the eldest son of Baba Gurditta and grandson of Guru Hargobind. The sixth guru chose his younger brother, Har Rai, as his successor, after which he started his own guruship (Kaur 1995). In view of the fact that Dhir Mall died much before the tenth guru founded the Khalsa Panth, it seems that Baba Dip Singh might have met one of his descendants. It may be noted that the original copy of *Guru Granth Sahib*, which was authored by Guru Arjun Dev is still in the possession of his descendants at Kartarpur in Jalandhar district.
5. The CPI was supporting the emergency as it had alliance with the Congress in the earlier elections.
6. The legend is that the Kashmiri Brahmins approached the ninth guru to help save Hinduism, which he did by sacrificing his life.
7. In his opposition to emergency, Sant Kartar Singh Bhindranwala has no rival in the history of that time. It also implies that from him began the entry of a seminary chief into a political space. His successor Jarnail Singh exploited that space effectively and with the tactical ability of a politician created an unforeseen political instability in Punjab.

8. There are some scholars, notably among them is Gurtej Singh – a former IAS officer – who claim to be 'Sikh scholars'. They have honoured Jarnail Singh Bhindranwala as the greatest Sikh of the 20th century. Along with the 'Sikh scholars', some Sikh fundamentalist organisations in India and abroad have also joined to designate him as the greatest Sikh of the 20th century.
9. The author is grateful to Malkit Singh – a well-known artist of Punjab – for giving this information.
10. *Nanaka dheri* comes to exist in village when a family does not have a son and the daughter who along with her husband settles in her parental villages inherits the land. As a result of this and also due to the *gotra* exogamy practiced by the Jats a new *gotra* group emerges in the villages. It is called *nanaka dheri*.
11. The entire discussion in this section is based on the following sources: Kaur et al (1984), Tully and Jacob (1985), Jeffrey (1986), Jafar (1988), Brar (1993), Jain (1995), Narayanan (1996), Chadda (1997), Gill (1997), and Puri, Judge and Sekhon (1999).
12. The Damdami Taksal did not accept the death of Jarnail Singh Bhindranwala till recently. It is on the 19th anniversary of the Operation Blue Star that the SGPC declared him martyr thereby acknowledging his death.
13. See Chapter 4.
14. It has been indicated by Puri, Judge and Sekhon (1999) on the basis of an empirical study conducted in 28 villages of Amritsar and Gurdaspur districts.

3

Reconstruction of Sikh Identity

The politics of reconstruction of the Sikh identity, as it evolved over a period of time, could be historically linked to the fundamentalist assertions of Jarnail Singh Bhindranwala and, after his death, to the militant leaders with the similar efforts of the Singh Sabha movement in the late 19th century. The militant movement in Punjab spanning 15 years addressed to the question of the Sikh identity forcefully and tried to impose it with the power of the gun on the Sikhs in Punjab (Sekhon 1999). Threatened by the militants, the common Sikhs in rural areas, where the militancy was strong, tried to follow their edicts. It also implies that the common Sikhs, who were informed and ordered by the militants to follow their notion of the Sikh identity, were not living in strict accordance with what they thought to be the Sikh religious tradition. It is because of this reason that in the case of the Sikhs, the question of identity emerged and still continues to be the most dynamic, challenging and contentious issue. Beginning in the late 19th century, "the Sikh" has been defined time and again. Even in the present century, the controversies with regard to who is Sikh have not been amicably settled. As a special case of its kind, the identity discourse among the Sikhs requires a rigorous analysis.

The present chapter aims at identifying the multiple and diverse streams of the politics of construction and reconstruction of Sikh identity. Accordingly, the discussion has been divided into four parts. In the first part, various theoretical issues regarding identity have been examined whereas the second takes stock of the historical genesis and evolution of the politics of Sikh identity. In the third and fourth parts the fundamentalist articulation and the enforcement of the Sikh identity by Bhindranwala and later on, by the militants respectively are analysed.

I
POLITICS OF IDENTITY

Explaining and understanding the notion of identity has always been a difficult exercise in conceptualisation. Though the sociological distinction between the religion and the community is a very useful device to handle the issue of religious identity, yet it is equally important to understand the dynamics of interaction between the two. Uberoi (1996), while referring to certain writings on Sikhism in the 19th century, mentions a view that if we map the tremendous variety in Islam all over the world, then Sikhism could very well pass for a variant of Islam. The implication of this observation is quite clear, that is, the community and religion interact in such a way that what we call a religious tradition gets entwined and mixed up with the local cultures and transforms it into a formation characterised by diversity. This makes the effort at conceptualising identity difficult, as Touraine (1988) points out that the appeal to identity entails the rejection of social roles. In other words, the articulation of identity is always a conscious activity and may turn against an actor's role in social situation. The concept of role in sociology has been a very useful analytical tool to locate the person in a social space. At the same time, however, it is a secular and neutral concept. Except for psychology, the issue of identity did not occupy the central position, as is the case now. To turn to the notion of role, it would be worthwhile to refer to Nadel (1957), who related the integration of individual with society in terms of the number of role performances an individual has to make. The person, who is performing multiple roles, is more integrated with the society than the person who has limited roles to perform. In the contemporary discourse on identity, the similar kinds of ideas have been mooted. It is generally stated that a person has multiple identities, which are to be examined and posited in terms of his/her occupational, ethnic, regional, caste and gender positions.

Since the concept of role is a neutral conceptual basis to locate people in social space, the question of why sociology should take up the issue of identity for the same purpose inevitably emerges. In actual practice, the concept of identity is not brought into play for the purpose of replacing the notion of role. Identity is used for the articulation of creating an assembly of persons on the basis of single criterion. This observation reinforces the position of Touraine and we may argue that the question of identity is political and its purpose is invariably influenced by the need for the mobilisation of the collectivity at a particular moment of time. It may however be added that the identity may not necessarily be the endeavour in the direction of the construction of only the 'self', it may also involve the construction of the 'other'. In present times, when there is a phenomenal rise in the study of identity issues, many researchers confuse between role and identity. Occupational roles are now stated as components of multiple identities, which is not an appropriate conceptualisation. Identity and role differ from each other in one fundamental respect, that is, the former is consciously constructed to demarcate boundaries in relation to certain other collectivity, whereas the latter is a part of the position and mobility of the individual in the horizontal and vertical social spaces. It may also involve the objective of excluding certain individuals and groups from a collectivity.

Sometimes the purpose and intention of the construction of identity may involve the reinterpretation of history by "inventing some traditions". Anderson (1991: 7), while defining a nation as an imagined political community, explicates the notion of community thus: "[Nation] is imagined as a *community* [emphasis original], because, regardless of the actual inequality and exploitation that may prevail in each, the nation is always conceived as a deep horizontal comradeship." Even if nation were replaced with religious community, Anderson's comment would remain valid. The articulation of religious identity always involves the blurring of heterogeneity that exists within it in terms of class and, in the context of India, caste. Thus, the construction of identity on the basis of any criteria, other than occupational and class positions in which heterogeneity exists, is basically an ideological process in the political space.

When the politics of identity is examined in the Indian context, the immediate reference to caste and/or religion is inevitable. Caste is regarded as a major indicator of a person's status in society, but in recent times, we are witnessing politics of caste identity, particularly in the case of dalits. The construction of religious identity in India has its roots in colonialism. For the British, the notion of society was historically rooted in the evolution of moral community where the central place was accorded to the common religion among the people. The understanding of the Indian society presented a set of problems, as the country of a sub-continent size in regional, cultural and religious diversities could not fit into their notion of society. Placed in this context was the construction of the Indian society consisting of religious communities. Grewal (1996: 51) rightly points out: "The colonial rulers, in spite of their professed religious neutrality, thought in terms of religious communities, thereby obliging members of the middle class to think as leaders of religious communities." He continues to emphasize the political consequences of this colonial perception thus: "... The newly sharpened articulation in the professed interest of communities and their culture became the basis increasingly of political articulation." Placed in the larger Indian context is the Sikh identity whose construction began as a political project in the colonial period. The next part deals with the process of the emergence and evolution of the politics of the Sikh identity.

II
SIKH IDENTITY AND ITS ARTICULATION

To examine the articulation of religious identity among the Sikhs, we may approach the issue by tracing its origin in the 19th century, which is the usual practice among the historians. Gupta (1997) has made a distinction between the construction of Sikh identity in peaceful times and crisis situations. This distinction is useful, but one has to constantly remind oneself that the identity construction in the crisis situation may not be independent of its construction in peace times. In other words, the crisis may be a consequence of the way the identity was articulated in the normal times. In the case of the Sikhs, there is a reasonable basis to argue that the way the identity politics was played it contributed to the making of crisis. However, in the case of the Sikh community, the issue of identity has had many dimensions, which involve the definition given and accepted by the SGPC, the colonial construction of the Sikh identity, construction of religious boundaries in relation to Hinduism, the post-independence rhetoric of discrimination against the Sikhs bordering on the creation of fundamentalist discourse, the definitions of the Sikh that evolve during the SGPC elections, and finally the efforts of the Sikh diaspora that have been articulating Sikh identity with different objectives and in different circumstances.

Sikh Rahat Maryada is the official publication of the SGPC and it was first published in 1950[1] to define who is the Sikh and to regulate the religious affairs of the Sikh community at the levels of both the individual and the collective (panth).[2] The definition provided in this document is as follows: "The man or woman who has faith (believes) in one God, ten Gurus (from Shri Guru Nanak Dev Ji to Shri Guru Gobind Singh Sahib), Shri Guru Granth Sahib and the writings and teachings of the ten Gurus and baptism of Dasmeshji [Guru Gobind Singh], and does not believe in any other religion is Sikh" (1973: 9). According to this definition, any of the words 'faith' and 'believe' has been both specific and general.[3] It is specific with regard to the Sikh gurus and their writings and preaching, but it is general when the issue of baptism of the tenth guru is stated. There is a reason to think that since all the Sikhs have never been baptised (*amritdhari*), the idea was to include all those people who had faith in the gurus and their writings. Keeping in mind this textual definition, which is available in the official document of the SGPC, it would be worthwhile to see how historically the Sikh identity was articulated. It is relevant to begin from the colonial construction of Sikh identity.

How did the British construct the Sikh identity? What were the consequences of this construction of identity for the Sikh community? It may be reminded that Punjab was the last state to be annexed by the British in India in 1849. This annexation proceeded after two Anglo-Sikh wars in which the Sikhs lost. It may seem natural and obvious that the British paid special attention to the Sikhs. Predictably, the objective of this attention was the establishment and consolidation of the colonial rule. The first systematic work on the Sikhs was authored by Bingley (1985), but his work may be understood as a contribution of ethnography in the service of the imperial power purely for the purpose of recruiting the Sikhs to the army. Fox (1987: 7) brings out the issue of the colonial and pre-colonial Sikh identity rather well thus:

> The terms Sikh and Sikhism refer to several cultural or symbolic identities prevalent in the Punjab during the nineteenth century. These identities subsumed a range of quite different religious beliefs and social practices. Because the boundary between these several sorts of Sikh identities was indistinct, a self-denominated

> Sikh might follow an amalgam of religious and social practices drawn from different points along the range of identities. Quite against the actual diversity of belief and observance, the British usually treated one Sikh identity, the Singh or Lion one as the only true Sikhism, and they often used the labels "Sikh" and "Singh" interchangeably.

Fox makes it clear that the colonial rulers recognised the Khalsa identity as the only Sikh identity and now we know that for the recruitment to and service in the army, there were strict rules for the Sikhs, which underlined the Khalsa identity. The British rule consolidated and recognised the singular tradition in Sikhism for the imperial interests. However, Fox's observation regarding several "cultural and symbolic identities" within Sikhism requires explication. In this regard, Oberoi's (1994) work acquires a great significance. He points out that the issue of religious identity came to be recognised quite late, as there was a composite religious tradition in Punjab, which is evident from the fact that in the first census in 1881 a considerable number of people recorded themselves as the followers of Sakhi Sarvar – a Muslim Pir. Joginder Singh (1997) has shown that in the first two decades of the 20th century, when the population of Punjab showed decline due to epidemics, like plague and influenza, the Sikh population showed a considerable increase. This could only be possible if persons, who did not earlier record themselves as Sikhs in the census enumerations, started doing so due to the persuasions of the leaders of the Singh Sabha movement.

The colonial construction for the purpose of recruitment to the army was evident, as a particular identity of the Sikhs was recognised, encouraged and nurtured. Fox (1987:10) observes: "The British Indian army nurtured an orthodox, separatist, and martial Singh identity among Sikh rural recruits to its regiments and companies. They served as the lions of British India." In the colonial construction of the Sikh identity, the anthropological theories of race might have contributed too. It is only recently that the validity of physical anthropological theories propounding unique features of every race have been seriously questioned. The recognition accorded to the Sikhs as martial may be explained in terms of the anthropological discourse, but the emphasis on the Khalsa symbols as the only identity for the recruitment to army had an altogether different context. A careful reading of Bingley unfolds still another mystery when he extensively analyses the cultural and physical traits of each caste among the Sikhs. Not only that when he identifies the Jat Sikh as the best soldier, which he might have done by following the famous comment of Bacon that the yeoman makes the best soldier (cf. Durant 1976), he also identifies regional variations among them. He particularly distinguishes between the Majha and the Malwai Jats. For the British, all Sikhs were not martial and thus could not be recruited to the army. The colonial rulers preferred the Jat Sikh to other caste groups within Sikh community. The Jat Sikh fitted perfectly in the notion of the western yeoman, as he was a landowner as well as independent cultivator. The other occupational groups like traders and artisans could not be spared for war as soldiers.

The colonial construction of the Sikh religion in the form of Khalsa Panth coincided with and complimented by the Tat Khalsa in the Singh Sabha movement. The Singh Sabha movement constructed the Sikh identity with the purpose of creating demarcation from Hindus. Kahn Singh Nabha (1973) wrote his polemical work, *Ham Hindu Nahin* (We are not Hindus) in 1898 and the time coincides with the rise of Tat Khalsa within the Singh Sabha movement. The British emphasis on the Khalsa symbols for the recruitment to the army and the position of the Singh Sabha movement seem to be synonymous with each other, whereas the purposes of the two were different. In the former case it was to create a class of loyal subjects, whereas in the case of latter, the objective was to purge Sikh faith of all other identities except that of the Khalsa. This purge was essential for the creation of a distinct religious identity, particularly from Hinduism. The construction of a distinct religious identity also created the need for the invention of a separate tradition, for which the martyrdom of the gurus and the devout Sikhs became rallying point for the Sikh leaders. Fenech (2000) has analysed the tradition of martyrdom in Sikhism. The Singh Sabha leaders faced the task of articulation, consolidation and enforcement of one tradition with one identity. It required rewriting and reinterpretation of *History*, which the movement did with the help of printed material. On top of all this, the *kaveeshars*, *dhadis* (bards) and preachers carried out the work of popularisation and internalisation of the myths, tales and Sikh practices, as invented and articulated by the Singh Sabha ideologues among the masses.

The construction of the tradition of martyrdom as the singular and the dominant process in the Sikh history has two interesting features whose consequences could be seen in terms of the construction of the 'other', that is, the Hinduism. It was argued, preached and sung that the Sikhs struggled against the Muslim rulers and sacrificed their lives, but the purpose of this argument was to create a demarcation from the Hindu religion. It is in Nabha's famous polemical work referred above that we find how the two seemingly contradictory constructions are synthesised with each other to create the Sikh identity. For Nabha (1973), the Sikhs sacrificed their lives to save Hinduism, but they are ungrateful. He also makes it clear that social structure of the Sikh community is different from Hinduism as there is no caste among the Sikhs[4] (Judge 2002).

The colonial intervention that followed the determined and non-violent struggle of the Sikhs for the gurdwara reforms proved decisive in creating a durable demarcation between the Sikhs and the Hindus. The Gurdwara Reform Act, 1925 permanently changed the status of Sikh shrines by bringing them under the control of the SGPC. From this period onwards, the politics of identity took a qualitatively different trajectory. The Akalis and the SGPC have remained synonymous from the day of the creation of the latter. Before we discuss the way the SGPC has been creating, articulating and enforcing the identity issue, it is important to just take stock of the definition of the Sikh as provided by McLeod. The definition he (1989) attempted earlier is long and tends to cover all digressions within the Sikh community. Later on, he (1995: 107-8)) provided a more precise definition by identifying five varieties of Sikh identity. These five varieties are: amritdhari, kesdhari, sahajdhari, khalsa families but cut their hair also called mona Sikhs, patit (fallen) Sikhs are those amritdharis "who have committed one of the four kurahits". Pashaura Singh (2004: 103) has recently provided a slightly modified version of McLeod's categorisation. According to this categorisation, the worldwide Sikh population of 22 million can be divided into five categories, which are as follows: amritdhari (15-20%), kesdhari (70%), and other three that constitute 10-15 per cent are ichhadhari, sehajdhari and bikhidhari. In these categories, the patit Sikh of McLeod has been replaced by bikhidhari, in which 'bikh' is a negative term literally meaning poison. Both the patit and the bikhidhari Sikhs seem to be those who commit heresy and are unorthodox by virtue of their deviation from the basic Sikh code of conduct. While defining the Sikh, there is a strong emphasis on his appearance. Contrarily, the patit or the bikhidhari Sikh seems to combine the physical appearance with some doctrine. The question can be raised, that is, which of the two does form the primary definitional principle of the meaning of the Sikh? If we implicate doctrine with the appearance, then the categorisation will have to change into a more complex pattern than what has been presented. Possibly, it is assumed that those who claim to be Sikhs have to be divided on the basis of their appearance. It is the plurality of appearances and expediently injected presence or absence of the doctrine that has significantly contributed to the political dynamics within the Sikh community.

In actual political practice, the manifest attempt to define who is a Sikh has been a never-ending phenomenon since the

Tat Khalsa dominated the Singh Sabha movement. To illustrate and clarify this observation, let us take two official definitions of "the Sikh". The first official definition of the Sikh could be found in the Sikh Gurdwara Act of 1925 according to which the Sikh was "a person who professes the Sikh religion", adding that the following declaration should be required if any doubt should arise: "I solemnly affirm that I am a Sikh, that I believe in the Ten Gurus, and that I have no other religion" (Pashaura Singh 2004: 96). The above definition may be compared with the one provided in the Delhi Gurdwara Act 82 of 1971, which is as follows: "Sikh means a person who professes the Sikh religion, believes and follows the teachings of Sri Guru Granth Sahib and the ten Gurus only *and keeps unshorn hair.*" The declaration was framed in the following manner: "I solemnly affirm that I am a *kesdhari* Sikh, that I believe in and follow the teachings of Sri Guru Granth Sahib and the ten Gurus only, and that I have no other religion" (Ibid.: 99). The change in the emphasis on what makes a person Sikh is quite obvious and need no explication. The underlying logic of this change is political as the exclusiveness is functional in the elections of Delhi Sikh Gurdwara Management Committee (DSGMC).[5]

The SGPC, which is governing body of the Sikh religious affairs, has been consistently emphasising the Khalsa identity as the only identity of the Sikhs. However, the grudging recognition to the sehajdhari Sikhs has also been accorded, whereas the DSGMC has excluded them. For the SGPC, the issue of identity has become a political trap. In fact, the continuous debate on the issue of identity has a lot to do with the nature of Punjab politics. The SGPC is a democratically elected governing body of the Sikhs. It looks after the management of most of the historical gurdwaras in Punjab as well outside Punjab with noticeable exceptions, such as Delhi Sikh Gurdwara Management Committee and the Pakistan Gurdwara Management Committee. The SGPC also looks after the religious matters of the Sikh community, but it is controlled by the Akali Dal, which is a political party. What happens is that whereas in the SGPC elections, the Akali leadership takes up the Khalsa identity, in the legislative assembly elections, it talks about the Punjab farmers' economic interests. Among the farmers the Sikhs are an overwhelming majority. Not only that within the Sikh farmers the Jats constitute a majority. What McLeod calls as patit Sikhs or mona Sikhs largely belong to the Jat caste.

Among the Jat Sikhs, if we make an empirical observation, the digressions from the Khalsa identity may be found to be the maximum. There is also a popular joke on the Sikh identity of Jats thus: "Once a *mona* Jat was standing rubbing lime and tobacco when a kesdhari Khatri passed by him. He just asked, "Sardarji, where are you going?" "To Gurdwara", he replied. When he was gone, the Jat commented thus: "When did the *Bhapas* (a pejorative term for Khatri Sikh) become Sikhs!" The digression among the Jats may be understood in the light of the power they hold within the Sikh community. Thus, it does not make a difference to their identity of being Sikhs whether they are kesdharis or not. The Jat as a caste has certainly contributed in the shaping of the Sikh community. One may interpret the discourse of Sikh identity in terms of the domination of the Jats, both numerically as well as politically, in the community.

It may be stated succinctly that at cultural level the Sikh community and the Jat cultural forms have become synonymous over a period of time largely due to the domination of this caste in the community. It, however, does not imply that alternative cultural practices have been eliminated by the dominant discourse. The marginalisation of other cultural practices has occurred, but these are still persisting. One of the significant areas, in which the dominant identity has failed to intervene despite the support from the religious orthodoxy, is the homogenisation of the marital practices. However, the identity question remains the most contentious issue within the Sikh community and interestingly most of the digressions come from the members of the Jat caste.

community is a little problematic. For example, Bhagat Singh has a unique place in the history of the struggle for independence of India. He still inspires the youth in the country. Interestingly, just before he was martyred he wrote that he was an atheist. Is it possible to characterise him as a Sikh martyr? Thus, a question could be raised, that is, did the persons who sacrificed their lives for the country do so because they were Sikhs? In recent years, we have witnessed an interesting process of appropriation of Udham Singh. We all know that Udham Singh went to England to avenge the deaths of people killed in the Jallianwala Bagh massacre in 1919. He belonged to the Kamboh caste and grew up in an orphanage in Amritsar. Suddenly, from a national hero the members of his own caste have transformed Udham Singh into a Kamboh martyr. What we find is the appropriation or reclamation of heroes by the caste or religious community in the country as a whole. There is no denying the fact that some people's heroic deeds could be identified with their communities, but to transform the secular into communal is an altogether different phenomenon.

At what point of time the appropriation of the national heroes by their caste and religious communities began is not known. This is a post-colonial process that started acquiring prominence with the rise of communal and caste conflicts in India. It may be regarded as a process of identity assertion among the communities, but simultaneously it also entails the regimentation of the society. The case of the Sikhs is both unique and part of this all-India phenomenon. In Punjab, there were three major religious communities, of which the Sikhs came the third in numbers. The Singh Sabha movement and later the Akali movement for Gurdwara reform changed the dynamism of Punjab. In spite of the limitations of numbers, the Sikhs demonstrated tremendous commitment to the nationalist cause. The only ideal example of non-violent *satyagraha* outside the activities of Gandhi is the Akali struggle for reform in the Sikh Gurdwaras. Simultaneously, the Sikhs were in majority in the British Army. No other religious community in the country had such a large proportion of soldiers in the army. Still another side of the support to the colonial rule were the titles, which the British gave to the people. Thus, we have in Punjab titles such as, the 'Singh Bahadur' for the Sikhs, the 'Khan Bahadur' for the Muslims, and the 'Rai Bahadur' for the Hindus, whereas the 'Sarkaria' was a common title. The prominence of Singh Bahadur tends to belie the fact of small number of the Sikhs in Punjab. Sarkaria has almost become a surname among some of the Sikh families. There is no such thing as hiding the colonial past that these families supported the British. There seems to be a great pride in showing, exhibiting and suffixing with name the signifiers of loyalty to the British rule. The third dimension that may question the construction of the Sikh as the one who sacrificed his life for the country is the existence of the structure and practice of information to the police. In popular expression, a police informer is called 'police tout'. Various militant movements in Punjab for the freedom of the country always targeted the police tout as number one enemy. The Babbar Akalis, Ghadar Party leaders, Shaheed Bhagat Singh and his comrades, and later on the Red Communists and the Naxalites all identified the police tout as one of their enemies (Judge 1992). Thus, an attempt at highlighting one aspect of the historical facts, that too in an exaggerated form, is a construction of religious community in a particular image.

As a corollary to the above, it may be argued that every religious community in this world has heroes, martyrs and quislings. There is nothing important in this, because every community has a social structure in which the intricacies of interaction are always present. The deprived and ambitious individuals behave differently. The dialectics of rebellion and loyalty go hand in hand and Sikh historical and mythological narratives amply demonstrate this aspect. Bhindranwala's speech on the question of the contribution made by the Sikhs in the historical context is just a construction of one tradition in order to establish the exclusive trait of the community. He is also referring to the three wars that India fought after independence.[11] In these wars, the Sikh soldiers' sacrifices are also part of his narrative. One may raise a query as to how he could work out the proportions of the sacrifices of the Sikhs and others. All these ideas and proportions seem to have emanated from the folk sources in which the valour and sacrifice of the Sikhs are frequently highlighted. In this speech, he is not only constructing martyrdom, but also emphasising that the share of the Sikhs in the territory of India should be in proportion to the ratio of their martyrs if the question of Khalistan emerges. The simplistic nature of the argument makes it a strong demagogic weapon when the congregation is comprised of the rural Sikhs.

To come to the basic issue of the demands of the Sikhs he expressed and articulated, there is a great degree of ambivalence in his narrative. It is not clear that he was demanding Khalistan. He made it clear that he was quiet on the issue of Khalistan. This quietness has no basis in Wittegenstein's (1961) emphasis on silence in those matters and situations where one cannot speak, because he was speaking too much. By remaining quiet on the issue of Khalistan, his discourse on liberation seems quite confusing. What was meant by liberation if he was not demanding Khalistan? Was it a demand for recognition to the Sikhs as a distinct community? We have already examined and noted that he was not simply emphasising the distinctive character of Sikhism from Hinduism. The Singh Sabha leaders, particularly Kahn Singh Nabha, had already done it. There is still another contradiction in his arguments. Constitutional recognition of Sikhism had nothing to do with the empirical reality. At the time of Bhindranwala there was no ambiguity about the distinctness of the Sikh religion. Various movements, such as the Arya Samaj and the Singh Sabha in the colonial period and Punjabi Suba in the 1960s, had significantly contributed to the emergence of Hindu-Sikh divide without any manifest conflict. The constitutional change could bring certain reorientation of the government policy, particularly with regard to the scheduled castes among the Sikhs. In fact, the protest actions of the Akali leaders with regard to the Article 25 of the Constitution were political gimmicks. They could never afford to lose the support of a sizeable scheduled caste population in the Sikh community. Bhindranwala did not seem to be having such a deep understanding of political dynamics in which the issues could be raised and exploited for electoral gains without necessarily resolving them. The Akali Dal invariably found an issue that could mobilise the Sikh masses without its resolution. Placed in this broader context was the Anadpur Sahib Resolution about which he spoke many times. It is adequate to know what he had to say about it. In his 21st speech, which he delivered on July 16, 1983 (Singh 2003), he mentioned the Anandpur Sahib Resolution in the following manner:

> I have got a copy [of the Anandpur Sahib Resolution]. If whatever is written in it is accepted, then we.... There is no need for us to struggle. In case we achieve less than what is demanded, I shall keep the watch. However, you will have to fight for it.

However, he also expressed his lack of faith in the promises of the Indian government. In his 38th speech, he was forthright in his views on this issue thus:

> ... At the time of independence of India Mahatma Gandhi gave the statement. Have they stood by their statements and promises? In this part of Punjab, he said that this would be such a zone in which the Sikhs would enjoy freedom. We are enjoying the freedom in Punjab! How they have degraded the Sikhs. How they have insulted the Sikhs. How many religious places of the Sikhs have been violated? Is it enjoying freedom?

He did not give any example of the enslavement of the Sikhs in the above-mentioned speech. Rather, he went on to talk of the demands of the Sikhs clearly. He mentioned Punjabi Suba and the Punjabi-speaking areas. He emphasised that in spite of the fact that the Punjabi Suba was formed, all the Punjabi-speaking areas were not included in it. We now come to certain concrete demands that were referred to by Bhindranwala. These included the rewriting of Article 25 of the Constitution to recognise Sikhs as a separate *qaum*, inclusion of Punjabi-speaking areas in Punjab and the complete implementation of the Anandpur Sahib Resolution.[12] We do not come across any articulation of his notion of freedom, but if we go by the fundamentalist discourse, it becomes obvious that he viewed the then condition of the Sikhs as second-rate citizens. Though he dismissed any contention that he was demanding Khalistan, yet he remained silent on the issue and called for struggle for freedom. What kind of freedom he stressed remained ambiguous as a result of which it gave tremendous room for his opponents that he was talking of Khalistan. It was an interesting example of demagogy in which the others constantly reminded him that what he wanted was Khalistan not the implementation of the Anandpur Sahib Resolution. Was it a conspiracy to project only him as the symbol of Sikh separatism? There was no such thing, as there is a need to go into the structure of narrative that was created by him.

Bhindranwala was not the only leader of the Sikhs. Much more important were the leaders like Harchand Singh Longowal, Jagdev Singh Talwandi and Sukhjinder Singh. It was the Akali Dal, which was leading the Dharam Yudh Morcha. After his initial phase of association with the Congress, Bhindranwala was enjoying his honeymoon with the Akali Dal. The Akali Dal was responsible for exposing him to its mass base and his forthright and candid way of stating the various issues won him the followers. Sukhjinder Singh, who was an Akali leader, raised the demand for Khalistan on the stage of the Dharam Yudh Morcha. Bhindranwala never took any position of no return and chose to remain quiet in his own way on the issue of Khalistan. However, there is a reasonable basis to argue that he supported the issue of Khalistan. For him the Sikhs were a separate nation and he remained firm in his convictions. In the process of arguing for the Sikh sovereignty, he reinterpreted the Sikh history and blurred the distinction between history and mythology. It is here that one uncovers his mixing of the past and present in a way that was never done on a political platform. He transformed the political stage where anything said could form a part of history to a congregation of devotees who would listen his sermons with intense devotion.

After the death of Bhindranwala in 1984 in the Operation Blue Star, the Punjab scenario began to change in a radical manner. Various militant groups came into existence and carried out the campaign of violence. The formation of Panthic Committee and the organisation of Sarbat Khalsa were the major occurrences in the post-Operation Blue Star period. The announcement of Khalistan by the Sarbat Khalsa in 1986 completed the entire process initiated by the Singh Sabha movement that began the construction of boundaries between Sikhism and Hinduism. The rising militant violence in Punjab created a situation where the state seemed to be helpless in handling the situation. In various press statements, the militant leaders clarified their positions with regard to the objective of the movement. They made it clear that their struggle was for the achievement of an independent and sovereign state of Khalistan.

The suppression of the militant movement has not brought an end to the idea of Sikh nationhood, which is still being articulated openly by certain sections among the Sikhs. Ballantyne (2004) refers certain websites created by the Sikh diaspora in which the expression 'Sikh nation' is frequently used. Notably, on the 20th anniversary of the Operation Blue Star, *Sikh Shahadat* – a pro-Khalistan magazine – published a message of Tejshadeep Singh, President of Sikh Students' Federation (Nabha Unit), and the first paragraph is reproduced below:

> The guns of the army of Hindustan turned to the Akal Takhat of the Sikh *qaum* in June 1984. Those innocents were massacred who had not yet learnt walking. Blown with bullets were those turbans of the old people that had come to pray. The Khalsa has

> learnt the lesson of tit for tat from the tenth Guru. Within a few months it was made clear that the head, which would oppress the *qaum* of the tenth Guru shall be cut. Brave warriors have protected the honour and turban of our *qaum*.

The above statement makes it clear that nationhood is a project and for a section of Sikhs it is linked and related with the Khalsa tradition. The word *qaum* could be interpreted as either nation or community, but if the contestation and struggle is against the Indian Army, then its meaning is singular, i.e., nation.

In sum, it may be pointed out that the construction of religious nationhood was a process that began with the construction of religious boundaries in the 19th century by the Singh Sabha movement. The formation of Pakistan in 1947 gave a boost to the idea of Khalistan that could be articulated any time. The politics of power in Punjab in which the Akalis and the Congress competed with each other led the Akali Dal to take more and more fundamentalist position. However, owing to the Indian Constitution and their participation in the electoral process, the probable and possible actions that the Akali Dal could undertake were limited and the Akali leaders had flexible approach. Even then, when they were out of power, they passed the Anandpur Sahib Resolution, which was interpreted as secessionist document by the opponents of the Akali Dal. It is on the grounds of this resolution that the fundamentalist like Jarnail Singh Bhindranwala began his discourses and started articulating Sikh nationhood. In the post-Blue Star Operation period, the militants made it clear that they were fighting for nation. It still goes on among certain sections of the Sikhs both in Punjab and in the Sikh diaspora.

In the beginning of this chapter, it was clarified that Smith's (1976) conception of the ideals of nationhood would be the basis of the discussion of militant movement. It was also stated that all the three ideals identified by Smith would not be examined. In this chapter, we took up two ideals for understanding the construction of Sikh nationhood in the militant movement, namely, distinctiveness of the Sikhs and demand for autonomy and self-government in federal set up. Smith (ibid.) makes it clear that this autonomy does not always imply 'sovereign state'. In the case of the militant movement the trajectory of the construction of nationhood moved from the relative autonomy to the sovereign state after 1984. In the proceeding chapters, the construction of nationhood would be further examined in terms of sharpening of the distinctiveness, creating solidarity though the construction of Sikh identity has already been the subject of analysis in the previous chapter, and finally the construction of unique culture and history of Sikhs.

Notes

1. In the existing literature the idea of nation and nationalism has been dealt with by a variety of scholars across the world. However, the purpose of having precise discussion is only to explicate the notions of nation and nationhood without subjecting these to critical assessment.
2. Some aspects of the construction of nationhood have been dealt with in the next two chapters too.
3. See Chapter 1 for discussion on what Nabha wrote on the fundamental distinctions between Sikhism and Hinduism.
4. The couplet of Kabir is as follows: *Sunnat karai turk jo hona tau aurat ko ka kahye, aradh sariri nari na chhootę tate Hindu kahye.* (If circumcision is the basis of the identification of a Muslim, then what should we call a women. Without circumcision she remains Hindu).
5. Even in this contention Bhindranwala is not right and shows no familiarity with cultures across the world. The argument that women are not circumcised is incorrect, as the practice of circumcision of women exists in Africa.
6. Varinder Walia, "Vedanti Opposes the Orthodox", *The Tribune*, January 3, 2003, p. 1. Subsequent to this reporting by Walia, a considerable controversy cropped up about what is preached in Sikhism and what is actually practised with regard to gender equality.

7. Bhindranwala mentions here the story of the founding of the Khalsa Panth by Guru Gobind Singh in 1699.
8. Nishan Sahib can be found an integral part of every Sikh Gurdwara. According to Singh (1997: 239), "Thus Nishan Sahib in the Sikh tradition means the holy flag or exalted ensign. A synonymous term is Jhanda Sahib... The Sikh pennant, made out of saffron-coloured, occasionally out of blue coloured, mainly in the case of Nihangs, cloth is triangular in shape, normally each of the two equal sides being double of the shorter one. The pennant is stitched to the mast sheath at the top which is also of the same cloth. On it is commonly printed or embroidered the Sikh emblem, comprising a *khanda* (two-edged sword) and *chakras* (an edged circular weapon, a disc or quoit) and two *kirpans* which cross each other at the handles, with the blades flanking the *chakra*."
9. Interestingly, in one of the cassettes of the speeches of Bhindranwala there is also a recorded speech of an Akali leader Sukhjinder Singh who made it clear that there is no other demand of the Sikhs than that of Khalistan.
10. The Chambal area of central India is identified with the dacoits. What Longowal was saying is obvious.
11. Mention is made of Indo-China war of 1962 and Indo-Pak wars of 1965 and 1971.
12. The Anandpur Sahib Resolution of the Akali Dal began the controversy as it was regarded as a document of separatism, whereas the Akalis claim that it only highlighted the autonomy to the states.

5

Self and Others

Any attempt at constructing the identity of the collective self is simultaneously a process of the construction of others as different and sometimes contentious identities. In continuation with the last two chapters, this chapter is aimed at understanding how the fundamentalist discourse of the militants, particularly Bhindranwala, constructed the others, for in the reconstruction of religious identity and construction of nationhood, the presence of the 'other' is invariably discursively and consistently subsumed. Das (1995) has rightly pointed out that in the construction of the positive 'self' there is also the simultaneous construction of the negative 'other'. Who is the 'other' that is constructed in the negative image? It seems that there are two-fold purpose of this negative construction. First, the 'other' is shown to be so obviously distinct from the 'self' in which the contexts of identity and nationhood become crucial, and secondly, the 'other' is shown either to be shorn of certain essential qualities or having done some harm or injury to the 'self'. This process is generally more pronounced in that religion in which the need for showing how one's religion is better than other's is strongly felt. Once the fundamental discourse reconstructed religious identity and created nationhood, the identification of the others as distinct identities and/or enemies was thought essential. Guha (1983) is of the view that there is no such thing as spontaneous peasant insurgency. He argues that the peasant resorts to revolt after exhausting alternative means. The similar thing may be stated about the construction of the 'other'. It entails a long-drawn process in which, to use Hobsbawm's expression, "traditions are invented" and then shown to be actual historical occurrences. In this effort, an event or an act of an individual is generalised for the entire community. The construction of the negative 'other' may include three kinds of people. The first includes the construction of the self, whereas the second covers the group or community from which the demarcation is constructed. In the case of the Sikh militant movement, this 'other' that was constructed was Hinduism largely due to the obvious reason that Muslims are no more overwhelmingly present in the Indian Punjab. The Indian Punjab has two major religious communities, namely, Sikhs and Hindus. The Hindus who are a minority in the state are a majority in the country, whereas most of the Sikhs are concentrated in Punjab.[1] Thirdly, there are individuals who may be regarded as the enemies. These individuals may belong to the constructed 'other' in which the attempt is to reinforce their negativity. However, such construction could be inwardly and its intention may be to purge the community from the renegades and traitors. The present chapter has been accordingly divided into three parts.

I
CONSTRUCTING THE 'SELF'

The moment Bhindranwala constructed the Sikh community with a distinct space, it was important to describe the existing condition of the faith and the community. In a situation where the 'Hindu majority' rules over the country, the narrative was to shift to the enslavement of the Sikhs. In fact, his favourite topic of speech was the discrimination against and/or the enslavement of the Sikhs. Starting from the first speech to the end the treatment given to the Sikhs by the Hindu rulers remained the important issue for him. The kinds of issues he raised, as we shall see, shared a lot in common with the fundamentalists of other religions. It would be worthwhile to start with his first speech, which he delivered in February 1983 (Singh 2003), thus:

> How are we slaves? I want to make the educated students aware of this fact. In the population of 66 crores when eighty years' old Lala Jagat Narain is killed, its inquiry is completed within three days. But if one and half dozens of young Sikhs like you are killed, then its inquiry is not even completed in a year.
>
> Out of the population of 66 crores Lala Jagat Narain was killed, post mortem examination of his body was carried out and it was handed over to his son Ramesh. .... But the dead bodies of turbaned persons were not returned. This is the sign of enslavement.
>
> Born in the family of Brahmins, she became the Prime Minister of India. Indira Gandhi was sent to the prison in 1977, because she was punished for her actions. Her assistants Pandeys hijacked a plane to protest against her arrest. Khalsaji, they got positions in the assembly. But if my father Guru Granth Sahib was burnt and my brothers Gajinder and others hijacked the plane, then they got the exile. This is the chain of slavery around our neck. When the plane is hijacked for the daughter of Brahmin, it becomes patriotic action, but if a Sikh hijacks the plane for his religion, then it is anti-national activity.
>
> Tobacco was thrown in the Golden Temple. When the Hindu boy is caught, Khalsaji, no case is registered against him. Here is Rajinder Singh Mehta. Jaswant Singh contractor is gone outside. .... We are not in favour of putting the head of cow. Some Sikhs in temple... though we are not in favour of killing the cow. We do not regard cow as guru. We think that it is a good animal.

The priest did not see anybody, but these students were harassed.

Evidences of slavery of the Sikhs he provided have not ended yet. In order to break the monotony, it is worthwhile to see what is meant by "slavery of the Sikhs in the country under the rule of the Hindus". There is a powerful political content in the first speech, which he delivered at the Golden Temple immediately after the beginning of the Dharam Yudh Morcha in August 1982. He was sharing the platform with Sant Harchand Singh Longowal, who had been appointed by the Akali Dal as the dictator of the Morcha. The level of the content of the arguments does not go beyond the perception of a common Sikh who as a peasant has been encountering many difficulties in his everyday life as a result of his interaction with the state and its apparatus. The convincing logic in the case of the hijacking of the plane captures the thinking process of a common man. Interestingly, the question that should have been raised was that if the hijacking of the plane was an illegal act, then why Mrs. Indira Gandhi rewarded some hijackers after coming to power in 1980. The Pandeys, who have been mentioned in his speeches time and again, as is clear to most of the analysts, were not rewarded because they were Hindus. It may be argued that had the hijackers been Sikhs in that case, Mrs. Gandhi would have rewarded them.

For him discrimination implied enslavement and Sikhs had to struggle to get their demands accepted. He refers to four demands, which according to him, should have been accepted without any struggle, because they were reasonable for a community. These were as follows: recognition to Punjabi language, demand for Punjabi Suba, naming the train on the name of the Golden Temple, and giving the sacred status to Amritsar city. He argued that for each demand to be accepted 86 thousand Sikhs should court arrest and 113 sacrifice their lives. Even then, Indira Gandhi would not concede. He called her hypocrite. He then posed a question thus: "Do you find even a single Hindu ever gone to jail for speaking Hindi, for getting the Hindi-speaking areas or to name the train on some temple?" The discrimination against the Sikhs, according to him, did not even end there. He said:

> If a Sikh is 17 years old and his father dies, then he has to pay the tax. Chhalli Ram and Gulli Ram become the owners of 40 lakh [rupees] worth property of their father at the time of their birth without paying any tax. We the turbaned people cannot become the owners of our parental property even at the age of 17. Why this discrimination, Khalsaji, why?

Bhindranwala then narrated the case of his nephew and since it was an incident that involved personal experience, it could not be invalidated and questioned. At the time of his delivering this lecture, he was 36 years of age. Most of his life was devoted to farming, recitation of Gurbani and meditation. His educational level was low. He was a married person. The confluence of all these biographically determined conditions gives us a better insight into the way he interpreted the external world. Popper pointed out that the observation of facts by scientists could not be done without a point of view (Magee 1973). A person whose primary responsibility is to preach religion and give sermons, we should least expect that he would speak without a point of view. What is his point of view? Bhindranwala is here referring to the existential experience of the Jat Sikhs. How does it form the point of view? We may answer this question by raising a commonsensical query. Is it that only the Sikh peasants had to pay the tax at the time of the inheritance of the property? The answer is no. The law of inheritance in the state is applicable to all landowning families. It implies that the comparison he made between the Jat landowner and the Hindu shopkeeper is untenable, but the issue of tax at the time of inheritance is applicable to both the cases. It is not the case of discrimination but the manipulation of the law in which an urban trader is more capable, but equally smart could be his Sikh counterpart. The issue is thus more existential than communal.

Much more serious issue is raised by Bhindranwala when he points out that whenever the Sikhs demand something, they have to struggle as well as make sacrifice. In comparison to the Sikhs, the Hindus have never sacrificed for any demand they raised. The sense of history in him zoomed on the question of Punjabi Suba for which the Akali Dal launched an agitation. The linguistic reorganisation of the states in India took place with the sole exception of Punjab. In Punjab, as pointed out earlier, the politics of language entailed communal overtones. The objective of the Akali Dal was more to create a Sikh-majority state than the Punjabi-speaking state. The overlapping of the Punjabi language with the Sikhs on one hand and Hindi with the Hindus on the other was one of the consequences of electoral politics. The struggle for getting Punjabi Suba turned into a long-drawn fight for the demand that ultimately succeeded after the Indo-Pak war in which, as is alleged by many, the Sikhs showed patriotism for which they were rewarded.

In both the examples that he put across, the purpose was to establish and substantiate the belief that there was discrimination against the Sikhs in India and the Hindu rulers were responsible for that. In spite of the historical references that are contrary to it, the logic of the argument is based on one firm and unchanging conviction that there is some conscious attempt to marginalise the Sikhs in the country. During the period he delivered his speeches from the public platform, such arguments were quite common among the Sikh masses. How such perceptions were articulated into a firm conviction is a matter for investigation.

Arguments in support of the view that the Sikh community/nation is slave in India are not yet exhausted. In his tenth speech, Bhindranwala elaborated at length how Sikhs were discriminated against in India. He repeated most of the arguments he gave in his very first speech and then he added new ones. Some of the arguments are given below:

> All Sikhs raise slogans regarding Hindu-Sikh unity. Both political leaders and all of us also do it. There was a convention here and they [Hindus] raised the slogan "Hindu-Hindu brothers"; nobody mentioned Sikhs. Sometime back there were slogans raised by the Hindus,
>
> *Kachh, karha kirpan,ehnoo bhejo Pakistan.*
>
> (Send the Sikhs to Pakistan)
>
> *Dukki tikki khehan ni deni, sir te pagarhi rehan ni deni.*
>
> (No Tom Dick Harry would be allowed to live, turban would not be allowed on the head)
>
> If Hindu raises a slogan, then it is patriotism. If a son of the Sikh says at the stage that we want our rights, then he is guilty of treason. This is the sign of slavery.

He kept on giving illustrations of atrocities committed on Sikhs by the Punjab police. Interestingly, he mentions a Sikh priest belonging to a village in Moga area who was tortured by police and a Hindu policeman sat on his chest, smoked cigarettes and threw tobacco in his mouth. Similarly, he referred to another case in which a person named Jagir Singh was also tortured. He also informed that 32 Sikhs had been dismissed from police, whereas no such thing had happened to the Hindus. Even the students who were put behind bars, he alleged, were Sikhs and then he challenged the gathering that whether anybody could tell him that a Hindu student was ever arrested. A case of a Sikh girl, he invariably mentioned, may be stated here in his own words thus: "A daughter of the Sikhs, a young girl was forcibly stripped off by the police and then forced to have intercourse with her father in public in Ghal Khurd police station. No action was taken against the police officer, because it happened to a Sikh girl." He also asserted that if a Hindu were killed, then the Hindu press would begin to demand for the imposition of President's rule. Nothing of the kind happened even when 200 Sikhs were killed. He concluded by saying that all these occurrences were the sure signs of the enslavement of the Sikhs. He ended his tenth speech by arguing that "We want to live in this country as citizens with equal rights".

In his 33rd speech that he delivered on September 9, 1983 at Deewan Hall, Manji Sahib to the members of All India Sikh Students Federation (Singh 2003), he spoke on the theme of the present condition of the Sikhs. Most of the examples were repetitions of earlier speeches. He also added the case of the discrimination against the Sikhs during the Asian Games in 1982 that were held at Delhi.[2] In the process of narrating incidents after incidents, he tried to convince the Sikh students who came to listen to his speech that in India they were second-rate citizens. His popularity among the Sikhs, particularly the youth, could be an indicator of the fact that he was touching the most sensitive cord of the hearts and minds of the Sikhs. Such kinds of impressions and convictions had been in circulation in rural Punjab.[3]

It may be pointed out that the language of fundamentalism is universal. In India, the fundamentalist leaders have been saying the same things. Kakar (1996: 208) has cited the speech of Sadhavi Rithambara out of which the following excerpts indicate how the logic remains the same, as it has tremendous resemblance with what Bhindranwala was saying:

> Why should there be two sets of laws in this country? Why should we be treated like stepchildren? I submit to you that when the Hindu of Kashmir became a minority he came to Jammu. From Jammu he came to Delhi. But if you Hindus are on the run all over India, where will you go? Drown in the Indian Ocean or jump from the peaks of the Himalayas?
>
> What is this impartiality toward all religions where the mullahs get the moneybags and Hindus the bullets? We also want religious impartiality but not of the kind where only Hindus are

> oppressed. People say there should be Hindu-Muslim unity. Leave the structure of the Babri mosque undisturbed. I say, "Then let's have this unity in case of the Jama Masjid too. Break half of it and construct a temple. Hindus and Muslims will then come together."

The ideas that echo in Rithambara's speech are similar to what Bhindranwala was saying. He was transforming the routine incidents into episodes in which the actors were identified in terms of their religion. All cases that he narrated had the quality of being interpreted in either way, that is, some of these could be cited as instances of police brutality, whereas the same could be interpreted as cases of atrocities on the Sikhs. The presentation of a community as a persecuted collectivity had not been a new thing. Scanning most of the written history of the emergence and evolution of the Sikh community after the institutionalisation of the charisma of the gurus, we find that an important element that emerges is the persecution of the Sikhs. In the stories of the persecution of the Sikhs, one essential element is the forcible conversion of the Sikhs to Islam.[4] The Sikhs struggled, sacrificed their lives for the faith and emerged victorious. In the times of Bhindranwala, as he saw it, the Hindu leaders had replaced the Muslim ruler and the persecution of the Sikhs continued without any change and interruption. Was he a Don Quixote fighting the windmills?[5] To a great extent there was a similarity between the two. Don Quixote perceived windmills as monsters out of his obsession with the knightly combat, whereas Bhindranwala constructed the enemy to unite the community. Interestingly, Rithambara has her successor in the form of Vishwa Hindu Parishad leader, Parveen Togadia who spoke the same language when the Chief Election Commissioner of India postponed the State Assembly elections in Gujarat in 2002 due to unsatisfactory rehabilitation of the Muslim riot victims. If the Hindu leaders are articulating the idea that the Hindus are being treated as second-rate citizens, then one should be curious to know the identity of the first-rate citizens. One may not find any religious community as the first-rate citizens. It is then clear that such rhetoric has different context, the purpose of which is not separatism, but 'perpetual hostility' to achieve and sustain a particular kind of unity in the religious community having political objectives in mind. However, in the case of Bhindranwala, the internal unity of a religious community could become the basis of forging nationhood.

II
THE HINDU AS THE 'OTHER'

Before discussing how the fundamentalist discourse constructed self and others as binary opposites, a little digression may be necessary. There is a need to make some comment on what I would call "body and belonging". We all know that humans vary tremendously within and across societies in terms of their bodily features. Such a variation is largely a function of nature through genetic diversity about which the biologists and evolutionists may explain better. However, there are two aspects of the body that have had significant bearing on the social relations and interaction. These are colour of the skin and the sexual differences between the male and female if we exclude the transvestites from our present discussion. Historically, these differences did not remain confined to the certitudes of identity without status and power. Racism emerged in which the colour of the skin created a system of hierarchy. It has been extensively examined by the social scientists that the emergence of racism was a function of domination and subjection, which got overlapped with the distinctions in the colours of the skin. Over a period of time, ideology of racism emerged and apartheid became its ugly side. However, the patriarchal domination in gender relations is older than racism; or so it seems. Both have two things in common, i.e., biological basis and ideological articulation of the biological differences.

It is, however, rarely noticed that some religious ideologies lay significant emphasis on the bodily appearance. In India, certain bodily characteristics are a product of religious ideology. For example, during communal riots in India, both the Hindu and Muslim rioters tend to identify a man's religious identity in terms of whether he had been circumcised or not. In the history of Sikhism, the significance of body occupied a crucial place when an attempt was made to construct its singular tradition of Khalsa. The Khalsa Panth was founded by the tenth guru of the Sikhs, Guru Gobind Singh, who according to the popular tradition, "turned jackals into tigers".

It has been argued in this chapter that in the construction of the differences between the Sikh and the Hindu, the fundamentalist discourse laid a great emphasis on the appearance of the body instead of the faith of the believer. An evidence of it could be found in our discussion of the reconstruction of the Sikh identity in Chapter 3. Such an emphasis on body could be traced to the construction of singular tradition in the Sikh history. It goes back to the founding of Khalsa on the Baisakhi day of 1699 by Guru Gobind Singh. The Khalsa was expected to keep five Ks (or five weapons) as symbols and signifiers of his being a warrior in the service of humanity.[6] Of these five symbols one was essentially a part of what constitutes body, namely, unshorn hair. The story behind the appearance of the Khalsa is also linked with the tenth guru. According to the legend, when the tenth guru came to know that at the time of the martyrdom of Guru Tegh Bahadur at Delhi no Sikh came forward, as all of them merged with the crowd, he said that he would give them such an appearance that even one Sikh would not be able to hide among thousands (Jagjit Singh 1985; McLeod 1975).[7] Pashaura Singh (2004:88) narrates the story in the following manner thus: "Tradition holds that the Sikhs who were present at the scene of Guru Tegh Bahadur's execution shrank from recognition, concealing their identity for fear they might suffer a similar fate. In order to respond to this new situation, the tenth guru, Gobind Singh, resolved to impose on his followers an outward form that would make them instantly recognizable."

The immediate point of reference for Bhindranwala was the comparison with the Hindus who were, as he saw it, were also the rulers. In Chapter 3, we found that in the process of constructing the Sikh identity, he also referred to Hindus and Muslims. There was no ambiguity left by him with regard to what he meant by Sikh and how those characteristics could be found missing among the Hindus as well as the Muslims. If we reverse this process, we find that there could be certain areas where weaknesses of a community – real or imagined is irrelevant – are highlighted and then it is possible to show how such things are absent among the Sikhs. The strategy is not new, but it is quite effective. In spite of the fact that we have already seen the narrative on Sikh masculinity, it is yet to be seen how he constructs a "coward and ungrateful Hindu". At the same time, those holding power in the country were Hindus. The dialectics between the perceived position of the Hindu as powerful and constructed image of the coward and ungrateful Hindu provides necessary dynamics to the narrative structure. Bhindranwala's narratives on Hindus in contrast to the Sikhs constitute the mechanism of negotiating identities. In the process, the Hindu is characterised in various ways.

The discussion may be started with the way he referred to the Hindus as the typified other. He invariably used two names to characterise Hindus as an abstract category. These names were Chhalli Ram and Gulli Ram. Literally speaking, the word 'chhalli' is corncob, whereas 'gulli' means a small piece of wood that is sharpened on both sides and is one of the items of street sport. The other item is stick called *danda*, which is used to hit the 'gulli'. One may like to go deep into the symbolic implications of the expressions he used to denote the Hindus for which one has to analyse the metaphors used. Metaphors are not simple categories of description, but these are linked with deep unconscious forces from where the prejudices emerge. As a matter of general expression, what he was doing is a simple act of denigration of the Hindus. It was perhaps a way of brushing aside the majority community by characterising them feminine (as it has happened earlier) or lacking any courage. In his 37th speech, he elaborates on how Sikhs are unique in comparison to Hindus and Muslims. He criticises the entire controversy over the issue whether Sikhs are part of Hinduism. He refutes the assertion that Hindus are like elder brothers to the Sikhs. Bhindranwala spoke on the visible identity of the Hindus as well as the Muslims. According to him, a Hindu should have 12 marks (*tilak*) one each on forehead, chin, chest, armpits, ears, cheeks, neck, etc., keep *bodi*, cap, nine threads of *janeu* and take *charnamat* (handful of water believed to be sanctified) of Shiv Lingum. His following observations may provide an insight into the degree of abhorrence he had against Hinduism:

> First you ask them [Hindus] how the Shivling was born. They will never tell you in spite of your continuous insistence. How can a person be right if he does not tell about his father? When God Shiva had sexual intercourse with Parbati, God Vishnu through his weapon (*sudarshan chakara*) cut the penis into 12 pieces. It is how that Shivling came to exist. If this is proved wrong, I will get my head chopped off. In spite of the evil from which Shivling came to exist, they say that they are right. Even then if a Hindu worships Shivling and rings the bells and does not smoke tobacco, we do not hate him.

To what extent the revelations made by him are correct about the mythology with regard to the Shiva's lingum. It also seems that though he was a head of a Sikh seminary, he was not aware of the Hindu mythology what to say anything about comparative religion. What he picked up could be the populist stories that aim at titillating the audience in private conversations. At the same time, he did not recognise the diversity that exists in Hinduism. Interestingly, the normative judgement on the question related with sex to show that it is something that is vulgar and thus repugnant turns the entire observation into polemics against the Hindus. The significance of sex and the construction of sexuality in the life of individuals depicted through mythological stories may be understood in terms of the way the reproduction of the species has been stressed in the society. Fertility and fertility rites are universal in the case of traditional societies.

Bhindranwala also had something to say about the Muslims thus: "If a person is a Muslim, he should be a committed Muslim. He should read *namaaz* five times a day. .... He must be circumcised and should not be smoking tobacco. That Muslim is our brother". Something that seems obviously common in his comments on both the Hindus and the Muslims is that they should be strictly following their religious codes and must not be smoking tobacco. He did not say whether smoking tobacco is prohibited in their religions. He did not state that a sure sign of the Sikh was that he did not smoke tobacco. The fundamental basis of unity is only possible among all the three religions if people do not smoke. Bhindranwala delivered his 37th speech sometimes between February and April in 1984 (Singh 2003) when he had already developed his differences with the Akali Dal, but he had not shifted to the Akal Takhat. At this time, his popularity among the Sikh youth had peaked and he had become more forthright in what he was saying. However, in his speeches, he continued to talk about the identity of the Sikh in contradistinction to the Hindus. He always held the view that man is born Sikh and kept on arguing that others become Hindus or Muslims and accordingly he would try to interpolate his views on the Hindus. The following remarks in his 37th speech are reminder of how the Sikhs at the folk level perceive Hindus, particularly when they mix it with some elementary education thus:

> What is the sign of the Hindu? The Hindu in fact is an Arabic word, which means thief. If they want to remain thieves, they can. If we look like what we were at the time of birth, then we shall be called Sikhs. In order to become Hindu, you will have to use scissor and razor. By cutting hạir and shaving beard with scissor and razor one becomes Hindu and by getting circumcised one becomes Muslim, whereas we become Sikhs by remaining

> the way we were born. If we put on sword, then we become Singh. When we walk on road, we are Sardar and a Hindu is called Babuji, Lalaji, Chhalli Ram, Gulli Ram. All have originated from the Sardars.

The above lines of the speech are important in many ways. Bhindranwala makes a distinction between amritdhari and ordinary Sikh. The distinguishing feature is that the former is called Singh, whereas the latter is known as Sikh. Despite this distinction, his construction of the Sikh identity remains fixed and inflexible, that is, a Sikh must be *sabat soorat* even if he is not an amritdhari. We hardly know whether there is such an Arabic word by which a Hindu is called thief. It may be reminded that all the conquerors called the conquered and subjugated people as barbarians, pagans, etc. with the exception of China, which was generally regarded as more civilised than some of its rulers who came as conquerors. The word 'Hindu' could be possibly derived from the Indus river. Such alternative possibilities do not exist for him, because his primary concern is to denigrate Hindus and Hinduism and brush aside Islam.

As a corollary to the above, how a person is addressed becomes most crucial for Bhindranwala. In what way the word *sardarji* is superior to *babuji* or *lalaji*, is a matter of contention. As such there is no reason why one is lower in status and the other is respectable. In spite of the fact that the word *sardar* also means leader, but as a mode of addressing the members of a particular religious community when they have beard and turban, it ceases to have any distinction. However, it is not the semantics as such but the social psychology of the community, which is to be investigated to understand the distinction between *sardarji* and *babuji*. One has to be a Punjabi and a Sikh to experience it as an everyday life reality.[8] In the rural Punjab, the word *sardarji* is regarded as more honourable than the *babuji* and to dissuade the youth from cutting their hair, it is used as an argument. There is also a joke that when an old man was telling his grandson that if you keep the hair unshorn and wear turban, then people respect you and give the way, the young man snapped back by saying that people always give the way to dangerous persons. What Bhindranwala is doing is that he is articulating the common Sikh's perceptions about the glory of Sikhism. It may be pointed out that virtually in every religion good things about it and bad things about others are told, articulated and made part of the process of religious socialisation. The perception about the defined other invariably entails the negative elements, because it is believed to be the only way to hold the members of the religious community with the sacred system together. In what respect a community constructs the other varies from one religion to the other. In the case of Bhindranwala, we find the expression and articulation of the prevailing folk understanding whose roots may possibly be traced back to colonial period. The Singh Sabha movement and the policy of the recruitment to army brought definite shift in the definition of the Sikh. The two created the similar image of the Sikh.

In his fifth speech, Bhindranwala began an uninterrupted process of appealing to the Sikhs to bear arms (*shastardhari*). For him, a real Sikh was not simply an *amritdhari* but also a *shastardhari*. This, for him, would make the real difference. It was also the wish of the tenth guru. In his seventh speech, he argued that when all other means are exhausted, the Guru had given the right to the Khalsa to use sword. His rhetoric on getting armed invariably involved the Hindus. He spoke in his 11th speech in the following manner:

> Many inform me that the licenses to get firearms are not issued. If Pawan Kumar can have 230 grenades, then why should you need the license? The believer of that God who tells that only at the time of war he should have arms otherwise bear the thread (*janeu*) only to tie the keys and keep the balance and weights is keeping 230 grenades. In the case of the Sikhs where the father had told the son that he would be like sheep if he did not keep the weapons, no crisis occurs in his keeping weapons.

The reference is obviously to the tenth guru of the Sikhs. He not only tried to legitimise the keeping of weapons among the Sikhs in this speech, but also built an image of the Hindus. The Hindus, for him, could only arm themselves in the time of war; otherwise they are expected to keep the keys and the balance to weigh the things. What does it mean? It is a well-known fact that in Punjab most of the upper-caste Hindus are traders and shopkeepers. In the cities, the Khatris constitute the major section of the traders, whereas in the rural areas the Banyas are more numerous. As pointed out earlier, the Hindu shopkeeper and the Sikh peasant are stereotyped categories. During the Punjab crisis, this issue emerged as one of the explanatory variables. The general argument that was advanced was that it was the exploitation of the Sikh peasant in the hands of the Hindu trader that is the underlying factor in the emergence of the Punjab problem. We now know that the Punjab crisis was too complex to be explained in the light of one factor, but the fact remains that the Banya has been one of the most hated, despised and feared class in the rural Punjab for centuries. Bhindranwala is simply interpolating his folk consciousness as a peasant to argue that waging a war is not the work of the Hindus. They are supposed to be shopkeepers. If the Hindus can keep arms, as he consistently and continuously refers to Pawan Kumar, then there is no need for the Sikhs to even seek permission of the government to keep the arms.

One may discern what a Hindu in the 15th speech of Bhindranwala means. He said: "We are being called *kesdhari* Hindus. The Brahmins told our father Guru Gobind Singh that he was a part of them. Our father, Guru Gobind Singh, declared that he was not the Brahmin, but the son of a Kshatriya." These lines are an interesting case of both defiance and acceptance of the Hindu tradition. He talked in the language of caste system to reject Hinduism, whereas talking of caste in this way would mean the acceptance of the Hindu values. However, the speech here is not as simple as we think it to be. One must raise the question why did Bhindranwala identify Brahmin with Hinduism and Kshatriya with Sikhism? The contradiction is so obvious that one tends to dismiss and reject such an argument. He referred to *Bachitar Natak* in which it is alleged that Guru Gobind Singh mentioned that he belonged to the Kshatriya caste. This could be the obvious reason for Bhindranwala to give the line of argument by identifying Brahmins with Hinduism. Since the Brahmin as a priest is regarded as the agent of sustaining, articulating and transmitting Hindu values, the negation of Brahmin signifies the end of Hinduism. However, as pointed out in the first chapter, it may not necessarily be the case. In Punjab, the Brahmin never occupied an influential position, but Hinduism along with the caste system had existed. It was found in the empirical study of 28 villages in Amritsar and Gurdaspur districts that most of the Sikhs referred to upper-caste Hindus as Brahmins (Puri, Judge and Sekhon 1999). For a certain section of the Sikhs, the upper-caste Hindu is Brahmin. There could be two reasons for this kind of perception and its manifestation. First, there is a complete exclusion between the Sikhs and the Hindus. This may not be true of the entire Punjab, but may be valid in the case of those villages in the Majha region where most of the people are Sikhs. Secondly, the distinction between the Brahmins and other upper-caste Hindus has disappeared, which may be case, for Brahmin lacks ritual prestige in Punjab. There is also an exception to this rule, namely, Banya, who figures in the folk songs of Punjab as moneylender. It seems that when Bhindranwala was making a distinction between the Brahmin and the Kshatriya by overlapping them with the Hindu and the Sikh respectively, he was essentially articulating and expressing the folk perception of the social reality. The defined 'other' is designated with single nomenclature, that is, Brahmin. At the same time, the categories of identification are derived from the caste system. In his 18th speech, which he delivered in July 1983 (Singh 2003), he defined the 'other' as renegade and ungrateful. The following part of the speech makes it clear:

> I have been saying it for a year. The person responsible for the martyrdom of the fifth guru belonged to their [Hindu] community. The man who poisoned the sixth guru belonged to them. The person responsible for the martyrdom of Sahibzadas [sons of the tenth guru] was also one of them. It is for the protection of frontal mark and sacred thread that the ninth Guru sacrificed his life. Today, these people have published a book according to which the sacrifice of Guru Tegh Bahadur was a result of personal reasons and he did not do anything for the Hindus. What can we expect from a community, which has become so ungrateful!

The martyrdom of Guru Tegh Bahadur marks a watershed in the Sikh history and "it is believed to have led to the creation of the Khalsa in 1699" (Fenech 2000: 124). It is important to mention that the general understanding among both the common Sikh masses and the Sikh religious leaders is that the ninth guru sacrificed his life to protect Hinduism after the Kashmiri Brahmins approached him. Even the Sikh historiography tends to support the prevailing view. Any attempt at any kind of alternative explanation has been facing aggressive reaction from the Sikh religious leadership. The recent incident involving Gurbax Singh Kala Afghana – an extremist Sikh and believed to be close to Jarnail Singh Bhindranwala – may be an illustration of the entire issue. He, in his book, alleged that Guru Tegh Bahadur did not sacrifice his life for the Hindus and in reaction to this statement, the Akal Takhat declared him guilty. Interestingly, what Kala Afghana was trying to construct was a more demarcated and exclusive past of the Sikhs which the Hindus could not transgress.[9] His speech in fact gives us an indication of the established and unquestioned explanation of the martyrdom of the ninth guru. The immutability of the reason for sacrificing his life to save Hinduism has provided a basis for another construction of the 'other'. This 'other' is weak, cowardly and incapable of protecting himself. Not only that the Muslim ruler is also posited in the situation who is oppressor and coercively converting the Hindus to Islam. In this situation, the agent as a saviour enters and intervenes effectively to save the oppressed and cowardly. In such a construction of history, it is not only the Hindu but also the Mughal ruler who is portrayed in negative terms. If after such a sacrifice of the Sikhs the Hindus do not acknowledge and express their thanks, then they are ungrateful.

Bhindranwala did not confine his arguments to establishing the already available view that Hindus are ungrateful. He went beyond this construction in his speeches. He argued that the Hindus had been betraying the Sikh gurus. He referred to the martyrdom of the fifth guru. The story of Gangu Brahmin is well-known to all the Sikhs that how he betrayed the two Sahibzadas (younger sons of the tenth guru) to the governor of Sarhind, who were then martyred. The betrayal of the Hindus is a constant reminder that they are not to be trusted. Once it is understood that he was preaching and spreading hatred, one may feel like getting into the heart of the fundamentalist. Mixing history with mythology and believing both to be the same constitutes the hallmark of fundamentalism because from such an affirmation emerges the conviction that truth is only one and that belongs to 'self'. In the absence of his comprehensive understanding of the Indian history, Hinduism and its plurality, composite religious tradition of the people, Islam and Sufism, the teaching of the gurus and saints, and presence of eclectic space, what he constructed was largely derived from impression and imagined stories as believed to be the ultimate truth. He did not stop even after characterising Hindus as ungrateful. Kahn Singh Nabha had already tried to argue along the same lines (Judge 2002).

It seems interesting that in the construction of the 'other', the history mixed with mythology is evoked and most of it is against the Muslim rulers. Knowing that he was duly trained in the Taksal to memorise and know Gurbani and Sikh tradition, Bhindranwala's comprehension and articulation remains at the level of the common Sikh perception. Most of the understanding has been the creation of *dhadis* and *kaveeshars*, who in order to eulogise the Sikh tradition, invent stories to show the valour and sacrifices of the Sikhs and they contribute to the negative construction of others in the process. The popularisation of the oppression of the Muslim rulers and cowardice of the Hindus has remained the main outcome of such activities. Two of the popular expressions about Guru Gobind Singh directly relate to the construction of the Hindu as a coward. One, it is popularly stated and said that Guru Gobind Singh turned jackals (*gidarh*) into tigers (*sher*). Obviously, the reference to the Hindu past of the Sikhs signifies the jackals. It may also imply that those who became Sikh turned brave, whereas those who did not become Sikh remained coward. Two, another popular saying is that had there been no Guru Gobind Singh, everybody (men) would have been circumcised. The presentation of the Guru as the saviour is without doubt a part of the universal religious tradition. Starting from Zorathastara and Buddha to the present-day saints, we invariably find that the religious leader is characterised as saviour. Such a phenomenon is powerfully presented in the Jewish tradition of the arrival of the prophet as well as the tradition of Vaishnav Hinduism regarding the incarnation (*avatar*) of Lord Vishnu. What is unique in the presentation of the tenth guru as the saviour is the simultaneous construction of Hindus as helpless and Muslims as oppressors. In the ultimate sense, the struggle and valour have been shown against the oppressor owing to which the closeness of the fighters with the helpless and oppressed was a natural outcome. It is here that the need for demarcating the space over a time was felt strongly. The saviour and the saved do not constitute the lord and the worshipper; rather, the latter is excluded from the moral community so long as he/she retains the old identity. The complex dialectical process that ensued in the making of Sikh folk consciousness created a necessity for a continuous and unabated effort to say that "we are saviour, but we do not form a part of the saved".

Placed in this context was the construction of communitarian closeness between the Sikhs and the Hindus. It was argued that the relationship between the Sikhs and the Hindus was marked by the exchange of "*roti* and *beti*", that is, common food and intermarriages. The upper-caste Hindus did not accept food from and dine with the Muslims, whereas the Sikhs and the Hindus did not have such taboos on the exchange of food as well as strong restriction on intermarriages. Numerous marriages have been taking place across religions among the Sikhs and Hindus. It is interesting to note that during the Punjab crisis an attempt was made to show that the Hindus and Sikhs have lot of things in common, whereas the Sikh militant discourse made every effort to convince that Sikhs are a separate community/nation. As the violence escalated, such attempts began to decline. The reason was obvious, that is, the Sikhs began to be recognised as a distinct religious community. Later on, the Blue Star Operation in 1984 and anti-Sikh riots following the assassination of Mrs. Indira Gandhi strengthened the demarcation.

After the death of Bhindranwala in 1984, the militant movement emerged again within six months with a vengeance, as the death toll began to rise with the passage of time. Many militant organisations emerged which carried the campaign of violence to higher and higher pitch. Though the activities of the Sikh militants were inwardly oriented towards the Sikh community and outwardly towards the state and its coercive institutions, yet the constructed 'other' remained unchanged. Threatened by physical elimination, the Hindus migrated to cities in Punjab and outside the state. The militants, in their warnings, remained ambivalent towards the Hindus. In certain warnings, they ordered the discontinuation of the teaching of Hindi, but later on, declared that learning any language was useful. In some cases, they warned Hindu students against seeking admission in engineering colleges of Punjab.[10]

III
CONSTRUCTING THE ENEMIES

Bhindranwala spoke on a large number of current issues and personalities and most of his comments were not just negative but derogatory and lacked in respect for the person. He seemed to have got the right to speak on anyone in any manner he wished. It is difficult to deconstruct and unfold the contents of his speeches to make logical sense out of the contents. Mostly his mentioning the political leaders and then criticising them in an abusive tone and language did not suit a 'saint'. Since he sustained his language and expression till the end, he could create excitement among the Sikhs gathered to hear him. He commented on a large number of personalities from different walks of life. Anyone of importance who spoke on his extremism and terrorism became the target of his violent criticism, but the politicians remained his favourite topic of discourse. In terms of criticism and the frequency of references, Mrs. Indira Gandhi remained *numero uno* for him. In the second place were the then Chief Minister of Punjab, Darbara Singh and the President of India, Giani Zail Singh. There were many others even among the Akali leaders, but Parkash Singh Badal, the former Chief Minister of Punjab, may be regarded as another leader who remained an object of his criticism and ridicule. An attempt has been made in the proceeding pages to construct from his speeches the enemies of the Sikhs he identified.

As mentioned earlier, Mrs. Indira Gandhi remained the main target of his attack. He referred to her as '*bibi*', and '*bahmni*', but in most of his speeches, he always mentioned the caste status of Mrs. Gandhi in one way or the other. He also mentioned her as the ruler of the country and for him the queen and the prime minister was one and the same thing. In the case of Mrs. Gandhi, he was perhaps right in the sense that as a prime minister of the country, she exercised her power in the manner of a queen. The imposition of emergency in 1975 has remained a black chapter in the country's history of democracy. Bhindranwala remained ambivalent towards her in the sense that he expressed both the hatred and fascination for her. The kind of power she symbolised and her ability to come back in power in 1980 after her defeat in 1977 became the focal point of his fascination. Simultaneously, she was an oppressive ruler for him who was not giving the Sikhs their due. He reacted to every statement that Mrs. Gandhi made on the Sikh issue and tried to show that she was telling a lie.

For him, Darbara Singh, the then Chief Minister of Punjab, was the agent of Mrs. Gandhi. He was always referred to as Zakaria Khan – one-time governor of Punjab during the Mughal period and responsible for the oppression on the Sikhs. In this way, he automatically equated Mrs. Gandhi with the Mughal rulers and the chief minister hailing form the ruling party became the stooge of the ruler. Interestingly, the person who is regarded as the creator of Bhindranwala phenomenon in the Sikh politics, namely, Giani Zail Singh, was also not spared from his scathing attacks. He said that Giani Zail Singh including and another Congress leader from Punjab were cleaning the chappals of Mrs. Indira Gandhi. However, the most interesting remark on Giani Zail Singh could be found in his 18th speech thus:

> Khalsaji, in this world, only that man's face is blackened who has committed a sin. Or has tried to outrage the modesty of a woman. Such person's face is blackened. But some people develop this habit that when they reach the old age, they blacken their face to hide the grey hair. I want to ask them that even if your face looks like a radish, how will you bring the light of youth? Though the beard would be black.

It is clear from the above remarks that Bhindranwala did not separate politics from personal life while attacking his opponents. There was no notion of what in civil society culture is called 'personal'. In his view, every aspect of a person's behaviour and conduct could be commented upon.

Bhindranwala went to the extent of referring to the *rahat maryada* to denigrate Giani Zail Singh's act of dyeing his beard. Parkash Singh Badal became his target of attack when his daughter was married to the grandson of Partap Singh Kairon. He reminded the audience that the latter persecuted the Akali leaders, particularly Mohan Singh Tur. It seems that he forgot to mention that in the beginning of his political career Kairon was an Akali, and notably Badal was in the Congress Party. In one of his speeches, he also threatened the then Chief Minister of Haryana, Bhajan Lal. He declared that come what may Bhajan Lal would be eliminated by the Singhs.

Besides the numerous political leaders of his time, he also commented on the writings and actions of the journalists, particularly when they wrote on him or the Punjab crisis. The notable among them were Lala Jagat Narain and his son Ramesh, Giri Lal Jain and Khushwant Singh. So far as Lala Jagat Narain and his son Ramesh who succeeded him as the editor of *Punjab Kesari* were concerned, there was nothing but contempt and hatred expressed against them. However, Giri Lal Jain and Khushwant Singh were given special treatment by him in his own characteristic way. In 1983, Jain wrote a piece in *The Times of India* the title of which was "One Hour to Midnight".[11] Bhindranwala reacted to it in the following manner:

> What was the name of the editor, which was just told. ... There is one Giri Lal Jain. He has given the news that it is 11 p.m. and one hour is left to 12 O'clock. He has not met me, otherwise he would not have written this. I request the journalist to publish my reaction. .... Giri Lal, you do not know when your 30,000 girls used to go, then the turbaned people brought them back. ... These Sikhs have made 90 per cent of the sacrifices for the country and those who tell us to leave it, I will tell later on.

After this response, Bhindranwala did not end the matter there. He went on to explain the significance of 12 O'clock in the Sikh history. He said: "The people have made it a joke.

Sikhs in the month of December used to attack the invader [allusion to Ahmed Shah Abdali] at the midnight when his armies would rest. They used to secure the release of girls belonging to Giri Lal and his like."

Khushwant Singh, another journalist of eminence and also a Sikh by religion also became his target of attack. Sometimes, in the beginning of 1984, Khushwant Singh wrote about the extremists in the Golden Temple. Bhindranwala responded to his article in the following way:

> There is a Khushwant Singh. I had his glimpse once. He is from Delhi and is close to Indira. He has given a statement that there are about 300 extremists and they can be eliminated. Khushwant Singh is somebody from Delhi.

After stating what Khushwant Singh had said Bhindranwala went on to clarify that he was doing his duty, as he had been fighting for the freedom of the Sikhs. He also explained that he was bringing the misdirected youth to the fold of Sikhism.

He kept his anti-Hindu stance quite clear as he tried to posit the valour and struggle of the Sikhs on the "historically established cowardice and impotence of the Hindus". He did not bother to inform the historical basis of such construction, as he took it for granted. He inherited a tradition set by the popular construction of the Sikh history at the folk level as well as the discipline of the seminary where he learnt Gurbani and *sakhis.*[12] We also find that the construction of the Hindu as coward and incapable of fighting to save his honour is consistently present in his speeches. It is also interesting to note that a person, who was hardly educated up to primary level, was reacting to various opinions and views, which had been appearing at that time in English newspapers. It implies that he was well briefed before he would deliver the speech. Since doubts were raised time and again on his integrity and interests due to his earlier association with the Congress leaders, particularly Giani Zail Singh, he consistently and frequently defined himself and his duties and functions. He always explained and clarified that he was a person who was devoted to Sikhism and was initiating the youth to get baptised and get rid of the path of addiction. He always argued that he was working for the unity of the *panth* and he had no other profane objectives in his mind. He went to the extent of claiming that he would never accept any position other than what he was – the head of a seminary.

In spite of the fact that his mode of presentation lacked any in-depth knowledge of history and his manner was rough, Bhindranwala became popular among the youth. Towards the end of his life, that is, before the Blue Star Operation, he was the most powerful person in Punjab. His threat could terrorise any person of importance and he played the game of death freely. However, in him were combined the Sikh folk perception and stereotypes and the narratives of the *dhadis*. This combination along with his status as the head of the Damdami Taksal provided the basis for his legitimacy and influence over the people. Added to it was the public platform provided to him by the Akali Dal. All these things combined proved to be dangerous, as he began to meet words with actions. At the time of the Operation Blue Star in which he was killed, he had already become hostile to the Akali Dal. The Akali Dal was also put into the category of the 'other' and he highlighted the inability of the leaders of the Akali Dal to be part of the Sikh tradition – an issue that would be taken up in the next chapter.

The identification and construction of enemies in the post-Operation Blue Star period began occurring at much larger scale than the earlier period. The emergence of many militant organisations also meant the active attack on the enemies. In the previous chapter, it was pointed out that contrary to the ambivalence of Bhindranwala towards the issue of Khalistan, the militants opened a new phase in the movement in 1986 when Khalistan as the goal of their struggle was announced in the *sarbat khalsa* in the Golden Temple. This brought them to the immediate confrontation with the Indian state. Still another class of people who became the target of the militants' attack were communists. Bhindranwala spoke on the communists only once criticising them for their lack of religious faith, but the militants identified them as enemies next only to the state and its coercive apparatus.

The construction of the 'other' in relation to the 'self' is an important project in building nationhood. It is like killing two birds with one stone. At the first place, the 'other' is identified as a homogeneous collectivity and all sense of discrimination within it is eliminated. Simultaneously, the 'other' is pitted against the 'self' whose cohesiveness is derived from the identification and the construction of the 'other'. Within the larger context of religious nationhood, the task is accomplished through the continuous efforts of the leaders and intellectuals over time and in space. Bhindranwala is located in this space at a particular historical juncture when an uninterrupted intellectual effort was put into the construction of the 'other'. The 'other' is important in relation to the 'self' in the sense that the one can only exist exclusively if it is able to identify the nature of separation from the other. For the militants' construction of nationhood the Hinduism was the constructed 'other', because it was politically essential due to Article 25 of the Constitution of India as well as close ties binding the two in certain respects of intimate relations. The construction of the Hindus as the 'other' was like severing off the umbilical cord to be free from all possible relations. Bhindranwala tried to do it effectively and in order to sustain it, he identified all those opposed to him as enemies of the constructed 'self'.

Notes

1. The other religious communities are Christians and Muslims, but their number is too small to be effective in political and social life of the state except for the Christian educational institutions. There is

also a small population of Ahmadiyas living in Quadian town of Gurdaspur district.

2. It is one of the major turning points in the history of the Punjab crisis. During the Asian Games, the Sikhs were not allowed to enter Delhi. They could not cross Haryana state. In the escalation of Punjab crisis the Government of India or the state government of Haryana contributed to the process of holding the entire Sikh community responsible for the trouble in the state.
3. Various interviews of the people in the villages conducted by the author along with his colleagues indicated that there was a widespread view that there was discrimination against the Sikhs. See Puri, Judge and Sekhon (1999).
4. Bhai Vir Singh's (2003) well-known novel *Sundri* revolves round the theme of forcible conversion to Islam.
5. Cerventes (1981) in his world famous novel has depicted a character who after reading lot of novels on knight errantry began to imagine himself as a knight and moves out to fight imaginary battles.
6. See Chapter 3 for the explication of the meaning of Khalsa and five Ks and its position in the Sikh history. It is now clear that the construction of the five Ks occurred during British rule.
7. Jagjit Singh (1985: 98-99) refutes this argument about the creation of Khalsa. However, the story is quite well-known among the Sikhs.
8. Most of the discussion is based on the observations and personal experiences of the author. The objectivity of the facts stated here is beyond doubt.
9. The case of Gurbax Singh Kala Afghana (Walia 2003) remained in the news in the recent past. But this is not the only controversy that has emerged in the recent times. The NCERT book on Indian History also mentioned certain non-religious reasons behind the sacrifice of the ninth guru and the Sikh community across the country branded it as a blasphemy and finally that part of the book was spiked. One of the problems in the views and description of the martyrdom of the ninth guru is the simultaneous construction of the Mughal emperor Aurangzeb, which is continuously challenged by the writings on the period. A recent addition to such work is that of Puniyani (2003: 60) and it is worthwhile to quote him on this issue thus: "The truth is that Aurangzeb ruled India for almost 50 years and, during this long span, he kept changing his policies depending upon the needs of the situation. His primary goal was to keep on expanding his empire all the time. The fact is that during the latter part of his rule, the number

of Hindus in his service was larger than ever before... The number of Hindus serving the Muslim emperor rose from 24 per cent during Shahjahan's reign to 33 per cent during Aurangzeb's rule."

10. Chapter 7 covers the issue and its analysis of the way the militants constructed the moral community of the Sikhs and posited the 'other' in that construction.
11. Since the complete reference is not known, it is difficult to say whether there was something provocative against the Sikhs. The title of the article was found offensive by many Sikhs, as it alluded to the jokes on the Sikhs with regard to 12 O'clock.
12. *Janam Sakhis* are based on the stories of the lives of the gurus.

6

Militancy and Martyrdom

In the previous two chapters, it was argued that the nationhood in the Sikh militant movement was a project, which meant that motive, intention and purpose were implicated in this construction. Identity entailed the construction of the 'self' as well as the 'other'. Following Smith's (1976) views on the ideals of nationhood, it may be pointed out that the project would not have been completed had the construction of distinct culture, tradition and history not carried out. In the present chapter, an attempt has been made to look into how the discourse of the militant movement constructed distinct culture, tradition and history of the Sikhs both as a community and religion. The discussion has been divided into four parts. The first part begins with the understanding of the Punjabi culture and its trajectory towards the construction of the Sikh tradition and culture. The second and the third parts respectively deal with the way Bhindranwala interpreted Sikh history and worked out the trajectory of the militant movement. In the last part, the construction of martyrdom in the post-Operation Blue Star period has been examined.

I
CULTURE OF MILITANCY

It may not be our purpose to find explanation for the alleged prevalence of the belief in the valour, bravery and militancy of the Punjabis from which the tradition of martyrdom is believed to have emerged, but one invariably comes across views strongly expressing these traits being a result of continuous invasions from the northwest frontier as well as the Sikh movement. The well-known Punjabi poet, Puran Singh (1964), expressed these views in the following manner:

> *"Beparwah jawan Punjab de*
> *Maut nu makhaulan karade*
> *Maran theen nahin darde."*[1]

> (The careless youth of Punjab make fun of death, as they have no fear of death).

Characterising Sikhs and/or Punjabis as militant, brave and aggressive is a common practice and attitude. It is generally believed that continuous invasions from the northwest India and the Sikh movement have contributed in making the militant personality of a Punjabi in the positive sense. Something that is invariably ignored and not given proper attention is the role of colonial construction of the communities in India as martial. To go still further back in history, one may argue that at one point of time when the caste structure was ideologically codified in *Manusmriti*, the assigned functions of each caste signified some ascribed abilities and skills of the people. What was more important in the colonial construction of martial races was that it claimed to have *scientific* origins, namely, physical anthropology and biology, and later on psychology when it invented IQ tests. This was the phase of the domination of theories of race.[2] The confluence of many forces has created an understanding that the Punjabis in general and the Sikhs in particular are militant and valorous. Some of the indicators that are empirically available to establish the militant tradition are as follows: (i) a large-scale recruitment to the British Indian Army took place from Punjab – a trend that continued after independence till recently; (ii) in order to keep the honour of the family, killing the enemy has been the norm among the peasants; (iii) vengeance is a part of the keeping of honour of the family as a result of which inter-family enmity is perpetuated for many generations; (iv) resolving the conflict through violence was powerful tradition instead of choosing the legal path; and (v) the construction of a rebel has also taken place in which bandits, like Dulla Bhatti, Sucha Surma and Jeona Maur, are treated with veneration. In the same way, the images of Shaheed Bhagat Singh, Kartar Singh Sarabha, etc. are seen in continuation with the rebellious tradition of the Punjabis.

There is a need to look into this issue of militant culture and tradition with a degree of ambivalence. There is no denying the fact that various scholars, who have studied the solidarity and feuds among the tribes and peasants, would find that some of the indicators mentioned in the preceding paragraph are quite prevalent all over the world. One is immediately reminded of Bourdieu's (1979) study of Kabyles of Algeria. The sense of honour and shame form the core elements in their social life. What has remained unnoticed is that solidarity and feud are confined to the inter-family or inter-group interactions within the peasant social life. In the case of the Punjabis, the valour and heroism are invariably limited to the peasants, particularly to the Jats. It is very difficult to observe the same valour and aggression of the Jat in some formal and informal interactions. A Jat never shows his militant and aggressive self in relation to the Patwari – the lowest level revenue official in the village – and the moneylender or Banya, who are indiscriminate in their exploitation of the peasantry. Patwari is rather a eulogised character in the village cultural life, whereas the Banya is despised. The following couplet highlights the way the Patwari is perceived:

"Balle Balle bai ladooan ne pind pattia
Teri tor patte Patwari."

(The people of the village are mad after sweetmeat, but the Patwari is mad after your walk).

However, the following story of earlier 20th century shows the high status, which the Jat peasant had accorded, and still continues to do so, to the Patwari:

> Once a Jat got implicated in a case. He appeared before the judge in the court. When the judge asked him to give the statement, he said to the judge, "May God make you Patwari, I am innocent, and kindly release me".

This makes the heroic elements of the peasant, both social and personal, in relation to his own class and caste of people. He was not showing this militant and aggressive behaviour towards the *kamins* related to and dependent on him under the *jajmani* or the *sepidari* system. If we examine the history and culture of feuds in Punjab, we find that the two caste groups predominate in the acts of violence, namely, the Jat and the Mazabi. In fact, it is the internal dynamics of the relationship between the Jat and the Mazabi that involves the latter in feuds. The Mazabi belongs to one of the lowest castes in the social hierarchy. He is dependent on the Jat for his survival. Earlier, and to a great extent, even now in most of the parts of Malwa, he is still working under the old *jajmani* system. Basically, the Mazabi is showing solidarity with his master in his feud.

It may look paradoxical that the Punjabi society, which is economically one of the most developed in the country, has not kept pace with the economic development. The fact that the tendency and practice to resolve conflict through violence still persists indicates the gap between the economic development and the culture. Does this gap create conflict between development and culture retarding the former? According to Nahar Singh (1999), there is no conflict between the two, for the Punjabi culture promotes consumerism, which is the dynamic force of the modern development. He is of the view that in Punjabi folk culture, which is a mirror image of the dominant mentalities of a society, the notions of death and consumption co-exist powerfully as the two are interlinked and united, but constitute opposite poles in the perception and thinking of the people. One is immediately reminded of the famous proverb in Punjabi whose origin may be dated back to the 18th century thus:

> *"Khadha peeta lahe da, baki Ahmed Shahe da."*
>
> (Whatever you have eaten and drunk is yours; the rest belongs to Ahmed Shah).

The proverb mentioned here only suggests that in the face of the invading forces what you have consumed is what belongs to you, which also implies that consumerism that is mentioned by Nahar Singh might have been the result of continuous invasions from the northwest. However, what he refers to is the following couplet:

> *"Do din khed lai, maujan mann lai,*
> *Tain bhajj javana, kangana kach dia."*
>
> (Enjoy and seek pleasure in your life, ultimately you will break like a bangle made up of glass).

Since there is no definite time for death, it is important to enjoy life. This kind of perspective is very much located in the space where the culture creates no contestation against the consumerism of modern developed society.

Over and above the militant Punjabi and/or Sikh is the construction of a tradition of martyrdom in Sikh history. The following couplet captures the essence of the martyrdom in Sikhism:

> *"Khalse the jit taan yakeeni hundi a,*
> *jang jadon larhada."*
>
> (The victory of the Khalsa is assured when he goes to war).

The above couplet is taken from a song sung by *kaveeshars*. *Kaveesharee* is one of the popular modes of singing the epics and folktales that also extend to the historical events and personalities invariably presented by mystifying the reality and the event. Various fairs at religious places, which are annual affairs in Punjab, provide the best platforms for the *kaveeshars* and other kinds of singers to put across these messages. Fenech (2000) has extensively dealt with the tradition of martyrdom in Sikhism where he has pointed out the role played by *kaveeshars* and *dhadis* in popularising the Sikh myth of martyrdom among the people. If there is an unshakeable faith in the martial and ever conquering spirit of the Khalsa, then it is also assumed that he is always willing to sacrifice his life for the faith and righteous cause. The stories of martyrdoms of the fifth and ninth gurus of the Sikhs and four sons of the tenth guru as well as of various Sikhs are the basis of the construction of the tradition of martyrdom. With the history and mythology mingling freely, the framework of perceptions is also aimed at constructing the other. Interestingly, this 'other' is not the Muslim community in spite of the fact all the tales revolve around the atrocities and cruelty of Muslim rulers.[3]

Within the Sikh community, the belief in the tradition of martyrdom in the construction of the 'self' is imputed through both the informal and formal channels of religious socialisation. Family and fairs may be taken up as informal settings, whereas the religious congregation on various occasions, such as marriage, death, birth and Akhand Path[4] constitute the formal settings. The construction of the tradition of martyrdom is internalised through the most powerful agency of socialisation, namely, family. All other agencies reinforce the same discourse. Fenech (ibid.) has rightly pointed out that among the various martyrs the martyrdoms of the ninth guru, Guru Tegh Bahadur and Baba Deep Singh occupy the central place in this discourse. However, it may be added that the stories of the sacrifices of the fifth guru, four sons of the tenth guru, many followers of the gurus, particularly Bhai Mati Das,

Bhai Taruji, etc. are narrated in various settings. One may trace back this phenomenon of the creation and transmission of the discourse of martyrdom to the Singh Sabha movement in the 19th century. More than a century of continuous articulation and transmission of the discourse has created a symbolic universe of the Sikhs in which martyrdom has become the value in Sikhism, which distinguishes it from other religions, particularly the Hinduism.

Smith (2002: 83) points out that "cultures involve the lived inter-subjective symbolic relationships through which we understand the conditions in which we live". In a way, the militant, aggressive and brave character and the tradition of martyrdom constitute the elements of the inter-subjective and lived experience that has been presented to the Sikhs through both the formal and informal agencies uninterruptedly for more than a century. It may be reminded that certain trajectories of culture are the function of the hegemony of a particular group. In this regard, a conscious creation of a discourse of particular kind is aimed at perpetuating the dominance. As pointed out earlier, the numerical superiority of the Jats in the Sikh community has qualitatively altered its character. It may also be noted that Punjab is predominantly based on agrarian economy. The Jats are the peasant proprietors and they dominate in agriculture. The two combine to provide them the political power. In such a situation, the cultural domination of the Jats may be regarded as a foregone conclusion. Within the Sikh community the Khatris and Aroras are the other important castes and they control the trade. The trading activities are against the spirit of aggression and violence. In fact, variations in the Sensex Index (Mumbai Stock Exchange) at the national level are largely dependent on the presence and lack of threat of political instability. In a situation of any threat of war, the index dips to lower levels. On the contrary, the peasants have always been involved in the feuds and wars. Bacon was of the opinion that yeoman made the best soldier (c. f. Durant 1976). At what historical time the

Jat culture, which has been described by many historians and anthropologists, has come to be identified with the Sikh community is a matter of further investigation. This is in spite of the fact that Sikhism was essentially a part of the Bhakti movement within which it was close to the sant tradition. Most of the works on Sikh history tend to associate the construction of militant tradition with the politics of identity to create demarcations from other religious communities. Bhindranwala could be regarded as the major figure that contributed to the construction of Sikh history with the singular purpose of highlighting militancy and martyrdom in the Sikh religion. The proceeding two parts of the chapter are based on his discourse of militancy and martyrdom.

II
CONSTRUCTION OF HISTORY

Bhindranwala frequently evoked the Sikh history in his speeches to clinch an issue. He remained confined to three gurus of the Sikhs, namely, Guru Hargobind (sixth), Guru Tegh Bahadur (ninth) and Guru Gobind Singh (tenth). There are minor references to other gurus if any in his speeches. Is it possible to make sense of why he chose only the three gurus? The fifth guru, who was martyred by the rulers of the day, drew his attention only once. It thus becomes difficult to argue that whereas the sixth and tenth gurus were evoked in order to valorise the Sikh tradition, the ninth guru symbolises martyrdom in the Sikh history. As we proceed to examine the narrative structure of his speeches, the motive or intention may become clear. It may also be added that in addition to the gurus, he also refers to the stories of the brave and sacrificing Sikhs. The best way to approach his narrative on Sikh history is to make the chronology of the events and the gurus. His first narrative on the sixth guru could be found in his second speech. In this speech he made allusion to the martyrdom of the fifth guru without referring his name. Let us see how he stated the 'historical facts' thus:

> [The fifth guru] had to sit on hot iron plate. Sacrificed the life by sitting on the hot iron plate. What were the prohibitions at that time? Jehangir had prohibited the Sikhs from keeping the arms, riding the horse, tying the turban, eating in the metalled utensils, beating the drum, flying the flag and keeping the army. All these chains had been put round the necks of the Sikhs. It was an enslavement of the Sikh community.

The above observation about the condition of the Sikhs at the time of Guru Hargobind has tremendous resemblance with what he had been saying about the conditions of the Sikhs in the contemporary times. In other words, only the rulers have changed, the condition of the Sikhs has not undergone any change. In the process, he misses the period of the British rule. Obviously, the period of Maharaja Ranjit Singh was the Khalsa Raj. One may ask a question whether all the Sikhs were allowed to keep the arms during the reign of Ranjit Singh. For him, the eternal objective of the martyrdom of the fifth guru was to give rights to the Sikhs. The Sikh historians would never agree with him on the circumstances that led to the martyrdom of Guru Arjun Dev. He is, in fact, inventing history to construct a tradition. The common sense perception is that no ruler allows the common people to keep arms. Even at the time of Bhindranwala keeping firearms required license and it never signified the enslavement of the Sikhs. We now have one image of the Sikh, that is, the one who keeps arms. There is no need to have any evidence to argue that at no point of time every Sikh would like to keep the weapons. Even if a stranger comes to Punjab the only thing he would notice is turban. So far as the weapons are concerned, a minuscule minority might be keeping arms with the conscious assertion of being the Sikhs. Most of the people who keep firearms are those who have rivalries or feel threatened. A common Sikh never kept arms. A baptised Sikh would invariably keep a small sword shaped knife called *gatra*. Neither Bhindranwala nor a common Sikh had the knowledge that the tenth guru insisted on keeping five weapons instead of five Ks for the Khalsa (see Pashaura Singh 2004). What Bhindranwala preached and insisted on was the tradition largely invented by the Singh Sabha movement by compromising with the British on the question of weapons.

In the same speech, he narrated the story of how Guru Hargobind decided to punish Chandu who was responsible for the martyrdom of the fifth guru. As he told, the Guru was 11 years old at that time. Chandu, according to him, was a minister of Jehangir. In his narration of the declaration of the sixth guru regarding the revenge from Chandu, Bhindranwala simultaneously constructed the present scenario. Immediately after succeeding the fifth guru, the sixth guru declared and swore to take the revenge. There was a reaction of the Sikhs, as the idea of revenge made some of them petrified thus:

> Even these days when there is minor heat, many start sweating. ...This is not right. On one side is the government and on the other side are the common Sikhs, we the people. That time also such people went to Mata Gangaji and pleaded to her. ...They told her that he spoke in excitement. Many a time Singhs say that I speak in excitement without applying my mind. If the Sikhs could say that about the Guru, then....

The project, consciously or unconsciously, directly or indirectly, is revealed right in the beginning of the narrative. And it is obvious. Only time and the rulers have changed, but the landscape of the oppression of the Sikhs remains unchanged. Even at the time of the Guru Hargobind, there were Sikhs who became anxious when he said that Chandu would be taught a lesson. The times of Bhindranwala also had such Sikhs. Comparing oneself with the guru has two implications that remain hidden in the narrative and could work, to use Jung's phrase, at the level of 'collective unconscious'. First, it highlighted the phenomenon of unending oppression on the Sikhs. It traces the time when it began and it still continues. Secondly, as and when the leader of the Sikhs (at that time the sixth guru and now Bhindranwala) begins to talk about revenge and sword, a section among the Sikhs starts thinking that he has gone out of his mind. The second implication in fact is legitimising process. It may be argued that since there are no differences in the two conditions, it is therefore essential to tread the path that was chosen by the Guru. He used the story of the sixth guru more to legitimise the actions and strategy he had adopted to fight against the 'oppressive' regime. The similarity was obvious for the common Sikhs. During the reign of Jehangir, a Sikh could not keep the sword and in the rule of Mrs. Indira Gandhi, the Sikhs could not keep firearms. These parallels looked obvious and unambiguous to the common person without understanding the underlying differences. Even if we accept that the two conditions are the same, we have to examine the relationship between the state and the individual or a group. As we have pointed out earlier, it is not the similarity between Jehangir and Indira Gandhi, but in the logic of governance in two distinct political systems. The threat to the political system in the situation where a common man can possess arms is believed to be more than if the restrictions on keeping them are put. It is only the differences in the kind of weapons from one period to another.

Since the narrative of the second speech of Bhindranwala essentially revolved around the punishment of Chandu, the story is told in an interesting manner. The tension between the ruler and the Guru is narrated with interjections making the story significant in the contemporary context. Bhindranwala did not mention the period of imprisonment of the Guru, but makes it forced confinement. The emperor is troubled and has nightmares and he tells the Guru to leave the prison, but the Guru refuses to go unless the other 52 prisoners are not released.[5] Guru is released after the emperor agrees to free 52 more prisoners. Thus, the nightmares of Jehangir come to an end and he also hands over Chandu to the Guru. We may now present how Bhindranwala narrated the subsequent story of punishment to Chandu that he got from the Sikhs thus:

> *Nakel* [nose string] was put in his [Chandu] nose and was paraded in the streets of Lahore. But when he (sixth guru) swore, many were saying it was impossible. "It is not possible" is expressed on the stage many a time. Many say that this boy [Bhindranwala] is speaking, has no wisdom, creating schism in the panth, he is not educated, and does not know politics. When they are struck on the ear, they say that he was talking sense and we should have agreed to him.

In one speech, Bhindranwala tried to hammer on the conscience of the Sikhs who had come to hear him that whatever he was saying was not of less importance than what the sixth guru had said. In the case of the sixth guru, the situation was characterised by revenge and punishment to Chandu who was responsible for the martyrdom of the fifth guru. It is time and space that become ambiguous, blurred and fuzzy in the trajectory of his narrative. The story of the Guru Hargobind becomes a medium to send the message across the addressee. The referent is primarily a veiled, hidden and coded message in which the addressee is expected to be aware of the story and its implications. The sender of the message is primarily reminding that the time and space in which the addressees are living is not different from the times signified in the story. The style typically resembles that of the *kirtani jathas*, but the content is political.[6] The political implications of the narrative are worked out and ordered in a way that the sender of the message is trying to claim the righteous place of being the leader of the community. Some of the followers had doubts and lacked faith in the Guru, but they were proved wrong. Similarly, in the contemporary period, some Sikhs have doubt, but they are wrong.

It is obvious that Bhindranwala narrates the story of the sixth guru in order to establish the validity of his own arguments. Logically, it is not the appropriate way to do this, but it does not matter to him. In his other speeches, he mentioned Bhai Bidi Chand, who was a loyal Sikh of the sixth guru. The stories from the lives of ninth and tenth gurus remained the main topics in his speeches and the pattern of presentation remained the same, that is, after a long story there would be a comment on the contemporary situation. Two motifs emerge from his narratives on the ninth guru. First, highlighting the plight of the helpless and oppressed Hindus who had lost their will to fight against the Mughal rulers. In his 36th speech, he drew a picture of the condition of the Kashmiri Brahmins approaching the ninth guru for help. In his narration of the story of the martyrdom of Guru Tegh Bahadur, he narrated a situation when somebody informed the emperor that the guru had said that he would destroy Delhi and Lahore. At this moment, he said: "There are many such persons among us. Please don't mind. There are many among us sitting here who will inform and exaggerate the things. But I don't care."

He so far followed the pattern well established by *ragis* and *kirtani jathas.* He mixed Gurbani, mythology and popular stereotypes well along the lines that had already been treaded. His frequent references to the contemporary conditions blurring time space distanciations had roots in the tradition of singing devotional songs and preaching. His most referred and frequently quoted guru is Guru Gobind Singh – the founder of the Khalsa Panth. One may make a conjecture that there is a universal pattern in depicting and describing the birth of a great guru or a prophet. He refers to *Bachittar Natak* allegedly written by Guru Gobind Singh. His narrative is simple and revolves round the story how the God approached the Guru who was meditating at Hemkunt Sahib and told him to go to the *mat lok* (human world) and do the good. He narrated what was expected from the Guru in addition to do away with the evil thus: "...to prepare to sacrifice life for religion. He was not only to prepare people to sacrifice life but also to punish those who were responsible for this." The narrative is typical of the divine birth, but it is the story of Bheekhan Shah that takes the narrative closer to the story of the birth of Christ. He said that Bheekhan Shah bowed in the direction of Patna Sahib at the time of the birth of the tenth guru. Bheekhan Shah's curiosity to meet the Guru and see his divine ability took him to Patna Sahib and he returned satisfied.

In the same (36th) speech, Bhindranwala also gave a new interpretation to the story of the founding of Khalsa Panth on the day of Baisakhi in 1699.[7] He said:

> When the Guru took the volunteer to the tent, he was beheaded. I shall tell our writers and *dhadis* that it is often remarked that goat was slaughtered. Can in history somebody tell the price of the goat? Can somebody tell who brought the goats? From which market were the goats purchased and how did they look?

What he emphasised in this speech was that after the five volunteers were beheaded, the Guru revived them to life thus establishing the divine origin of the tenth guru. In his 41st speech delivered on May 13, 1984, he again evoked the story related to the tenth guru. It was one of the most aggressive of the speeches. When one hears this speech, it becomes obvious that he was very angry and the contents of the speech make it clear that why he was angry. His close follower, the apprentice from the Taksal and the main mercenary, Surinder Singh Sodhi, had been killed. He was upset and spat fire. At this moment he narrated how the tenth guru punished Cheto Masand for deceiving the Guru. His legs were tied and hot *halwa* was poured on his head. The pattern of the presentation of the argument by Bhindranwala becomes predictable and could only be understood if we know the tradition of singing and sermonising in Sikhism. Since most of the preachers try to create impression among the common masses, they use simple language and argue in the traditional way in which narrating a story or quoting religious hymns from the sacred book are the most effective and persuasive methods for the purpose. The choice of the gurus for the construction of a narrative is one of the interesting aspects of his speeches. When one Gurdial Singh was shot dead by Punjab police, Bhindranwala, in his second speech delivered on February 27, 1983, narrated the story of how the tenth guru sent Banda Bahadur to punish 'Wajida' who was responsible for the martyrdom of the sahibzadas.[8] In his 31st speech, he responded to his critics in his own characteristic way when they stated that his actions were against the Sikh tradition. He narrated the story how when the tenth guru was informed that the Mughals were looting the *sangat*, he ordered that the Sikhs should loot them.

His 14th speech is one of the model examples of how the history is constructed. Sometimes, in May 1983, Bhai Balwant Singh, belonging to Mukerian, approached Bhindranwala that Kewal Krishan – the local Congress leader – harassed him. He informed him that his wheat crop had been forcibly taken away on the orders of Kewal Krishan and now he would also auction his house. After narrating the woes of Balwant Singh, he said: "We have no enmity with any caste, but I wish to tell that the ancestors of Kewal Krishan were Lakhpat and Jaspat who killed the Sikhs."[9] It is irrelevant whether the contemporary events and conditions come first or later for illustration. The important thing is that the story of the tenth guru could act as an explanatory variable if we express the matter in positivist sense. There is no evidence to argue that Kewal Krishan had some relationship with the two 18th century personalities who were responsible for the atrocities on and massacres of the Sikhs. Incidentally, we do not find the reference to Deewan Kaura Mal, who was a Hindu but helped the Sikhs in the same period.[10] Two things emerge from this. One, the story of the lineage of Kewal Krishan is concocted. Two, if we assume that there could be some linkage, even then he could not be held responsible for the crimes of his forefathers. It is clear that Bhindranwala's illustration of harassment of Balwant Singh at the hands of Kewal Krishan cannot become the basis of establishing that he has been anti-Sikh. There is a tremendous parallel between the language of Bhindranwala and that of the 'Hindutva' forces, which have been making the Muslims responsible for the alleged demolition of some Ram Temple in Ayodhya.

In the end of this part of the chapter, it may be pertinent to refer to Bhindranwala's 27th speech in which he gave long discourse on the story of Botā Singh and Garja Singh, believed to be characters from the Sikh history, which epitomises how time and space could be blurred to the extent of making them immutable and unchanging. The story he narrated referred to the 18th century period when the Sikhs were persecuted and they fought guerrilla battles. We have already mentioned Bhai Vir Singh's novel, *Sundari*, in this regard. Bota Singh and Garja Singh, Bhindranwala spoke, heard people saying that the Sikhs had vanished. In order to establish the presence of the Sikhs, both of them put a check post and started charging tax on the people. After narrating this story he moved on to the contemporary situation and stated the following:

> Thus, the rulers were surprised that in a situation when the Sikhs could not be found even if they are searched, these two had formed their own parliament. The Khalsa is very strange. The God blessed them and they could establish their rule for seven days. Two Singhs established this rule. They did it when it was difficult even to mention the name of the Sikhs. Now, there is nothing. There is a need to have the courage. Those who are talking in a different language have not read the Sikh history.

At many places, in his various speeches, Bhindranwala betrayed his real intentions in a stream of consciousness. Hearing his speech provides a better insight into how he could have arrived at the establishment of Khalsa Raj. We find that he got excited and raised the pitch of his voice. He did not mention the name of his target of attack and criticism, but it could be discerned that he was critical of the Akalis. Three things combine to make this speech insightful. First, even when the Sikhs had to hide to survive, they could establish their rule. Second, the phenomenon of rulers oppressing and killing the Sikhs is not new. It is as old as the history of the Khalsa. This second aspect clearly brings out the mixing of the past and present. The persecution of and oppression on the Sikhs have not deterred them from their objectives. We all know that the struggle of the Sikhs culminated into their rule over the region that led to the emergence of Ranjit Singh in the 18th century. Finally, there is an imposition of contemporary concepts on the past. One such concept is 'parliament'. Since he mentioned this word to emphasise that whenever and wherever the two Sikhs sat together and took a decision it became a parliament. The explanation of the parliament is very close to what is called *gurmata* in Sikhism.[11] The only common thing between the two is taking decision together after proper deliberations.

History, mythology and folk stories merge together in the speeches of Bhindranwala to give new interpretation to the contemporary period. There was no question of anybody asking him whether all these things he was saying could be authenticated with some documentary evidence. He seemed to be having complete faith and conviction that whatever he was saying was the truth. It was the conviction of a fundamentalist who was trained to be a preacher of faith. His mode of preaching was to be the legacy of more than two hundred years and traced its roots to the tenth guru. The moment Bhindranwala entered the politics and surcharged it with his own brand of extremism, the Akalis, who were primarily interested in electoral gains, felt threatened and withdrew and dissociated from him. By the time this happened, he had already established himself as the militant leader with a large following among the Sikh youth. As he got isolated from the Akali Dal, which was also controlling the SGPC, his very presence in the precincts of the Golden Temple was threatened. He thus used his coercive power to stay in the temple. For him, the Sikh history, as he presented, interpreted and understood it, and the contemporary conditions, were not different, that is, there had been oppressive rulers and the traitors and they were still there. Since the present was not different from the past, it was of paramount importance for the Khalsa to find the ways and means of fighting not only against the oppression, but also for freedom. Oppression and freedom emerge as binary oppositions and the struggle for freedom would end all oppression. What are the methods and modes of this fight? In the light of his conception of Sikh history, he spelt out his plan of action and in the next part, the discussion is mainly focussed on this issue.

III
STRUGGLE AS CONSTRUCTED TRADITION

The oppression on the Sikhs could only be ended if they acquired freedom, but how it would be done was an equally important question. All consciously planned movements are characterised by well-thought out strategy and tactics. Was there such a case with Bhindranwala? How did he articulate his strategy and tactics? In his speeches one hardly finds any element of articulation of his strategy. Despite all this, he talked about how to achieve the goal, which for him was 'freedom' for the Sikh community. Since we know that he did not clearly state that the purpose of his struggle was to achieve the sovereign state of Khalistan, the notion of freedom remained fuzzy in his conceptual scheme. The road to freedom was to be found in and legitimised through the construction of the religious tradition. In a way, what is called righteous path was to be the strategy and tactics of the struggle for freedom. The Akali Dal was not faced with such limited choices. Its leaders were seasoned politicians and knew that in political space flexibility of the methods was essence of the success. They would have liked to use the issue of the Sikh autonomy the way it had been articulated in the Anandpur Sahib Resolution to the extent it could get them votes. Bhindranwala belonged to a different tradition and the legacy of Baba Deep Singh kept his choice of alternative methods limited. Even then, he learnt the art of political rhetoric rather well.

When the Dharam Yudh Morcha was started in which he collaborated with the Akali Dal and accepted Sant Harchand Singh Longowal as its 'dictator', he also accepted the non-violent means to be adopted for achieving the goal.

Simultaneously, he organised killing squads and initiated revenge murders. The targets of these attacks were the Nirankaris in the beginning and as the time passed, they not only began to increase but also covered anybody who could be opposing him or his movement. His speeches deliberated on the entire issue of peaceful struggle and preparedness for the armed struggle. In his sixth speech, he spoke on the peaceful path. This speech provides us the way he understood non-violence as he said: "Since the avatar of Guru Nanak to present times the Sikh community has been passing through a severe struggle.... It suffered during its period of non-violence." He then narrated the story of the sixth guru how he decided to take the revenge of his father's death. What he was hinting at was that the fifth guru adopted the peaceful path and faced oppression. He was alluding to the non-violent nature of the Dharam Yudh Morcha. It has already been pointed out that he was very selective in his choice of the stories from the Sikh history and mythology. In his 15th speech, he spoke on non-violent method of struggle in his typical style. He said:

> Khalsaji, be united, work together and arm yourself. Though it has been told to us to remain peaceful and I also support it, but I do not support such a peace in which the daughters of the Sikhs are insulted and then it is said we should be peaceful.

As the time passed, his disdain and disregard for non-violence as a method of struggle began to become visible. His differences with the Akali Dal and his total rejection of non-violent methods surfaced simultaneously. In August 1983, he openly turned against non-violent means of struggle adopted by the Akali leadership. In his 30th speech, he made fun of non-violence. Treating it as a farce, he regarded it as if it was something like a feminine object. He then shifted to the Sikh history to show how non-violence could be situated when he said:

> In the history of the Gurus and the history of the Sikhs excluding that of the Akali Dal, there are no two generations that were non-violent. Let any educated person show that it is not the case. In the presence of the sangat, I swear that I will behead myself if somebody could prove that I am wrong. Except for the history of the Akali Dal, no two consecutive generations have remained non-violent in the history of both the Gurus and the Sikhs. Our history that we are now witnessing has been continuously non-violent for fourteen generations. Why? Are we Sikhs of Indira [Gandhi]? Why are you not telling whose Sikhs are you? If you are Sikhs of the Guru, then how long will this non-violence continue? An old man asked me, ... "Non-violence is now forty years old. When will she be married out?"

After this pun he proceeded to give evidence in both the history of the gurus and the Sikhs. Interestingly, he begins with the martyrdom of the fifth guru and the revenge in the next generation. Most of the stories he narrated of revenge are well-known in the Sikh folk history. After completing what he understood as evidence of his contention, he then mentioned the incident that occurred in 1978 on the day of the Baisakhi in which according to him, thirteen Sikhs were killed and 70 injured.

The critique of non-violence that is constructed by Bhindranwala has three dimensions. First, he argues that non-violent struggle is not the character of the Sikh movement in history. Quoting largely from the folk construction of the Sikh history, he tries to establish that the Guru believed in avenging the wrong done to them though in the next generation. Second, he tries to undermine the Akali Dal by arguing that it was not the legitimate heir to the Sikh tradition, as it had never abandoned non-violence, particularly after independence. Third, he regards non-violence as feminine and uses the metaphor of marriage of the daughter to discard it. He argues that the time has come to abandon the non-violent path.

In the process, he also constructs the gender by creating binary opposition of male/female corresponding with violence/non-violence. Mention should be made of his reconstruction of Sikh identity where he constructed masculine/feminine oppositions corresponding with Sikh/non-Sikh and brave/coward (see Chapter 3).

Even in 38th speech, which he delivered on April 1, 1984, he reiterated his position with regard to non-violence as if it was a female. In fact, he began with a joking expression by saying, "This non-violence, I don't know how many feet long it is". Then, he pointed out that he was joking, but there was an element of truth in it. After demolishing and dismissing non-violence as something, which was feminine and did not suit the people of honour, he went on to do the main job, that is, questioning and undermining the legitimacy of the Akali Dal as the party of the Sikhs. It was a coincidence that the then President of the Akali Dal was fourteenth in the line of succession and the same number belonged to Jarnail Singh Bhindranwala among the heads of Damdami Taksal. He challenged that there was not even a single president of the Akalis, starting from Baba Kharhak Singh to the present, who achieved martyrdom, whereas the founder of the Taksal, Baba Deep Singh, was a martyr. For him, non-violence was Gandhian and had no place in Sikhism.[12] Strategically, his objective was to marginalise the Akalis who remained insincere to their faith.

In the backdrop of such a rhetorical landscape, the trajectory of Bhindranwala's rhetoric logically moved towards the legitimacy of the use of violence to achieve the objective. Now, the question was what to do to the fight for freedom. It required preparedness. The best way to prepare is to get armed. He distinguished between the traditional weapons, such as sword and iron bangle, and the modern firearms that would prove effective and decisive in the struggle.[13] Even when he accepted the non-violent mode of struggle in the Dharam Yudh Morcha, he kept on hammering the idea of preparing for the eventual struggle that could be violent. He time and again emphasised the need for arming oneself against any such eventuality. He kept on repeating his appeal to the youth that they should keep firearms. In his 33rd speech, he emphasised that keeping the weapons is the order of the guru to the Sikhs in his characteristic way thus:

> Second, I talked about weapons. They said (they have heard from the CID) that we are carrying weapons. I want to ask whether the weapons are kept by the eunuchs. Weapons are kept by men (*marad*). We are not your Sikhs, Bibi. We are neither the Sikhs of Indira nor her father. We are the Sikhs of Guru Hargobind Sahib.

With regard to the firearms, he gave many clarifications. One clarification he gave was regarding the arms license. His favourite example was Pawan Kumar who, according to him, possessed 230 grenades. He argued that if a Hindu could keep grenades and was not punished, why should the Sikhs bother about license. He also pointed out that come what may keeping arms was indispensable for the Sikhs if they believed in the tenth guru. In his 30th speech, he suggested the ways to get the firearms while speaking on the entire issue of licenses for arms thus:

> The licenses in the villages are only issued to the Hindus. I received reports yesterday that when the Sikhs applied they were refused. Don't worry. You don't have money to pay the revenue and how will you buy firearms? Let the Hindus get the licenses and at the right opportunity snatch these weapons from the Hindus. Don't wait for my orders to do so at that time.

The construction of communalism in his discourse was quite obvious though on certain occasions he tried to argue that he had nothing against Hindus. In the process of convincing the Sikhs that they should buy firearms of the best quality, he revealed and betrayed his construction of both the Indian state as controlled by Hindus and the Hindus as cowards. At the level of common sense, one could ask what is expected from the state if a religious and political leader appeals to his followers to get armed and talks of freedom? The legitimacy of keeping weapons was derived from the Sikh gurus, rightly or wrongly is irrelevant. The gurus are portrayed as aggressive, militant and well-armed in the construction of discourse. It is an example of choosing a singular tradition from the essentially synthetic or composite religious creed. Bhindranwala, in the process of legitimising his own position with regard to the use of weapons, simultaneously decentred the Akalis who, according to him, had not followed their gurus. The Akalis lost ground to Bhindranwala, but owing to their long political experience and enlarged network, they could withstand his efforts to demolish them.

One riddle that has remained unsolved was regarding the views of Bhindranwala on the possibility of attack on the Golden Temple. He frequently mentioned it in his speeches. Could he anticipate such an occurrence? Or was he the person who gave the idea to the government to attack the Golden Temple? It is very difficult to assert which one of two is an adequate query to be raised. There is also a third possible question – a revised form of the first query. Did he really anticipate such an occurrence? This third question has arisen because one could say that when talked about the possible attack on the Golden Temple, he only meant police action. However, the events of June 1984, that is, the launching of Operation Blue Star, indicate that he in fact had prepared himself for the army attack. There could also be an argument that Bhindranwala was sure that the government would not attack the Golden Temple due to the sentiments of the Sikhs. As he was trained in the study of Sikh scriptures, mythology and possibly history, he might have been sure on one ground, that is, attacking the Golden Temple could be a serious offence, which would lead to mass uprising of the Sikhs. However, such views can only be stated as conjectures though each point can be emphasised with ertain arguments.

In his 11th speech, he spoke on the possible attack on the Golden Temple at length and tried to take cognisance of various aspects of such an eventuality. He not only tried to warn the government, but also told the youth to get prepared for such an eventuality. He said:

> I understand that I am justified in telling the rulers who are planning while sitting in their offices and government quarters to find a way to pick up and kill Bhindranwala and Longowal. Pay heed to what I am saying. Many regimes tried to do the same thing with the gurus in the past. We are the sons of that father [Guru Gobind Singh] who defeated the army of ten lakh men only with forty Singhs. .... So far as Harimandir Sahib[14] is concerned, whether it is woman, a child or the Singh of the Guru, he/she prefers to be cut into pieces, but shall not tolerate the insult to the Harimandir Sahib.

After stating the possibility of the attack on the Golden Temple, he might have felt unsure, as he went on to appeal to the Sikhs in the following manner:

> Alert the sangat[15] in the villages. When in the boundary of the Golden Temple somebody with power tries to destroy the existence of the Sikhs, don't hesitate. As for Muslim nothing exists beyond Mecca, for the Sikh there is nothing beyond Sri Harimandir Sahib.

However, what the Sikhs would do in the situation of attack on the Golden Temple was best described and explained in his 30th speech thus:

> Many ask what is to be done? What is the objective? It should be explicitly told. The explicit is this that when you come to know that police has attacked the Harimandir Sahib, but you must confirm it. It should not happen that somebody spread the rumour and you start your action. The moment there is an attack on the Harimandir Sahib, the same day whether it is small towns or big cities, no person without turban could be seen. Remain sympathetic to the Muslims.

Of all the views he expressed in anticipation of the attack on the Golden Temple the above mentioned betrays his fundamentalist self clearly and unambiguously. In other speeches, he tried to emphasise the valour and aggression with which the Sikhs would face such an attack. It also becomes clear that he might have started preparing for an army attack quite late; otherwise he anticipated only the possible attack of the police. He made it clear that the Golden Temple was the most sacred place for the Sikhs and its violation would not be tolerated. Bhindranwala might have tried to convince himself that the government would not venture to involve army at a large scale to apprehend him. Even then, he had a lingering doubt, for he tried to give words to his thought about what was to be done in such a situation. The action he suggested was killing the people without turban and possibly sparing the Muslims. It is interesting to note that in his speeches he spoke at length how the gurus saved Hinduism from the tyranny and oppression of the Muslims. Understanding that the Hindus as rulers had proved to be oppressive and ungrateful, they were the real culprits and to be eliminated. In one of his speeches, he also talked about not to violate women, but to treat them as mothers or sisters. Thus, his orders were clear, but the problem was that there were a large number of Sikhs called *sehjdharis* who did not bear turban. Were they to be spared? Such serious and intricate issues were not the subject matter of the rhetoric of a public speech. However, even his notion of a Sikh was exclusive and it may be reasonably argued that in his scheme of things, the Sikh and Khalsa identities were coterminous. The achievement of freedom was only possible if the Sikhs become internally cohesive and pure. Arming oneself would only be effective if the Sikhs live according to the edicts of *rahat maryada*. Stopping the consumption of drugs and alcohol and getting baptised were the preconditions for the attainment of freedom. He emphasised the need for unity among the Sikhs that could become the basis for meaningful struggle.

IV
TRIBUTES AND THE CONSTRUCTION OF MARTYRDOM

This part of the chapter deals with the construction of martyrdom in the post-Bhindranwala phase. As mentioned earlier, Bhindranwala died in the Operation Blue Star in 1984. It is based on the messages that appeared in the newspapers as tributes to those militants who had been killed mostly in encounters with the armed forces. The nature and content of these messages were informative and denotative. The important aspect of these messages was that all these appeared as advertisements, as the militants paid the money to the newspapers for getting these published. It is interesting to note that the newspaper that provided a lot of space to the warnings and responsibilities of the militants earned money from the advertisements, which appeared as tributes. In terms of the contents of the tributes, these were monotonously the same. It seems that the newspapers brought out a standard version in every case.

The tributes were paid to the dead terrorists by the organisation(s) and militant leaders. In 1990, the militant whose death was mourned by all organisations and the maximum tributes appeared in the press was Toofan Singh Toofan of Cheema Khuddi village in Gurdaspur district. He was about 20 years old at the time of his death and was involved in 150 cases of murders. He was Lt. Gen. of the Khalistan Liberation Force (KLF). He died on April 8, 1990 in a police encounter.

The killed militant's actions and character were highlighted with praise and he was regarded as a great hero of the Sikh Panth in all the tributes. Most importantly, he was given the status of 'martyr' through these tributes and his martyrdom would be located in the Sikh tradition. Besides these tributes, there were advertisements regarding the *Antam Ardas* (Last Prayer) at the villages of the slain militants. Here also, we find two kinds of messages. In the first kind, it was stated that "In Sant Jarnail Singh Bhindranwala's initiated struggle *so and so* militant had sacrificed his life". The other kind stated that "In the present struggle *so and so* militant had sacrificed his life". In fact, these wordings are not unconsciously framed. There is an indication that some of the militant organisations did not accept Bhindranwala as the guiding spirit of the movement, whereas others considered him their leader. The Babbar Khalsa International, particularly, seemed to be opposed to Bhindranwala.

To illustrate various aspects of the tribute, one of the advertisements, given below, appeared on the front page of the *Ajit* (February 15, 1987), and issued by Manjit Singh, President of the All India Sikh Students' Federation, was different from the usual but the pattern was common. It was regarding the *Antam Ardas* of Sher Singh Sher and it carried a photograph of Bhindranwala and also another but smaller in size of Sher Singh Sher. The following is the translation of the advertisement:

> The Bhog of Akhand Path and the Antam Ardas of great warrior and immortal martyr Bhai Kanwaljit Singh Kamba alias Sher Singh Sher will be held on 16 February 1987, Monday at village Haruwal of district Gurdaspur. For this great and honourable warrior's antam ardas Baba Thakur Singh of Damdami Taksal, Baba Joginder Singh, Bhai Jagir Singh Masat and other workers of AISSF are coming.
>
> Programme: Bhog Sri Akhand Path Sahibji: 10 A.M.
> Kirtan: 11.30 A.M.
> Tributes: Till 3 P.M.

Such advertisements continued to appear during the militant movement. Sometimes there would be numerous advertisements on one slain militant, as it had happened for Toofan Singh Toofan mentioned earlier. Tributes also appeared as resolutions of the meetings or press statements, but the news about the *Antam Ardas* invariably appeared in the form of advertisement. The following is an example of the press statement:

> The All India Sikh Students' Federation (Daljit) expressing its sorrow over the martyrdom of Gurnam Singh Pehalwan (Sultanwind), Lt. General of the KCF, a few days back in Ludhiana and paid tributes to him. He [Daljit Singh Bittu] said that Bhai Pehalwan has been martyred at the time when the militant struggle is passing through a very sensitive phase (*Ajit*, June 1, 1990).

The common feature of all the tributes was designating the slain militant as martyr (*shaheed*). The militants were not killed only in encounters – fake or real – with the police or para-military forces, but also in inter-organisational fights. One of the major reasons was inter-organisational rivalry, whereas the other and equally important was labelling some militants as renegades. In such matters, there were controversies and contention about the exact status of the killed militant, that is, he was either *gaddaar* (renegade) or *shaheed* (martyr). If he was renegade for some, then his betrayal was not confined even to the movement. He would be designated as *qaum da gaddar* (the renegade of the entire community). The matter would become contentious when another organisation would designate the same militant as martyr. A classical example of such a situation is that of Harminder Singh Sandhu mentioned earlier. He was killed on January 24, 1990 within a week of his second marriage. His murder initiated and provoked a controversy among various organisations. It became known that the original Khalistan Commando Force, which was then called the KCF (Panjwar), had been responsible for his murder and the police claimed on June 1, 1990 that Gurnam Singh Pehalwan of Sultanwind village had killed Harminder Singh Sandhu.[16] Within a week of his murder, the four militant organisations of which the original KCF was one of the components had called Harminder Singh Sandhu as the renegade of the Sikh community, whereas the chief of the BTFK regarded him as a martyr. By the time the killer of Sandhu was shot dead by the police, the entire controversy surrounding his murder had evaporated.

Harminder Singh Sandhu was not the only one, who was killed by the militants, but there never arose such a fierce controversy over any other militant's death. Among the militants the issue of whether a particular militant was martyr or renegade began to occupy an uncontested space in most of the cases. When a militant was killed in fake or real encounter with the police, he became a martyr. Designating a person as a martyr is not a very serious matter in Punjab and it tends to transgress rigidly defined standards for any case of killing except for the person killed in inter-family or inter-faction fight. During the militant movement, the people who were killed in movement-related violence are designated as martyrs irrespective of who they were, how they were killed and who killed them. Lala Jagat Narain, the editor-in-chief of 'Hind Samachar' group of newspapers, has also been designated as martyr though he was killed by the militants, so has been the case of the son of Jiwan Singh Umranangal - an Akali leader. Maninderjit Singh Bitta, who escaped many attempts of the militants on his life was called as *Zinda Shaheed* - the living martyr. Similarly, the police personnel who died during militancy have also been honoured and remembered as martyrs by the police establishment. Beant Singh - the Chief Minister of Punjab, who is accredited as the person responsible for suppressing militancy in the state - is a martyr after he was killed as a result of a suicide bomb attack in 1995.

There is a need to examine the deep underlying structures of thoughts and perceptions in the society in which the dominant discourse revolves round giving the status of martyr to the person killed in militant movement. One is reminded of the Dark Age (or Age of Faith to use Will Durant's expression) in which the prophecy of the Hebrew bible caught the imagination of individuals and congregations. Prophets and martyrs are both different and connected. A prophet could be martyr, but a martyr may not necessarily be a prophet. Interestingly, the martyrdom has its roots in religions and their development. Fenech (2000) argues that in Indian religions, before the advent of Islam, the concept of *shaheed* did not exist. He is right so long as he is mentioning the Indian religious traditions, but there was a concept of *veergati* that referred to the person who fought bravely and got killed in war. Over a period of time, the word *shaheed*, which has Arabic origin, has also become an acceptable expression for the person killed in war or some collective struggle. As we are primarily concerned with the martyr within the framework of religion, the need is to adequately contextualise the concept.

The first and foremost dimension of the concept of martyr is its inseparable relationship with violence. Martyrdom is a consequence of an act of violence. Klausner (1987:268) points out: "Violence, as a means, may serve religious values or, more typically, a blend of religious and economic or religious and political ends. Limited mundane conflict may escalate into violence when issues at stake are imbued with religious ultimacy. Violence may be rationalized by the perpetrators' claim to have exhausted the alternative of social negotiation." Klausner goes on to examine various examples from the European history including the crusades during the dark ages. All such people, who are killed in achieving the religious objectives, are generally called martyrs. A martyr is not necessarily and indispensably linked with religion, but the present discussion is confined to the religious space only though, irrespective of the space, whether religious or political, the phenomenon carries the same trajectory of meanings. Klausner (1987: 230) rightly comments: "The martyr and his slayer are delegates, champions or defenders of their societies. ...The societies of the slayer and the slain struggle to control the meaning of the slaying: is it to be understood by the world as martyrdom or as judicial retribution?" What characterises an act or occurrence, as a case of martyrdom, is also a question of on which side one is at the time of approaching it. Klausner is right when he argues that martyrdom is exemplary as well as political. It thus involves both a voluntary act to willingly choose death and a kind of punishment for a particular kind of preaching or action, which is thought contrary to the existing power holders in the society. Examining the entire issue from Weberian perspective, Klausner (ibid.: 230) writes: "Martyrdom imbues economic and political conflict with sacred meaning, subjecting it to what Max Weber called 'the ethic of absolute ends', the pursuit of goals with little attention to the cost. In fact, action guided by an 'ethic of responsibility', the value of the goal weighed against the cost of means, discourages martyrdom."

Martyrdom as a part of religious tradition becomes a powerful ideological force in which the martyr becomes the symbol of sacrifice and sometimes gets identified with what religion means. It also becomes a legitimising force in the sense that it is asserted that the person who chose death instead of life has to be right. The tradition of martyrdom, as studied by Fenech (2000), is dominant in Sikhism. McLeod (2002: 192-93) makes the following comments on the issue thus:

> The concept of martyrdom, evidently borrowed from the Islamic culture of the Punjab, is extremely important in Sikh history and tradition. Before the arrival of the British, all martyrs met their deaths at Muslim hands. ...The concept has continued to play a central part in the history of the Panth. Jarnail Singh Bhindranvale [sic] is widely regarded as a modern martyr, and there are many more besides him.

McLeod (ibid.) is also of the view that in Sikhism "it is justified on the grounds that it becomes inevitable when the Panth is resolutely involved in protecting the weak from oppression and the defenceless against tyrants". Talib (1997:61) holds the similar view regarding the place of martyrdom in the Sikh religious tradition. However, he is also of the view that in the Sikh tradition "the martyr must meet his end in perfect poise and in spirit shunning all intent to hit back". This view of martyrdom does not take cognisance of fight in battlefield and the attainment of martyrdom thereof. Uberoi (1999) strongly holds the view that Guru Tegh Bahadur was the first martyr in India. The implications of such a view are quite clear, that is, before Sikhism there was no concept and thus convention of martyrdom in the Indian religious tradition – a view that is close to what Fenech (2000) has stated. Interestingly, all these scholars agree on the identification of some major martyrs besides the two gurus in Sikh history.[17] The name of Baba Deep Singh tops the list of all martyrs. The tradition of martyrdom in Sikhism has been popularised by the professional singers (*dhadis* and *kaveeshers*) in Punjab to the extent that the tradition and the faith have become coterminous.

The emphasis on the tributes and labelling the militant, who has been killed a martyr in the case of the militant movement, could be understood as a part of the strong identity with the Sikh tradition. Pettigrew (1995: 96) has provided some glimpse of the way the Sikh militants stressed martyrdom in their struggle for Khalistan when she wrote: "The guerrillas claimed that the act of *shahidi* (martyrdom) would bring about Khalistan. Certainly it meant that the struggle never lost momentum. Martyrdom provided the cause with unlimited manpower." Pettigrew voiced her views on the basis of her study of the KCF (Zaffarwal). Wassan Singh Zaffarwal, for her, became a great revolutionary and it might be embarrassing for her to note that the same person surrendered to the Punjab police and talked about peace. The main flaw in her argument is that she based her views on particular individuals, who could have behaved in an unpredictable manner. If the militants were killed in action, then they automatically became martyrs and it becomes possible to state that they had a lofty ideal of achieving martyrdom. Similar kinds of things are also said about Bhagat Singh and his comrades.[18] The problem emerges when the militants, who remained alive, after a period of time, behave in a manner that does not correspond with the expected behaviour pattern as it has happened in the case of Wassan

Singh Zaffarwal. Another western scholar, who has dealt with the issue of martyrdom in Sikhism on the basis of extensive interviews with the militant Sikhs in the USA, is Mahmood (1996: 196), who makes the following observation:

> Unlike Islam, a religious tradition with an equally prominent tradition of martyrdom, Sikhs who die in battle do not look forward to an eternal life in paradise. Though some elements of heavenly aspiration and of reincarnation have crept into Sikh popular religion, on the whole this is a tradition focused on this life as the only life there is. G.S. Manusukhani, who wrote a popular primer on Sikhism, instructs that "those who know the art of true living also know that of true dying. True living is dying to the self, the ego, and living up to God. True dying is the privilege of the brave".

Interestingly, Mahmood has given the title "Playing the Game of Love" to one of the chapters that deal with the issue of martyrdom. Fenech (2000) has given the same sub-title to his book. This couplet is cited from Guru Nanak's writings. What has happened in the process is that these writers have made an attempt to construct a tradition of martyrdom in Sikhism whose roots, they consciously or unconsciously claim, could be located in the writings of the first guru of the Sikhs. It lends tremendous credence and legitimacy to the Singh Sabha movement and also the fundamentalist discourse that there is only one singular tradition in Sikhism.[19] The writings of the earlier gurus are interpreted in such a way that any symbol of sacrifice is associated with martyrdom. The sufi and sant traditions always emphasised that the path to achieve oneness with God was never an easy one as it entailed struggle and sacrifice. The tradition also produced its martyrs, but it corresponded with the idea and the commitment to the fearless surrender to the executioner.

However, martyrdom seems to be the reason for action in certain cases. The Sikh martyrs have always inspired certain young people and this inspiration is not confined to Sikh militants. Even in the case of the Naxalite movement in Punjab, some of them stated that the Sikh martyrs were their source of inspiration (Judge 1992). The exemplary character of martyrdom is quite obvious, as the martyr turns into a great force when he begins to live as a legend. These legends have become material force to evoke radical movements and cause social transformation. The Sikh movement has undoubtedly been regarded as one of such examples and the Sikh youth has time and again rose to militant action by getting inspiration from the way the Sikh tradition has been constructed for them. In the tributes published in the newspapers, the entire tradition of martyrdom was operating as the rationale and reason for actions. Making it sure that the killed militant is regarded as a martyr was also a way of inspiring the Sikh youth to join the ranks of the militants.

Notes

1. These lines of Puran Singh are taken from his poem "Jawan Punjab" (c. f. Randhawa 1964).
2. See Chapter 3 on how race was regarded as the central feature in defining the traits of individuals in the 19th century.
3. See Chapter 5. The 'other' is Hindu in the construction of 'self'.
4. An uninterrupted recitation of the *Guru Granth Sahib* is called 'Akhand Path'.
5. Fauja Singh (1996: 233) wrote on the imprisonment of the Guru thus: "Reports about the splendid style Guru Hargobind kept led Jehangir to pass order for his detention in the Fort of Gwalior. According to the *Dabistan-I-Mazahib*, the charge leveled against him was that he had not paid the fine imposed on his father. For how long he remained in the Fort cannot be stated with certainty... It seems that Guru Hargobind remained in the Fort for a few months during 1617-1619 whereafter he was required to stay in the royal camp under surveillance for sometime. ... As time came for Guru Hargobind to be released from the Fort, he came out on the condition that all other detenues were freed, too. He led fifty-two prisoners out of the Fort". Fauja Singh hereafter refers to the Sikh tradition according to which

the emperor delivered Chandu to the Sikhs and he met a violent death at their hands.

6. *Kirtani jatha* primarily means a small number of persons who sing and narrate stories of the lives of the gurus. They are also known is *raghis*, but there is a difference. Whereas the *kirtani jathas* narrate stories along with singing, the *raghis* remain confined only to singing the gurbani.
7. The legend says that on the occasion of Baisakhi in 1699 the Guru unsheathed his sword and demanded a head from the members of the congregation. One of the Sikhs stood up. The Guru followed this process five times. Later on, the followers discovered that Guru had not beheaded them. They were made *panj piaras* (five dear ones) and thus the new panth was founded.
8. The younger sons of Guru Gobind Singh were Zorawar Singh and Fateh Singh.
9. The story of two brothers, Lakhpat and Jaspat, is one of the most referred to by the *dhadis*. It seems that Jaspat was responsible for the execution of Bhai Mani Singh and the Sikhs avenged his martyrdom by killing Jaspat. Lakhpat vowed to avenge his brother's death and with the help of the Subedar of Lahore he unleashed violence against the Sikhs. These were the times of the invasions of Ahmad Shah Abdali. See Bhai Vir Singh's *Sundari*.
10. Bhai Vir Singh, Ibid. In the *Encyclopaedia of Sikhism* (1995), Deevan Kaura Mal is described as sehajdhari Sikh.
11. *Gurmata* basically means taking a decision according to the Sikh principles. Generally, in Sikhism, the *sangat* is believed to be the supreme. The decision taken with consensus in a congregation may be called *gurmata*. Detailed discussion on *gurmata* has been made in the next chapter.
12. There is every possibility that Jarnail Singh Bhindranwala alluded to the Gurdwara Reform Movement led by the Akalis in which they adopted the Gandhian *satyagraha* and remained non-violent throughout the movement.
13. His lack of knowledge of history becomes quite obvious in the light of Pashaura Singh's (2004) recent argument that Guru Gobind Singh insisted that his Khalsa should possess five weapons one of which was gun.
14. The Golden Temple is called Harimandir Sahib by most of the Sikhs. Still a large section of the Sikhs, particularly in Amritsar, also call it Darbar Sahib. The word *darbar* means court in its medieval usage.

The implications of this meaning are two-fold, that is, it could either be a court of the King or the God. The expression Darbar Sahib signifies the latter in this case.

15. His use of the word *sangat* seems either to be out place or it means he never distinguished between community and congregation. *Sangat* is an assembly of persons sitting in the presence of *Guru Granth Sahib*, whereas the Sikhs living in villages and cities and engaged in their profane day-to-day activities form a community. Transforming community into congregation is inbuilt into the discourse of Bhindranwala.
16. It may be interesting to note that the day AISSF's Daljit Singh Bittu paid tribute to Gurnam Singh Pehlwan the police confirmed his death and also stated that he killed Harminder Singh Sandhu (*Ajit*, June 1, 1990, p.7).
17. The two gurus who attained martyrdom were Guru Arjan Dev, the fifth guru, and Guru Tegh Bahadur, the ninth guru.
18. Bhagat Singh is called Shaheed-e-Azam to denote his status as the greatest of all martyrs during the national liberation movement.
19. The lines that signify Guru Nanak Dev's views are as follows: *"Je tau prem khilan ka chao, sir dhar tali gali mori ao"* (If you seek to play the game of love, then come to my path with head on your palm).

7

Creating a Moral Community

There is a general consensus among sociologists that it is not possible to permanently reorient and influence the behaviour of individuals in a society through the use or threat of use of violence. Individuals respond, adapt and accordingly change with the onset of certain forces that tend to threaten their existential conditions including physical liquidation, but permanent change cannot be achieved. Positivists would argue that there are certain factors that bring about social change. Some of the major factors that have been identified in positivist sociological imagination are industrialisation, education, legislation and communication. Most of these factors are themselves determined by the evolutionary process through which societies progress. Interestingly, there is also a widely acceptable view that revolutions transform societies in a sudden and radical manner. It seems difficult to accept that a religious community is homogenised with the coercive threat of some militants. We have a history of inquisitions, and witch-hunting in Europe. It was in this context that Huss was burnt at the stake that created the conditions for Reformation in the second decade of 16th century. In this chapter, an attempt has been made to understand how after the demise of Bhindranwala the militants tried to enforce and impose with the threat of the gun on the Sikhs a particular way of life, which they thought were the real path for the Sikh of the Guru. In this sense, their attempt at creating a moral community entailed an underlying assumption that nationhood implied homogeneous society – a moral community as defined by the religious code.

Still another aspect of this attempt was the prevailing view among the militants that there was a need for cleansing the community of quislings and traitors. The community of the pure was understood as a homogeneous collectivity mainly in line with the construction of the Sikh identity by the Singh Sabha movement as well as Bhindranwala. As the time passed, the militant violence escalated in Punjab and the failure of the state to handle it worked as a catalyst. New names and organisations emerged among the militants who began dictating their terms to the police, the political leaders and the common masses. Once the militants tasted power, they started sending messages through the medium of the newspapers dictating the others to behave in a particular manner. As stated in the introduction, most of the messages appeared in the *Ajit* – a Punjabi newspaper, which virtually became a 'letter-box' for the militants. These messages were called 'warnings' and the sender was the militant, whereas the addressee could be other militant (organisation), political leaders or the common masses. The nature of the messages varied according to the situation and circumstances.

The word 'warning' requires no explication though its meanings vary from caution or caveat to admonition. In common parlance, warning is given to the person(s) against or for his way of acting. As a narrative, warning could be prescriptive, proscriptive, denotative or attributive. There is also a special feature of the narrative structure of 'warning'. It entails power relations. If we ignore the usual encounter with the warning placard hanging on walls in certain restricted areas, then in the structure of everyday life the person/agency warning others against a particular kind of behaviour carries either an authority or power. Obviously, ignoring a warning would invite punishment or some action against the violator. There is a built-in logic in the warning coming from that movement that is based on the ideology of violence in which anybody ignoring or not paying heed to it must be eliminated. The situation is such that if the order is not complied with, the non-complier must be punished by death. The logic is built into the source of the power of the militants, that is, their ability to exercise violence by virtue of their ownership of means of coercion. This ability is the source of terror among others and the militants are aware of it. Non-compliance is akin to opposition and the very logic of perpetuating struggle requires that anybody doing so should be eliminated. It also depends upon the ideology of the movement and there could be certain movements in which killing or taking the life of somebody because of minor lapses or non-compliance are not preferred. Rather death sentence is carried out as the last resort. Ideologically, it seems fine, but it depends upon at which stage a movement has reached.

Violence for the purpose of creating terror has to be discriminatory failing which there is always a possibility of losing its effectiveness. The ability to commit violence as well as punish is the fundamental basis of a militant movement, which adopts terrorism as a tactic. Thus, warnings are not merely prescriptions and prohibitions, but are also a real threat of punishment going to the extent of physical liquidation. It is generally believed that most of the militants tend to give an exemplary punishment to derive compliance. Warnings, in that sense, have to be specific and must involve some kind of legitimising element. For instance, in the case of the Sikh militant movement, it is expected that the form and content of warnings that would be given lie within the framework of the Sikh tradition. Owing to the time-space distanciation between the two, not all warnings could be contextualised in the Sikh tradition, but a major component could even then belong to the legitimising tradition. Situating the act of violence in the Sikh tradition is a way of justifying it. Can we say that compliance and legitimacy are intertwined to result into a predictable behaviour of the people? There is a positive relationship between the two if we go by the Weberian notion of the authority, irrespective of what are the sources of legitimacy. The agents who seek legitimacy from a tradition, but at the same time use their ability to exercise the option of using coercion, it may not hold valid. From Weber's point of view, it is an exercise of power in which an agent (individual or organisation) is deriving compliance even against the wishes of those whose obedience is sought.

How do the militants come to know that their orders are complied with? It is difficult for the underground movement, as it has to rely on its contacts and informants. Once the warnings and threats cease to discriminate between the enemy and the friend, the political benefits disappear for the militants. In the case of the Sikh militant movement, any Sikh could be understood as the potential supporter and thus the base on which the movement was to be carried to the higher stages. The issue of the Sikh identity and the struggle for the achievement of the sovereign state of Khalistan were the underlying principles on which the movement was expected to develop. It is pertinent to remark that Jarnail Singh Bhindranwala never raised the demand for Khalistan openly. He seemed to be ambivalent towards the entire issue. The militant organisations that regrouped themselves after his death in 1984 never left an iota of doubt regarding their objective. The aim was the achievement of Khalistan and the means to attain it was by waging the war against the Indian state.

They still had to establish their sovereignty for which they were expected to mobilise the Sikh masses and involve them in a prolonged war with the Indian state. All this did not happen in any classical manner. Rather, a large number of militant organisations created a radically different kind of dynamism from the one that is expected from such movements.

Interestingly, the only way to know (other than the accounts of the militants) the actual operation of militancy is through the 'warnings' that appeared in the newspapers, particularly the *Ajit*. 'Warnings' constituted the prescriptive, proscriptive and denotative narratives of the movement. The proceeding discussion is based on 450 warnings collected from the *Ajit*. The data on number of warnings issued by the militants provides certain interesting features of the militant movement.[1] It may just be pointed out that the total number of warnings was much more than selected for analysis here. Though it is difficult to make an exact estimate, but these are about 20 per cent of the total warnings appeared in the newspaper. It may be interesting to note that the largest number of warnings appeared in 1990, whereas there was a dramatic decline in 1991. The main reason for this decline was that in the beginning of 1991 when O.P. Malhotra, the then Governor of Punjab, imposed censorship on newspapers, these messages began to decline, but at no stage these disappeared till the end of 1992. Warnings almost disappeared in 1993. With the death of Gurbachan Singh Manochahal on February 28, 1993, the Punjab situation changed so radically that it became difficult to imagine that a few months ago there was terrorist violence in Punjab. Only the assassination of the then Chief Minister, Beant Singh, in 1995 reminded that militancy could again come back. It seems in the retrospect that even if the militants might be sending the warnings to the newspaper, the dramatic decline in the movement might have given the option to the editor to ignore them.

The discussion on various aspects of warnings has been divided into five parts. In the first part, an attempt has been made to trace the place of origin of the warnings as it was thought important to know the concentration of the activities of the militants. The second part deals with the way these warnings were framed as press statements in the newspapers. It has been found that in the process of sending their messages, the militants also tried to derive legitimacy from the Sikh tradition for what they were doing. The quantitative estimate of the warnings in relation to various militant organisations has been made in the third part. It may be pointed out that among the people the perception of real and fake threat was based on the knowledge of the organisation that was sending the warning. The fourth part traces the background of the people who the militant thought were deviants and should be disciplined, whereas in the fifth part the kinds of punishments the non-compliers could have met have been described.

I
PLACES OF ORIGIN OF WARNINGS

The militant movement was more powerful in the Amritsar district and some areas of the Gurdaspur and Firozpur districts than other parts of Punjab. Most of the chiefs of various organisations belonged to the Amritsar district; for example, Sukhdev Singh Babbar, Gurbachan Singh Manochahal, Avtar Singh Brahma, Paramjit Singh Panjwar, General Labh Singh and Sukhwinder Singh Sangha. Wassan Singh Zaffarwal belonged to the Gurdaspur district. It was likely that the warnings would emanate from these strongholds of the militants. Places of origin of warnings may be examined in terms of regions and the names of cities and towns. The data indicate that 58 per cent of the warnings originated from the Majha region.[2] Malwa had 22 per cent share of the warnings, whereas 18 per cent of the same originated from Doaba. It clearly shows that Majha was the centre of militant activities in Punjab. In view of the fact that Amritsar is the centre of Sikh religion and, to a greater extent, Sikh politics, it was possible to foresee such a scenario. A further investigation of the main cities/towns from where these warnings were issued revealed an interesting picture. Of the total warnings, 251 (55.8%) originated from five cities/towns, namely, Amritsar (81), Rayya (58), Jandiala Guru (45),

Jalandhar (41) and Ludhiana (26).[3] One common feature of all these cities/towns is that these are located at the Sher Shah Suri Marg. In the case of Amritsar, it is self-evident that being the religious centre of the Sikhs it was the hub and the focal point of militancy. Jalandhar could be distinguished as the centre of vernacular press in Punjab and the *Ajit*, from which these warnings have been collected, is published from there. Similarly, Ludhiana is the biggest city of Punjab and the militant activities became noticeable during the period when the warnings began to appear in the newspaper. Rayya and Jandiala are exceptional cases, which require a degree of investigation and explication.

Both Rayya and Jandiala are at a distance of less than 20 km from each other and fall in the Majitha police district.[4] Rayya is also close to the area, which falls under the Tarn Taran police district. The area falling in the circumference of 20 km of Rayya was among the most disturbed in the Majha region. This fact may not suffice to give a reasonably satisfactory explanation of why Rayya and Jandiala were so prominent as sources of warnings. There could be two reasons for the centrality of these two places. First, as is evident from the data, some of the militant organisations that started sending the warnings were active in this area. Secondly, the journalists were willing to pass on these warnings to the head office. In fact, the first reason seems more plausible than the other. However, from January 1992 onwards, Sangrur and Ahmedgarh (Ludhiana) began to figure prominently. Batala, Moga and Kapurthala are other places from where the messages emanated. The Amritsar district remained the epicentre of the militant movement and it began to have its impact on other parts of Punjab. It may also be pointed out that the idea of sending the warnings through newspapers first occurred to the militants of Amritsar district and then others followed the example when they realised the actual effect of the threat on the people.

II
MODE OF PRESENTATION OF WARNINGS: SIKH TRADITION AS SOURCE OF LEGITIMACY

Most of the warnings from militants were presented in the form of resolutions passed in the meetings. Invariably one or the other chief of a militant organisation was shown to have chaired the meeting. Though even a novice could make it out that such a frequency of meetings of an underground organisation was impossible, yet each warning presented a case of typified text from which certain elements of the militant movement could be read. The following warning appeared in the newspaper[5] on January 12, 1990 thus:

> "Jandiala Guru. According to a press note from the Khalistan Liberation Force, an emergency meeting of the organisation was held at a secret place. In this meeting the Chief General of the organisation, Gurjant Singh Budhsinghwala, Lt. Gen. Bhai Nishan Singh Makhu, Lt. Gen. Tasbir Singh Tasbira (Jhander), Lt. Gen. Manjinder Singh Mand, Lt. Gen. Annar Singh Parha, Maj. Gen. Gurbachan Singh Ala, Maj. Gen. Dayal Singh Dhola Chiragwali, Maj. Gen. Balraj Singh Ala, Maj. Gen. Mukhtar Singh Saroowal, Maj. Gen. Jang Singh Janga Dubli and other 135 armed militants participated...(p. 3).

The above quoted news item provides us information about the Khalistan Liberation Force (KLF) in terms of (1) the names and villages of the major militant leaders, (2) the hierarchical positions of these militants thus betraying the organisational structure, (3) the large size of the organisation, and (4) the democratic process of decision-making in the organisation. One may begin to doubt claims of the underground movement for certain indiscretions of the militants. The meeting of the major leaders of an organisation, who had been working in different areas of Punjab, is improbable on a short notice. For example, Gurjant Singh Budhsinghwala was operating from Ludhiana and its surrounding areas; Nishan

Singh Makhu was active in Ferozpur district, whereas others were operating in different parts of the Majha region. In such circumstances, calling all the leaders for an emergency meeting at one place was impossible without wireless communication. At that time the mobile phones had not made any presence in Punjab. It should also be noted that to gather 135-armed militants at a spot was extremely difficult. The security forces could have noticed such a movement. The conclusion that can be drawn from the above arguments is that no such meeting could have taken place. The fact that virtually every other day the KLF was issuing warnings through resolutions of meetings it was impossible to have such a high frequency of meetings organised by an underground militant movement. Then, what was it? It was a simple and effective method of sending the referent – prescriptive, prohibitive, or denotative – by simultaneously showing that the Sikh tradition of *gurmata* was strictly adhered to.

The legitimation process through collective resolution was an important component of the mode of sending the message. Since the militants already possessed the coercive power, the demonstration of the fact that the resolution was an outcome of a meeting and not the order of an individual provided tremendous legitimacy to the referent.[6] Interestingly, the inability of the militant leaders to dictate terms to the Sikh masses could have been compensated had they been occupying some formal position in the clerical organisation of the Sikh community. They could then issue *hukamnamas* to the Sikhs. Interestingly, such an attempt was made time and again but without much success.[7]

The dialectical relation between *gurmata* and *hukamnama* remained the core basis of the creation of referents in the interaction between the sender and the addressee. Even when the militants possessed and were exercising coercive power, they could not derive legitimacy from the Sikh tradition for which they were compelled to show that they were following the practice of *gurmata*. Ganda Singh (1996) has pointed out that in the Sikh tradition a Sikh of eminence could issue a *hukamnama*. However, the militant leaders might not have acquired and achieved such a position in the Sikh community. Thus, the simple practice of *gurmata*, which the tradition informs could even be more effective than the *hukamnama*, was found to be the best and the effective mode of sending the warnings. In such a situation, *gurmata* was used not only as a substitute, but also as a negation of the *hukamnama*, as it carved out its own meanings and interpretation of how the matters were to be resolved. The language of the warnings does not indicate whether proper procedure was followed in arriving at the decision. We find that in many of the warnings, it has been mentioned that the resolution was based on consensus (*sarab samiti*).

Still another revelation of the form and content of militant movement that is made through the compilation of warnings is the existence or pretension (if it did not actually exist) of some kind of coordination among various organisations. The following news item that appeared in the *Ajit* (May 21, 1990, p. 3) indicates this reality:

> An emergency meeting was held a few days back in Amritsar at a secret place of the Khalistan Commando Force, the Khalistan Liberation Force, the Babbar Khalsa, and the All India Sikh Students Federation (Daljit) under the chairmanship of Bhai Paramjit Singh Panjwar. In this meeting Bhai Gurjant Singh Budhsinghwala, Bhai Sukhdev Singh Babbar and Bhai Daljit Singh Bittu were especially present. In the gathering of more than hundred armed militant Singhs, a unanimous decision was taken. ...

The above-mentioned portion of the warning indicates two dimensions of the militant movement, namely, the frequent use of prefix 'Bhai' and some kind of inter-organisational coordination. The names of the militants invariably carried the prefix 'Bhai' or 'Baba' to bestow honour to their own names. For both the common people and newspapers they were '*kharhkoos*' (heroic and brave), '*munde*' (boys), '*attbadi*' (extremists) or '*antakbadi*' (terrorists), but they had created enough terror to be referred as Bhai or Baba. Both the words carry an intrinsic respect – the former means priest and/or knowledgeable person or brother, whereas the latter that literally means grandfather was loaded with tremendous respect due to the Ghadar Party martyrs. During the interviews with the people, it was informed that as and when the militants would knock at the door of some house, they would always answer to the query that "Babas have come" (*babe aye aa*). From these simple facts regarding their names and the way they wanted these to be mentioned in the press, it may be inferred that the militants were megalomaniac and they had an elated notion about themselves. It becomes all the more important to understand it in the light of the fact that most of them were quite young (Puri, Judge and Sekhon 1999).

Singh (2002: 180), however, interprets the usage of these words in a somewhat different way when he points out: "The Sikhs not only looked at the militants with awe and some sort of inspiration, but reverently addressed them as *bhai*, brother and *baba* a respectable elderly person. Many Sikhs felt that they were contributing nothing towards the Sikh struggle in their routine life, when those *munde*, were laying down their lives for Panth..." Since Singh has forcefully raised the issue, one may like to grapple with it to position its relevance in the militant struggle. In fact, Singh (ibid.) does not tell us what 'many' Sikhs mean? Has he based his argument on some quantitative source to exactly estimate the meaning of 'many'? Secondly, 'Bhai' does not only mean brother, but it also refers to the Gurdwara priest. Similarly, 'Baba' was used for Ghadar Party revolutionaries as a mark of respect not necessarily meaning an elderly person. In the next sentence, Singh informs us that Sikhs also mentioned the militants as *munde*, which literally means boys and the word never acquired any respect of any kind during militancy. As a matter of fact, all of them were self-styled 'Bhais' and some of them began to call themselves

'Baba'. Whereas every militant was 'Bhai', the prefix 'Baba' was rare.

We may now move to examine whether various militant organisations coordinated their activities. Since the plausibility of holding a meeting has been put under suspicion, it may be inferred that there could not be any practical coordination among four organisations. In the mid-1990, these four militant organisations increased to five owing to the emergence of the Bhindranwala Tiger Force of Khalistan under the leadership of Sukhwinder Singh Sangha, who broke away from the main organisation headed by Gurbachan Singh Manochahal. Such alleged coordination in sending the warnings could also be found among other militant organisations. The collectively sent warning was not simply an indication of the emergence of a large federation of organisations, rather it articulated, reaffirmed and reinforced the Sikh tradition of *gurmata*, which holds tremendous religious sanctity. To seek and derive legitimacy from this tradition, it was also emphasised and asserted that the resolution was unanimous. Despite all this orientation and action, the militants, as we shall see little later, largely relied on their coercive power. In the process, the militants were creating an imagined community of the pure/people of god – the way the word 'Khalsa' could be interpreted.

III
MILITANT ORGANISATIONS AND WARNINGS

It has been observed that there was a competition among the organisations in issuing the warnings. It thus becomes important to know the number of warnings issued by each organisation. The data indicate that the KCF (P), known by the name of its leader, Paramjit Singh Panjwar, issued the largest number, that is, 70 (15.56%), of the warnings.[8] The next in the line was the KLF, followed by the KCF (Z). Since there was a practice among different organisations to coordinate while issuing the warnings, four militant organisations, namely, the

KCF (P), the BKI, the KLF and the AISSF (Bittu) issued the largest number of warnings constituting 16.88 per cent of total. Other organisations did not lag behind. Some of them like the BTFK (M) and the KCF (R) issued joint statements. In the later phases, some other organisations, namely, the Dasmesh Regiment and AISSF (Butter) also joined them.

The warnings continued to appear for a period of seven years and reading them became an everyday reality for the Punjabis, as a result of which some of the obvious facts remained ignored, consciously or unconsciously, by the people. Since the joint warnings were not any indication of any kind of coordination in their activities and attacks, each group was acting and operating on its own and it could be made out from the contents of warnings. Each joint statement/warning would list the chief/general of the each organisation and some other prominent leaders. Incidentally, many of them had already crossed the border and were living in Pakistan, for example, Wassan Singh Zaffarwal and Paramjit Singh Panjwar. Who were actually issuing the warnings? In most of the cases the local level leaders used to warn specific people on restricted issues. It also implies that the format of the statements to the newspaper remained the same in all organisations, but there was no evidence of any meeting of the militants of an organisation or of different organisations held with rapidity corresponding with the frequency of warnings issued by them.

It may also be added that some of the organisations, for instance, the Khalistan Mukti Fauj, the Malwa Kesri Commando Force, the Dushat Sodh Commando Force and the Khalistan Azad Force that issued warnings could be bogus, for their authenticity could be questioned. Though the warnings given by these organisations were not different from those of major militant organisations, yet there could be two possible objectives of their warnings. First, the police might have used it as a counter-insurgency tactic to confuse militants. The Sikh masses could not be confused, because there were already myriad militant organisations due to which another addition to the plurality would not have created any confusion. Moreover, these organisations' warnings had no qualitative distinctions from the others. Obviously, the target could be the other militant organisations. Such a tactic could prove to be effective in the light of the fact that most of the militant organisations had emerged from splits and splits within splits. Inter-organisational rivalry and conflict were the natural corollaries to these splits. Formation of new organisations could imply more challenge, competition and conflict. The second possibility seemed equally realistic. There could be some individuals who might have entertained the idea of making hay while the sun was shining. Adventurers and carpetbaggers – sometimes criminals and anti-social elements – tried to use the terror of the militants/insurgents to extort money. It is quite possible that such persons issued these warnings to make money. The probability of the latter was higher than the former, as most of the warnings of the major militant organisations were addressed to such elements.

IV
DISCIPLINING THE DEVIANTS

The militant organisations sent warnings to 73 different kinds of individuals and groups. It may be stated that between 1986 and 1992 they virtually warned most of the sections of the society. For the sake of focussed discussion, these 73 types of warnings were clubbed in a way to make 14 categories.[9] For example, warnings to police officers, jail officials and police force in general have been put under the category of 'police force'. It was interesting to note that out of 450 warnings the largest number (152) was issued to 'looters, extortionists or anti-social elements' and/or other militants. All these people claimed that they were militants, whereas for the other militants they were looters and extortionists and were defaming and giving a bad name to the movement. The second target of the militants was the police force in whose share fell 77 (17.11%) warnings. It was understandable in the sense that in their line of action they had to encounter the police force. Interestingly, 33 (7.33%) warnings were addressed to the eve-teasers. It seems that a movement fighting for a sovereign state had to give a serious attention to the menace of eve-teasing in Punjab.

Predictably, these categories of people were warned against various acts. For example, the police officials were warned against killing the Sikh militants in fake encounters, harassing the families of the militants, or torturing the arrested militants in jails. Sometimes, an individual police official would be warned. Interestingly, Jarnail Singh Bhindranwala also warned a number of officials, one of which was Bichhu Ram. In such cases, the militants would mention the name of the official and warn him to stop killing/torturing the militants. Sometimes, the Hindu police officers were also warned against harassing the Sikhs making it a kind of communal issue, the underlying rationale of which was that the Hindus were against the Sikhs though most of the police personnel in Punjab excluding IPS officers were Sikhs. The jail officials were also warned against mistreating, harassing and torturing the militants in jails.

We may now turn to the first category of the people who were warned most frequently by the militants. This is the category of the militants themselves. There is no denying the possibility and fact of some adventurers or carpetbaggers, as pointed out earlier, taking advantage of the uncertain and disturbed political and law and order environment during the movement. However, the fact that the largest number of warnings was given to the militants – real or fake – during the seven years' period remains an undisputed fact. Why did the militants warn the looters/extortionists "who pretended to be militants" or other militants? There could by many reasons. One and the most probable was that it was an image-building exercise in the print media. In today's terminology, it is called public relations exercise, whereas in the left insurgents' term it is keeping the aspirations and expectations of the masses in view. In other words, it may be stated that any insurgent movement requires funding and the best way to get it is through looting, kidnapping for ransom and extorting. The Sikh militants did exactly like this. They also carried out, as studies of Puri, Judge and Sekhon (1999) and Sekhon (2002) have shown, a large-scale extortion.[10] The warning could be understood as a form of legitimising discourse to absolve oneself of looting and extorting money in the eyes of the people. Things in fact did not end with looting and extortion. There were also cases of misbehaviour with women. Certain militants were also warned against using the name of a particular organisation. The major focus continued to be warning the looters and extortionists who pretended to be militants. It is evident from the fact that out of total 152 warnings to other militants, 131 were issued to the looters. Virtually every militant organisation warned 'anti-social elements' against looting and harassing people.

The fact that the targets of a majority of the warnings were the militants, it is quite clear that there were inter-organisational conflicts, as pointed out earlier, among them. These conflicts were also based on certain differences over various issues, one of which was the position of the Damdami Taksal. The Babbar Khalsa International came to exist independent of Jarnail Singh Bhindranwala and at the time of conflict between him and Sant Harchand Longowal, its leader sided with the latter. One issue that emerged among the militant leaders was whether they accepted the authority of Baba Thakur Singh, the acting chief of Damdami Taksal. In this regard, Gurbachan Singh Manochahal, the chief of the BTFK made his allegiance, though symbolic, clear. However, the Babbar Khalsa International along with the other three militant organisations referred to earlier remained cold towards this issue. Other leaders like Wassan Singh Zaffarwal showed ambivalence towards the issue. Another matter that might have led to certain warnings was the change in the affiliations of various militants from one to the other organisations. A classical illustration of it is Balwainder Singh Shahpur, who was an apprentice with a tailor in village Butala in the Amritsar district before joining the militant movement at the age of 19 years. He first joined the BTFK (Manochahal), then he became Lt. General in the KCF (Z), and after developing differences with Zaffarwal, joined the Dasmesh Regiment and became its deputy chief. When Sital Singh Mattewal was killed in the real encounter with the police, he became its chief. The evidence of inter-organisational rivalry was evident when the militants killed Harminder Singh Sandhu – a close comrade of Jarnail Singh Bhindranwala and student leader – in January 1990. After his murder the newspaper became the main medium through which various organisations expressed their views. It was the KCF (P), which made it known to others that it had carried out the last wishes of its former chiefs, Labh Singh and Kanwarjit Singh (*Ajit*, January 29, 1990). Confrontations, both verbal and violent, among various militant organisations became a cause of concern for many militants. In one such statement (*Ajit*, September 25, 1990), Gurbachan Singh Manochahal and Gurjant Singh Rajasthani appealed to and also warned other militant organisations against fratricide and emphasised the need for orienting the struggle against the Indian state.

The most interesting of all the warnings have been those that were issued to the eve-teasers. Various categories of people were warned against eve-teasing and predictably, it dramatically declined. There is no doubt that teasing and molestation of women/girls occur at certain public places, which entail disrespect and insult to them. The issue is certainly of a great concern, but what kind of effort is required to check it could be a matter of discussion. On October 21, 1990, the following news appeared in the *Ajit*:

> Amritsar. An important meeting of five militant organisations was held at Amritsar at some secret place. In this meeting the chief of the Babbar Khalsa International, Bhai Sikhdev Singh Babbar, the chief of the KCF, Bhai Paramjit Singh Panjwar, the chief of the KLF, Bhai Gurjant Singh Budhsinghwala, the chief

of the BTFK, Bhai Sukhwinder Singh Sangha and the head of Federation Bhai Daljit Singh Bittu and many other militants participated. According to a press release issued by Bhai Manbir Singh Babbar, the shop of Kakka [sic] at Chowk Baba Bhauniwala was warned against teasing the girls; otherwise there will be serious consequences.

The above-quoted warning, to make it clear at the outset, is not very different from others in terms of both form and content. It is a typified warning to the eve-teasers. Thus, it becomes important to make sense of the very magnitude and level of farce it presents along with some kind of tragic realisation of the expanded space of terror in the minds of the people. Let us first look into the farcical dimension of this warning. In this warning, we are informed that chiefs of five organisations held a meeting to discuss the issue of Kakka's shop in the narrow lanes of the old Amritsar city. Was this matter an important enough to draw the attention, time and energy of the chiefs of five militant organisations? Were there no important issues of ideological, political or religious nature for them to handle? The issue is, in fact, insignificant, irrelevant and unnecessary to require the meeting of five chiefs. Obviously, the five chiefs are not involved in this matter as leaders as well as individuals. What are involved are their names. It was pointed out earlier that warnings were given in the form of resolutions of the meetings, which could never be held owing to the nature of movement. If this is the case (in fact this was the case), then it could be concluded that Manbir Singh Babbar issued this warning, as he was operating at the local level and was more involved with the issues that concerned with the area in which he had been operating.[11]

Can we say that warning against eve-teasing was linked to the ideology of the militant movement? It may or may not be rooted in the ideology of the militants who wanted to achieve Khalistan. It could be interpreted as a part of their social reform programme. At the same time, it seems strange that a movement with such lofty ideals was concerned with such a trivial matter if we assume that Kakka was teasing the girls when they would come to his shop. Any sensible businessman/shopkeeper would not have teased his female customers. It thus implies that Kakka was not a wise shopkeeper, as he was harming his own business interests as a result of his behaviour. It seems least probable. Through the warning we do not know the religious background of the shopkeeper; nor are we aware of the nature of his shop. Since in Punjabi the word used is *hatti*, it denotes grocery shop in Punjab. It is a place where there is least likelihood of such behaviour unless the matter is personal between the two. As a conjecture, it may be pointed out that this warning involved two persons only, namely Manbir Singh Babbar, who issued the warning, and Kakka, to whom it was issued. Since the nature of the warning was proscriptive and related with objectionable behaviour of the addressee, it was important to know the source of this information to the sender of the message. In other words, how did Manbir Singh come to know about eve-teasing? Did women/girls tell him or complain to him? Or was he personally aware of this? The issue is so localised that it is difficult to know and then react unless there is some personal involvement of the sender of the message.

It has already been observed that such warnings against eve-teasing had its impact and it declined considerably during militant movement. However, all the warnings against eve-teasing were highly specific in which addressees were particular persons and/ or persons at particular places/localities. This general impact could have reinforced the behaviour of the militants in issuing such warnings. Unfortunately, the behaviour of the militants did not indicate any exhibition of idealism on their part. Stories and incidents of rape of women during militancy were widespread. Talwinder Singh's (1998) novel covers this aspect quite well.

Interestingly, the militants took interest in education and issued 27 warnings on this issue. Most of the warnings were confined to copying. During militancy, the incidents of mass copying increased tremendously. The militants warned both the students against copying and the teachers against helping the students in this illegal and unfair practice. The students were warned against using the names of the militants to indulge in this practice. The school teachers were also warned against coming late and not taking classes. We also find a warning against the teaching of Hindi language in schools; however, this was immediately withdrawn as the militants thought learning any language was good for the growth of knowledge.

The militants also tried to define the Sikh tradition through various warnings, involved themselves in creating the Sikh community in a particular mould. They warned people against selling liquor, meat or cigarettes (4.44%). On the social side they warned against taking dowry. They limited the size of marriage party to eleven persons (3.78%). They also warned young girls and women against being fashionable (2.22%). The girls were not supposed to wear pants, jeans or skirts, rather they were to wear *salwar* and *kameez* and cover their head with *chuni* (head cover). One is reminded of Taliban and other fundamentalist discourses, but with regard to their warnings against dowry and size of marriage party certain comments are needed. Both the issues are also treated as social problem, but at the same time it involves and determines the social standing of as family. Giving dowry and entertaining a large *baraat* (marriage party) are also a matter of prestige and economic status of the family. Liquor and meat are inseparable from the marriages among the Jat Sikhs unless the families involved are not vegetarians owing to religious convictions. The social reform programme of the militants might have been initiated with good intentions, but the main question always remained, that is, how to bell the cat. The militants used their coercive power to enforce the social reform. Knowing that they could punish the violators of their decisions, they warned people against violating the norms set by them.

It may be reminded that fundamental qualitative changes in the social and cultural lives of the people do not occur as a result of the orders of the powerful, irrespective of whether it is the individual, the state or the movement. The militants were mistaken in their opinion that they would be able to enforce their will on people. During the period of high tide of militancy, numerous stories of the militants punishing those people who violated their code of social conduct were circulating in Punjab. However, the militants could not stop the Punjabis from drinking liquor and organising big marriage parties in the cities instead of villages and giving dowry in a clandestine manner. It was the dress code that was observed during militancy and once the movement was over young boys and girls moved to fashion with vengeance. The unintended consequence of the social reform programme of the militants has been the mushroom growth of marriage palaces in Punjab.

Ironically, we still find some appreciation of the effort of the militants to bring change in the society of Punjab by removing certain social evils. There could be some beneficiaries of their actions. However, it should be noted that violence or threat of violence may change the behaviour of individuals, but for permanent change much more is required. One of the examples that come to the fore is that of the former Yugoslavia, which ethnically exploded after the collapse of communist system. When Marx commented that the ideas of previous epoch weigh like nightmares in the present, he was essentially referring to the resilience and perpetuation of certain cultural practices that adapt and remain unchanged even in those situations where these should have disappeared. The language of bullet may make a permanent impact on society, but to say that it would enable the holder of the gun to change social and cultural formations the way he/she desires is quixotic thinking. Moreover, drinking on certain occasions like marriages and festivals, such as Lohri and Diwali, are the main sources of enjoyment for the Punjabi Jats.

With regard to meat eating and enforcing vegetarianism there are serious problems. One can raise a query whether vegetarianism is a Sikh tradition. At the level of practice the baptised Sikhs are supposed to be vegetarian, whereas the non-baptised Sikhs could eat meat. This practice had been going on since the 19th century. The militants warned both the butchers and the people against meat eating thus enforcing Vaishnavism on the Sikh tradition. Whereas the warnings to the baptised Sikhs and priests (*granthis*) regarding meat eating and drinking liquor could be understood, the same to the common Sikhs proved to be a failure. The use of intoxicants by the militants was a well-known fact (Puri, Judge and Sekhon 1999). The consumption of tobacco is the only intoxicant whose prohibition is widely recognised and observed in the Sikh community. The militants warned the liquor contractors against selling the alcohol and, as we shall see in the next chapter, they responded to the warnings. Avtar Singh Brahma, the first chief of the KLF, warned the liquor sellers and also the distillers against indulging in the practice. There are certain cases of the militants clarifying their position with regard to the killing of a particular person by stating that he was distilling and selling alcohol. As a part of their effort at moral cleansing, they also warned the bus operators in Punjab (2%). In most of the warnings, the bus drivers and conductors were told to bring to an end the playing of the vulgar songs in the buses. They were asked to play religious songs. The bus conductors were particularly warned against misbehaving with the girls. These warnings were taken seriously and complied to.

The government officials were also made the targets by the militants for their objectionable conduct in public (4.44%). What is interesting to note about the warnings to the government officials is that most of these were directed or addressed to lower level personnel. The staff of the Punjab State Electricity Board (PSEB) received most of such warnings; the Patwaris (village level revenue official) came next, followed by doctors in the hospitals and the officials of Municipal

Committees/Corporations. The primary focus of the warnings to the governmental officials remained confined to specific issues. For example, the PSEB personnel were told not to harass the farmers. Besides government officials, the political leaders were told not to oppose the militant movement. Next in the category of warned was that of the police informers and touts. Created by the British as a social category, the police touts/informers continue to be an integral part of Punjabi society. The primary objective of keeping such people was to keep a watch at the grassroots level on the nationalist and/or illegal activities and report to the police. In lieu of their information to the police, such people used to have clout in the bureaucracy, which would make them useful to the village people too (Judge 1992). In the post-independence period, the police used these informers to keep an eye on illegal distillation of liquor. However, these touts proved quite useful during the Naxalite movement in Punjab from 1969 to 1972. Even in the Sikh militant movement, the informers proved their worth for the police force and the militants had to warn them against such activities, and there were also cases of their murders. The presence of informers and touts shows and indicates the perpetuation of the British legacy in the police functioning in Punjab.

The militants also warned the rich for various reasons. Among them were included factory/theatre/hotel owners, and businessmen including commission agents. However, they were warned for different reasons. Factory owners were told to pay the salaries of their employees or in the case of sugar mills give slips to the farmers,[12] the hotel owners were ordered to stop flesh trade, and theatre owners were told to stop showing vulgar (probably pornographic) movies. All such warnings were specific and without naming any owner the militants asked them to stop their objectionable activities. On the contrary, the commission agents and businessmen were warned against cheating the farmers. Finally, we may mention that there were about thirty warnings, which were issued to diverse categories of people. These were issued to some families, which were harassing the families of the militants, drug addicts, women running brothels, youth organisations, opponents of the reservation policy, Kashmiri militants, and the Hindus. The Hindu students were warned against applying for admission in engineering colleges of Punjab.

Before moving on to the final aspect of warnings, it is pertinent to make another observation about the contents of the warnings. Sometimes, the change in the general conditions in the state would evoke some response from the militant organisations. For example, from the month of March onwards to the end of April, a considerable number of warnings were related with the school/college-going students who were appearing in various examinations. They and their teachers were warned against copying. Towards the end of March, when the time of the auction of liquor contracts would start approaching, we also find warnings to the liquor contractors. During wheat harvesting season commission agents were warned against the harassment of the farmers. Similarly, during winter, warnings to sugar mills on the giving of slips or delay in payment to the farmers are considerable. Finally, most of these warnings were confined to the local issues. Sometimes, particular villages or individuals were warned against specific behaviour.

V
CONSEQUENCES OF NON-COMPLIANCE

As a corollary to the warnings against numerous actions of the addressee, it was equally important and essential to inform the addressee that failure to comply would provoke the militants to punish him/her/them. It was obvious from the claims of killings by the militants that appeared in the newspaper that one of the reasons for killing particular persons were related with these warnings. According to a police official, these warnings were taken seriously even by the police.[13] Police had graded various militant organisations and the response to the warning depended upon which particular organisation had issued that. For example, warnings issued by the Babbar Khalsa International, the Khalistan Liberation Force, the Khalistan Commando Force or the Bhindranwala Tiger Force of Khalistan had been invariably perceived to be serious threats. It was expected that these organisations would punish those who did not pay heed to these warnings.

What was the nature of punishment? In the context of the kind of threat given by the militants, if the warned person(s) failed to comply, all quantitative assessments and numerations failed to convey the reality. In other words, there is no need to inform how many times a particular threat of punishment was actually carried out. The reason is simple. All threats were different expressions of one punishment. Let us first see different kinds of threats given, which were mainly of five kinds. First, one of the ways to threaten was to inform that the non-compliance would be punished according to the Sikh tradition. The following news item appeared in the *Ajit* on, February 10, 1990 shows the way the threat was given in the warning as well as makes the Sikh traditions as perceived by militants more explicit:

> Moga. A meeting of the All India Sikh Students' Federation was held at a secret place. In this meeting Vice-President Bhai Kamaljit Singh, Bhai Nanak Singh, Bhai Gurdip Singh, Bhai Gurnam Singh and many other militants took part. In this meeting those college-going students were warned who tease girls in colleges and at bus stands. They were told to mend their ways; otherwise they would be corrected (killed) according to the Sikh tradition.

The militants also provided the definition of the Sikh tradition in the warning. In view of the fact that the warnings were issued as resolutions of meetings and thus constituted *gurmata*, the nature of punishment could also be legitimised. The history of the Akal Takhat at Amritsar giving punishment to someone who violated the Sikh tradition has remained quite clear. In most of the cases a public apology in the presence of the *Guru Granth Sahib* at Golden Temple and preparedness to accept any *tankhah* (punishment) with humility have remained the hallmark of the contemporary Sikh dynamics. In most of the cases, the punishment has taken the form of cleaning the shoes of the *sangat*, washing utensils in the community kitchen or cleaning the floor. There has been no death sentence to the violator. In his/her failure to appear before the Akal Takhat to accept *tankhah* has led to the ex-communication of the person from the Panth, as has recently happened in the case of Gurbax Singh Kala Afghana. However, such an institution was not available and accessible to the militants as a result of which they made their own decision by interpreting the Sikh tradition.

Secondly, the threat of death or annihilation was used and it was also carried out in many cases. The word used was *sodhna*, which also means correction or modification. In the case of militants it always meant death. The next three kinds of threat of punishment were almost the same, namely, 'action will be taken', 'stern action will be taken', and 'serious or danger consequences' shall be faced by the offender. However, there does not seem to be any consistent pattern in awarding the punishment in the warnings. We are hardly aware of the meaning of stern action or punishment according to Sikh tradition. However, when one scans through various claims and reasons for killing, we find that these involve selling or drinking liquor, or violating some Sikh norm. We also find police informers, renegades being killed by the militants. It is clear that informers and traitors are generally killed by the insurgent organisations (Judge ibid.). Interestingly, an incident occurred in village Ghel in Patiala district and was reported by the *Ajit* on February 18, 1990. The incident, which gives us an idea of militants' understanding of the Sikh tradition, was related with punishment given to a person who had raped another person's wife. The Khalsa Panchayat blackened this man's face and with a garland of shoes around his neck he was paraded in the village.

It is hard to believe that Khalsa Panchayat punished the rapist according to the Sikh tradition that meant that the guilty should be paraded in the village by blackening his face. In the same vein, killing somebody because he was selling liquor is not acceptable as a punishment according to the Sikh tradition. In the light of universal values, rape is a bigger crime than selling the liquor. Selling and consuming alcohol could be legal, but it is not so with rape. One hardly finds specification of what was meant by Sikh tradition as provided by the militants. Their most common action was killing the offender. We do not find any evidence of the gradation of offences. It is wrong to assume that the purpose of evoking Sikh tradition had anything to do with the actual offence; rather it was to appeal to the imagined community for legitimation. For disciplining the community was an essential corollary after the construction of nationhood.

In the end, it may be stated that all these messages constituted a narrative structure in which a particular conception of religion and nation was constructed. In comparison with the argument of Bhindranwala that Khalistan was not on his agenda, the militants later on made it clear that they were waging an armed struggle for the achievement of Khalistan. However, the way they defined Sikhism was not different from what Bhindranwala had already stated. They went beyond Bhindranwala to conceptualise a society of the 'Sikhs'. In the process of enforcing singular conception of religion and social life, they intervened in trivial matters marginalising their grand efforts. Once they treated the Sikh community as a collectivity of devotees, the militants thought it legitimate to intervene in the social and private matters of families and individuals. The intention, motive and purpose of the messages to minimise the eclectic space could not be realised. It was temporarily enforced, but the suppression of the militant movement brought it back to the normal condition. In the end, the suppression of the movement by the Indian state also ended all these constructions through the newspapers. The discourse has now shifted to its original place, that is, among the intellectuals.

Notes

1. This argument is based on author's conclusions after going through the newspapers from 1985 onwards.
2. The following table shows the region-wise origin of warnings:

Region	*Number of Warnings*	*Percentage*
Majha	261	58
Malwa	099	22
Doaba	081	18
Not Mentioned	009	02
Total	450	100

The Majha region consists of Amritsar and Gurdaspur districts; Doaba is comprised of Hoshiarpur, Jalandhar, Kapurthala and Nawan Shahar districts; and the rest of Punjab is called Malwa.

3. There were 48 cities/towns from where all the warnings were issued. The largest number of places from where the warnings had been issued were from the Malwa region (24), followed by Majha (15) and Doaba (9). In spite of this widespread, the major places were only the five of which Amritsar and Rayya are the most prominent.
4. During the militant movement one of the counter-insurgency measures by the state was to divide the entire Majha region into five police districts. Amritsar had three of these, namely, Amritsar, Majitha and Tarn Taran, whereas Gurdaspur district had two, namely, Batala and Gurdaspur, police districts.
5. The newspaper means the Punjabi daily the *Ajit*.
6. In the Sikh tradition only the Guru could give order (*hukamnama*) to the Sikhs. Later on, the places from where the Gurus had given orders were named *takhats*. Five *takhats*, particularly the Akal Takhat located in the Golden Temple, Amritsar have been recognised as the source of *hukamnamas* (Ganda Singh 1996: 289-91). Thus, within the

Sikh tradition the only way the militant could give orders without violating the Sikh tradition was through the institution of *gurmata*. According to Thapar (1996: 152-53), "Gurmata, a mata, i.e., counsel or resolution adopted by the Sikhs at an assembly of theirs held in the name of the Guru concerning any religious, social or political issue".

7. The militants tried to capture Akal Takhat is an example of this effort. Gurbachan Singh Manochahal and later Gurdev Singh Kaunke were made the Jathedars of Akal Takhat in the 1980s through the resolutions of the Sarbat Khalsa, but the SGPC continued to exercise its legitimate authority.
8. The following table provides information regarding the warnings sent by various organisations:

Organisation	*Number*	*Percentage*
KCF (P)	70	15.56
KLF	56	12.44
BKI	35	7.78
KCF (Z)	41	9.11
BTFK (M)	34	7.56
KCF (R)	26	5.78
BTFK (S)	13	2.88
Four/five militant organisations	76	16.88
BTFK (M) and KCF (R)	12	2.67
AISSF (all factions)	21	4.67
Others	66	14.67
Total	450	100.00

Note: Total number of organisations that sent the warnings= 30.
KCF – Khalistan Commando Force; P – Panjwar; R – Gurjant Singh Rajasthani; and Z – Wasan Singh Zaffarwal.
KLF – Khalistan Liberation Force.
BKI – Babbar Khalsa International.
BTFK – Bhindranwala Tiger Force of Khalistan; M – Gurbachan Singh Manochahal; and S – Sukhwinder Singh Sangha.
AISSF – All India Sikh Students' Federation.
Four militant organisations – KCF (P), KLF, BKI, and AISSF (Daljit Singh Bittu faction); and later on, BTFK (S) joined them in issuing warnings thus making them five.

9. The table given below provides information regarding the status of the warned:

Status of the Warned	*Number*	*Percentage*
Looters/extortionists/other militants	152	33.79
Police force	77	17.11
Eve-teasers	33	7.33
Educational Institutions/teachers/students	27	6.00
Liquor/meat/cigarette sellers or contractors	20	4.44
Government officials	20	4.44
Police informers/touts	18	4.00
Political leaders	18	4.00
Sikh violators	17	3.78
Factory/theatre/hotel owners	13	2.89
Fashionable women/girls	10	2.22
Bus operators	09	2.00
Businessmen/commission agents	06	1.33
Others	30	6.67
Total	450	100.00

Note: The categories have been arranged in descending order according to the frequency distribution.

10. In fact, the extent of extortions was much more than the study of Puri, Judge and Sekhon (1999) has shown.
11. The author visited the Chowk Baba Bhauniwala to inquire about the possible and probable effect of this warning. People were not willing to discuss the matter. However, they informed that Kakka had left for Delhi.
12. The sugar mills in Punjab issue orders to the farmers for the procurement of the Sugarcane. They do so by issuing the slips. During the glut period there is a tremendous competition among the farmers to procure those slips, which they do through questionable means.
13. An IPS officer was informally interviewed on this issue.

8

The Militant and the Meek[1]

Clarifications (*spashtikaran*) that appeared in the newspapers signified validation, effect and terror of warnings. It is here that the narrative structure is reversed, as the addressee becomes the sender of the referent. This reversal in the relationship occurred when it began to dawn on the people that militants could have and had undertaken actions, which they had been indicating in their warnings. The prescriptive and proscriptive character of warnings inevitably created conditions and circumstances that necessitated feedback in the form of explanation, apology or appeal. It was a relationship between the militant and the meek in a defined set-up in which the terror of the former weighed heavily on the mind of the latter to evoke a response. Reading an endless appearance of warnings in the newspapers might have given one impression that these could be fabricated. It is only when the clarifications began to appear that the reality of the warnings was adequately comprehended. Who belonged to the class of the meek? Were they individuals or groups? Were they Sikhs or Hindus? All these questions could be raised with regard to clarifications. One can only make a conjecture by pointing out that since a considerable number of warnings were directed against the violation of social reforms, there is a reasonable basis to anticipate that clarifications might have come from the Sikhs. All clarifications did not emanate from the meek, but also from the militants. Such clarifications were invariably addressed to other militants and sometimes these were of general nature.

All clarifications appeared in two Punjabi newspapers, namely, the *Ajit* and the *Punjabi Tribune*. It was evident from the contents of these clarifications that there was no qualitative difference between the two. Most of these clarifications were published as advertisements, which means that the person who sent the message to the militants also spent the money to get it published thus making it sure that it would reach the addressee. In terms of the region of origin of these clarifications, most of these, i.e., 206 (62.05%), originated from the Malwa region, followed by Majha (19.28%), Doaba (10.24%) and from Chandigarh and Sirsa district of Haryana (1.80%). In the case of 6.63 per cent of the clarifications, the place of origin was not mentioned. Within Malwa most of the clarifications originated from Ludhiana (23.80%) and Sangrur (18.07%) districts. It may be inferred from the above information that as compared to other regions the terror of the militants was strongly felt in the Malwa belt. The militant movement was strong in the Majha region of Punjab in comparison to other areas and most of the warnings were issued from this region. However, the text of certain clarifications from the Malwa region indicated that the militants distributed as well as pasted on walls the posters in which the people in the villages were warned.

We can make two broad divisions of these clarifications in terms of the sender. We find that some individual terrorists or organisations clarified their position with regard to a particular issue or situation. The second type of senders covers a large number of people or groups drawn from different walks of life. The analysis of clarifications has been accordingly divided into two parts.

I
MILITANT AS THE SENDER

When the militant was the sender, the addressee was invariably a militant or an organisation. However, there are cases of general clarification given to the Sikh masses. There were 332 clarifications, of which 67 that had been given by the militants. Out of these, 50 originated from the Majha region, followed by Doaba (10) and Malwa (7). These clarifications broadly covered four major issues. The first and foremost of the issues was regarding the primary objective of the armed struggle, which was clarified by repeatedly and explicitly stating that the struggle was for the attainment of Khalistan.

Secondly, there had been, as pointed out in Chapter 7, inter-organisational competition and conflict. Therefore, some clarifications were regarding a particular individual terrorist who had been considered by another organisation as hostile, traitor or doubtful character. Also included in this were the cases of responses of the leader of an organisation in a situation of accusations made by some other militant organisations. One may like to know about the nature of accusations made of which the following news appeared in the *Ajit* on June 1, 1990 is an ideal example:

> Amritsar, 31 May (PTI). Top militant leaders and members of the Panthic Committee Baba Gurbachan Singh Manochahal and Wassan Singh Zaffarwal have accused each other of embezzling the money that was received from foreign countries. Both the leaders were in Pakistan, but recently Baba Manochahal has returned to India in February. Baba Manochahal told that Bhai Zaffarwal has made a false accusation against him of embezzling crores of rupees. He told that when he was staying in Pakistan, Ragi Gurmail Singh of England gave him six lakh rupees.

Thirdly, clarifications were given in order to explain why a particular terrorist(s) was killed by the militant organisation. The following clarification by the Babbar Khalsa International, published (in the *Ajit* on October 21, 1990), amply demonstrates the intensity of the phenomenon of inter-organisational conflicts leading to even killings:

> A meeting of the Babbar Khalsa International was held at a secret place. Bhai Sukhdev Singh [Chabba] Babbar, the chief of the Majha zone, issued the press statement regarding the proceedings of the meeting. According to the press release, ...it was clarified in the meeting that by killing Bhai Hardev Singh Baba Bakala, Balwinder Singh Kirtewal and Baljit Singh Bantu the Babbar Khalsa has acted according to the *gurmat* tradition and they have been punished for their sins. There were serious allegations against these three Singhs. They had spread terror in villages around Balpuria and there were cases of unjustified killings. They raped a woman and shot her later on, but she survived and narrated her story to the Babbars. They also raped women at other places. Anybody having doubts can have clarification from even the people of the village.

In the case of clarifications in which the militants gave reasons for killing a particular militant, no addressee was specified and the above clarification is an instance of it. It may also be pointed out that either the addressee was implicated in the message itself or these were addressed to all. It now seems that in such situations, terrorists tried to kill two birds with one stone. In the first case, it was a warning to the comrades against betrayal and in the second case it was a public relations exercise to convey to the people of the purity of their cause and purpose. There is also something interesting that the above-mentioned clarification betrays, that is, even giving the prefix of 'Bhai' to the militants killed by another organisation. The issue of the use of the prefix of 'Bhai' has been already dealt with earlier in the seventh chapter, but its use for the killed militants on the part of the militants themselves tends to suggest that it was used indiscriminately. The clarification given above also indicates, substantiates and validates the cases of rapes of women by the militants.

Fourthly, sometimes, mystery shrouded the murder of a militant, as a result of which various militant organisations began to seek and give clarifications. The finger of suspicion would be raised against a particular militant. In such a situation, a militant might resort to clarify his stand to prove his innocence. One of the classical clarifications of this kind emanated from Sukhdev Singh Kakku, who belonged to the village Cheema Khuddi. A well-known militant of the KLF, Toofan Singh Toofan alias Jugraj Singh, belonged to this village and in 1990 he was killed in encounter with the police.[2] He was glorified as a great martyr to the extent that even the *kaveeshars* sang in praise of his bravery and martyrdom. In one of the narratives of a kaveesher, it was said that a traitor removed the clip of his AK-47 when the police encircled him. Sukhdev Singh Kakku gave the following clarification that appeared in *Ajit* on July 5, 1990:

> Bhai Kakku said that at the time of the martyrdom of Bhai Toofan Singh he was with him and Bhai Toofan Singh fired 60-65 shots from his gun. Bhai Kakku said that a general could not have given his gun for cleaning to somebody else and then kept with him without checking it. He also said that if somebody had any doubt he could remove it personally.

It may be informed that at the time of giving his statement, Sukhdev Singh Kakku was in the BTFK and later on he was killed by the militants. The case of Kakku explaining and clarifying the conditions at the time of encounter of Toofan Singh Toofan with the police was not the only type of such incidences. Sometimes, the family members of a militant were also made targets as the following instance (*Ajit*, February 3, 1991) indicates:

> The former President of the All India Sikh Students' Federation [Khalsa College, Amritsar] Baljit Kaur Fatahpur sought clarification from four militant organisations with regard to the killing of five members of a family on the evening of September

25 in Fatahpur by Bhai Nishan Singh Fauji Kasel. If they were killed due to personal enmity, then why do you make press statements? These murders prove these statements wrong. The eldest daughter of the deceased made this statement. The four organisations should answer it immediately.

Herself the leader of the AISSF at the local level, Baljit Kaur identified the personal enmity as the root cause of the murders of her family and had the courage to seek clarification. What makes this press statement important is that it betrays the gap between the claims and actual working of the militant organisations. It seems that the incidences of killings due to reasons other than ideological were quite noticeable. No militant organisation could completely justify the killing of children and women. We find that in certain cases the reasons given by the militants with regard to the killing of women were those of 'loose character' and 'police informer'. In the above press statement in which the sender and the addressee are unambiguously identified, it also becomes clear that such killing could not always be attributed to the Punjab police. Not denying the fact that even such acts of violence could be explained in terms of police conspiracy, these were too many to be justified. This issue would also come up when the meek would be sending the message to the militants.

II
MEEK AS THE SENDER

Most of the clarifications emanated from non-militants and signified the effect of the militant movement on the people. What forced the people to respond to the warnings of the militants was the terror in their minds. Militant and terrorist in this sense became overlapping expressions. The word 'militant' seemed to carry a positive connotation and was understood as the translation of the Punjabi word *kharhku*, which means heroic and brave. Defining the *kharhku* is also a process of constructing the "Robin Hood" image (Judge 1992). The equivalents of this image in Punjab are Dulla Bhatti and Sucha Surma.[3] There are many others, but these two approximate the constructed image of *kharhku*. The ability of the militants to create terror among the people was dialectically related with the ideology of the movement. The experts on terrorism generally argue that to achieve its objective, it must not create indiscriminate terror. Only the defined enemy should feel terrorised. It assumes that a movement must be able to mobilise the people. Since the goal of the militant movement was clearly stated as the achievement of the sovereign state of Khalistan, all the Sikhs could be defined as the potential supporters. Without the support – active or passive – of the Sikh masses, the militant movement could not succeed. Clarifications coming from people who were overwhelmingly Sikhs, that is, 299 (90.06%), provide an altogether different scenario. The movement seemed to have created an indiscriminate fear. As we would see little later, the militants in the movement got implicated in the issues related to the social and family life of the Sikh community under the excuse of social reform movement.

What kind of people did try to send their messages to the militants? What were the contents of these messages? We, of course, are aware of the fact that the fear or terror among these people compelled them to send the messages. The fear was that of being eliminated or liquidated if they failed to comply with the edicts of the militants. They were convinced that the threat indicated was real. In similar circumstances, the militants had carried out the act of annihilation. Besides the militants, who sent the clarifications, there were 31 different classes of people. We can broadly divide them into two groups, namely, the sender as an individual and the sender as a group. Among the individuals the most prominent number of 135 constituting 40.66 per cent of the total (332) senders were common people responding to the threat of various kinds. Among the groups the notable were village panchayats (29), Gurdwara managements (8), and liquor contractors (19). For the purpose of analytical understanding, the women senders were separated from the category of individuals and it was found that 16 women gave clarifications of different kinds to the militant organisations. In Punjab villages (as elsewhere in India), we find rural healers who use magical practices and are known by various names. These healers are exorcists, shamans, etc. There were ten such persons who felt threatened enough to give clarifications. We also find some prominent persons, namely, Prof. Darshan Singh, the former jathedar of the Akal Takhat, Kuldip Manik, a well-known Punjabi singer, publishing house of Bhai Chatter Singh Jiwan Singh at Amritsar, a leader of BSP, principals of colleges and a Doordarshan official.

So far as the contents of various clarifications are concerned, we find a tremendous diversity connected through one thread, namely, the religion and community as defined by the militants. Bhindranwala in his speeches condemned the consumption of alcohol and other intoxicants. For him, *nam japana* (praying to the glory of the God) was the best intoxicant in a metaphoric sense. After the Operation Blue Star, the militants grouped together and in the beginning of 1986, we find a considerable number of warnings, particularly from Avtar Singh Brahma, the chief of the then Tat Khalsa, and later on the Khalistan Liberation Force, to the liquor distillers, sellers and contractors. However, we do not find any response from them. The Panthic Committee (Dr. Sohan Singh) announced its social reform programme in 1987 in which one of the issues was the distillation, selling and consumption of alcohol. Since the state government's excise department has been auctioning contracts of liquor selling in the end of the month of March every year for many years, the warnings would invariably appear during that period.[4] The selling of liquor in the government approved shops and illicit distillation and selling never stopped in Punjab despite all these warnings and enforcement of the social reform programme on the part of the militants.

Interestingly, in the beginning of 1991, most of the liquor contractors in the state began to give clarifications with regard to the selling of country or English liquor. For example, Narinder Singh and Co. of Khanna issued the following clarification (*Ajit*, January 1, 1991):

> We are one of the parties of liquor contractors in Khanna. We request militant Singhs that we agree with their social reform movement. But we may kindly be permitted to continue our business till March 31, 1991. After that we shall not indulge in this activity.

Virtually, all clarifications given by the liquor contractors were identical. The liquor trade in Punjab is controlled by a syndicate of contractors and is one of the major sources of the revenue of the state. In spite of the fact that the liquor contractors had the capacity to face challenge as liquor trade is considered to be run with the support of the mafia, they capitulated under the real threat to their existence that was lurking in the environment of general fear in the state. What makes the above clarification more relevant for our understanding is the way the contractors also tried to send the message that they agreed with the social reform programme of the militants. At the same time, however, they pleaded that in view of their economic interests, they should be allowed to continue to sell liquor till March 31. Even after March 31 of any year the auction and sale of liquor never stopped in Punjab. Giving clarification was either a mode of vying for time, using personal connections or giving some amount of money to save oneself from being physically liquidated. Sekhon (2002) has noted the practice of kidnapping during the movement and the argument of the militants to justify their acts of getting money. Warnings to liquor contractors could be a way of getting the 'protection money'[5].

The second set of groups that sent clarifications was that of the village panchayats or the Gurdwara management committees. One of the organisations is formal, whereas the latter may or may not be formalised in most of the villages at the local level, but both are important in the social and religious life of the village community. The important and crucial aspect of these clarifications was that these indicated the all-pervading terror of the militants in the villages. In terms of the contents of these clarifications, most of them focused on explaining, explicating or informing how the edict of the militants had been followed or could not be complied with due to certain circumstances. Another fact that came to light in these clarifications was that in addition to sending the warnings through the newspapers, the militants also adopted the practice of pasting the same on the walls of a building in the village. The village panchayats and Gurdwaras received different kinds of warnings as a result of which they also gave different clarifications. Here is a sample of these appeared in the *Ajit*, on January 14, 1991:

> The village panchayat of Sooch, Tehsil Phool, district Bhatinda has unanimously passed 17 resolutions sent by five militant organisations. The people of the village have been informed of this decision. If any person fails to comply, then besides militants, the panchayats would also punish him.

It is clear from this clarification that there is a complete compliance to the 17-point social reform programme of the five militant organisations.[6] Whenever there was a case of the Gurdwara management committees giving clarifications, the issue largely remained confined to the Sikh principles. One of the significant dimensions of the warnings of the militants was that the people conducting the religious rituals and ceremonies must not consume, stay away from intoxicants and must be *amritdhari* Sikhs. The same thing was made applicable to the members of the Gurdwara management committees. Sometimes, the villagers had to swear by the good behaviour, conduct and character of an individual. The following appeal of the people of a village in the Sangrur district, appeared in the *Ajit* on December 30, 1991, shows how they used to do it:

> A few days' back four militants came to the *math* of village Gobindgarh Jejian. They accused the saint of that *math*, who is

> 60 years old, of being loose character and also of being discriminatory on the basis of caste. Perhaps the militant brethren have been wrongly informed. We appeal to the militant organisations that they could inquire about the saint from the neighbouring villages and the informer's identity be made public. It may also be informed that whether the individuals who came to *math* were militants or not.

The above clarification provides two important insights into the way the people have been living and perceiving the external world. The fact that the saint of a *math* is strongly defended, it shows the diversity in the religious world of the people of Punjab. The clarification does not indicate whether the saint is part of the Sikh or Hindu tradition. However, irrespective of the fact whether the saint is Hindu or Sikh, it indicates that people have been practicing the composite religious tradition. Secondly, despite the terror that the movement created, there is an indication that some people believed that militants were not bad; rather some anti-social elements were giving bad name to them. Otherwise the people of Gobindgarh Jejian would not have asked whether the warning had come from the real militants. Was it a consequence of militants' warnings to the looters and anti-social elements or common people's ploy to provide some elbowroom to the militants to withdraw their threat? It is difficult to know and ascertain what was the case.

The third category that needs our attention is that of women. Violence is generally regarded as having dehumanising effect on women, particularly when the entire society is facing tremendous violent tremors. In his lucid and comprehensive study of partition of India in 1947, Pandey (2002) has shown that when violence is used to construct nationalism through the religious communities, women become the symbol of disciplining the difference between them. In the process, women are not simply marginalised, because they are already located at the margins of the patriarchal social space, but are dehumanised and targeted to make them the symbol of the other community. The moment the religious violence engulfs the society, the distinctions among women as targets get blurred. The self-purification of the religious community is also seen as located in the purity of women. Violating women of the other and killing own women for honour or to purge the community emerge from the same perception, belief and world-view. In her study of women's experiences and perceptions of militancy in Punjab, Hundal (2003) has shown that there was a great degree of degradation of their conditions. In the process of protecting their honour, women were confined to their house that adversely affected their education, particularly among the peasant classes of Majha region. The militants as well as police contributed to the dehumanisation of women. Ignatieff (1994) has explicated and brought out the way women are objectified in ethnic cleansing in his journey into the emergence of new nationalism in the former Yugoslavia.

As a corollary to the above, the militants' orientation towards women entailed a different set of interests. However, it also involved a paradox. Jarnail Singh Bhindranwala had clearly said that even when the Sikhs had to annihilate the opponents, they must treat their women as sisters and mothers.[7] In Bhai Vir Singh's (2003) famous novel *Sundri*, the Sikhs warriors have been shown to be morally upright. They are projected as the saviours of the honour of women, rather than the violators. They have been shown as possessing great human qualities like compassion, love, sympathy and the conviction to fight injustice. It was, therefore, least expected from the Singh of that Guru whom Bhindranwala called "our father" and who founded the Khalsa to save and help the oppressed and persecuted that he would turn into an oppressor of women. In order to reflect the image of the Guru, it was expected from the militants to be the men of honour, character and conviction. As perpetual warnings to the looters and some clarifications regarding why a particular militant was killed began to appear in the newspapers, such an image was impossible to uphold.

The diversity of human life in any setting also reflected in the appeals and clarifications given and offered by women. These clarifications also signified the extent to which the militants could intrude and intervene in the moral, family and social lives of people. One Harbans Kaur in Sangrur district made the following appeal through the *Ajit* of January 15, 1991:

> In village Attarsinghwala, some brothers have accused me of being characterless. I apologise for any wrong act committed by me unwittingly and in future I shall not indulge in any such activity. I assure that in future I shall live a virtuous life.
>
> – Harbans Kaur wife of Balraj Singh, village Attarsinghwala, Tehsil Barnala, District Sangrur.

In this clarification, the appellant accepts that she has been living an immoral life. Since the appeal is clearly stated, it becomes obvious that the militant movement made an attempt to impose a particular kind of sexual morality. If it is so, then one has to reflect on and investigate certain issues. How did the militants come to know that a woman in a particular village is characterless or immoral? Did the militants have the right to make normative decisions and then punish the person? It seems that there must be somebody in the village who informed the militants that a particular woman did something wrong. There is a reasonable basis to suggest that the militants also killed women whom they labelled as loose characters or police informers[8]. It also implies that the punishment to any digression or deviation from the moral standards of behaviour would be physical elimination. Since such events had happened, the best way to save oneself was to submit to the authority of the militants and apologise. The language of clarification did not always follow the pattern of complete submission to the coercive power of the militants, but its origin always lied in the terror. The following clarification, published in the *Ajit* on November 8, 1991, is of this kind:

> I, Harjinder Kaur, widow of Hazara Singh of village Lakha, tehsil Jagraon, district Ludhiana, inform all brothers [militants] that I married my daughter six years ago in village Banjoodi. She had come to me, because she was battered there. Respecting all brothers [militants] I tried to send her through the mediation of Pritam Singh, the Sarpanch of Bajoodi, many times. After the decision through the panchayat I sent my daughter to her husband on October 31, 1991.

We find in the above clarification an example of the active intervention of the militants in the familial affairs of people. An equally important issue here is that the woman who is giving the clarification is the Sarpanch of the village and thus carries some political authority. Another clarification, also appeared in the *Ajit* on December 3, 1991, and seems to have combined the above two, is reproduced below:

> I, Sant Kaur wife of Marha Singh, village Tajoke (Sangurur) request the sangat that I have no relationship with Ruldu Singh Fauji, son of Sunder Singh. None of my sons indulges in anti-social activity. If any wrong has been done, then I apologise for that.

The intervention in personal and family life of the people became a routine activity for the militants. Touching the core of that life was accusing women of the household of being 'loose morals'. It was a process of transforming the private space into a public space. It can only be conjectured that this kind of intrusion in and transformation of the private space was never welcomed. Making a woman's behaviour public in a patriarchal society in particular involved the family honour. Women's clarifications did not remain confined to the personal and social relationships. Sometimes they tried to reach the militants to save members of their families. In the above clarification, a woman is trying to save her sons' lives, whereas the following, published in the *Ajit* on February 4, 1991, involves husband thus:

> I, Kulwant Kaur, village Bagha, district Hoshiarpur, request the militant organisations that my father, S. Ripduman Singh was killed and my husband, S. Gopal Singh was injured. We swear by Sri Guru Granth Sahib that we have never been police informers. Please do justice with us.

In the above case, the woman is making a desperate attempt to save her husband's life after the murder of her father. They are accused of being police touts/informers. Kulwant Kaur symbolises all such women whose family members were under the threat of the militants. Thus clarifications in the form of advertisements were turned into an important channel of sending the message to the militants. Since the militants were perceived as the Singhs of the Guru, the underlying idea was that women were secure in the movement.

The next category was that of prominent people who felt the threat to their lives. They belonged to different walks of life and included politicians, officials, educationists and artists. Two clarifications may be discussed here to highlight what the militants wanted from them. The first clarification, which is discussed here, came from Kuldip Manik – a well-known Punjabi singer – as a press statement in the *Ajit* on December 12, 1990 thus:

> Ludhiana, 11 December. Famous Punjabi singer, Kuldip Manik, gave clarification in a statement that his new cassette is the recording of a live performance at the stage programme. It has not been recorded and the slogan "*Bole So Nihal*" in its beginning and end has been recorded there. If some wrong been done, then he apologises and will keep this thing in mind in future.[9]

The public apology by Kuldip Manik did not go unnoticed and we find the following statement of the militants belonging to the KCF (Z) in the *Ajit* on December 25, 1990:

> The Khalistan Commando Force (Bhai Zaffarwal Group) has decided not take any action against the famous Punjabi singer

> Kuldip Manik after the publication of his apology and clarification in various newspapers.
>
> The organisation had asked Kuldip Manik to apologise when he shouted "*Bole So Nihal*" while singing a vulgar song on the occasion of marriage.
>
> According to the press note of the organisation that has been issued by Bhai Punjab Singh Chhapa, Bhai Pritpal Singh Bishanbandi and Bhai Balwinder Singh, since Kuldip Manik has apologised as per the news on December 14 [sic] for his mistake and has assured that he would not repeat this mistake, he has been forgiven.

The second clarification came from P.L. Trakharhu, the principal of the DAV College, Jalandhar on January 18, 1990 in the *Ajit* in which he stated thus:

> In our college, the course on Masters in Punjabi has been going on since 1986. Also BA (Hon's) in Punjabi is taught. For teaching Punjabi at every level and of every type 16 teachers in the college are working hard and with commitment. For the development of Punjabi the Punjabi Sahit Sabha of the college is quite active, which also organised a big seminar on February 18.

The above clarifications coming from prominent persons are connected with religion and language. Kuldip Manik was forgiven for his behaviour, as he rendered public apology. He was told to refrain from using the Sikh religious expressions in 'vulgar' songs. The clarification from a principal of a college governed by the Arya Samaj management provides an interesting case in understanding the politics of language in Punjab. The fundamental basis on which the notion of identity of a particular people may be established is language. The language, as we know, is not only a means of communication but also a vehicle of culture. It may be stated that the Punjabi language is the first distinctive aspect of Punjabi identity. It is here that a serious problem comes in. In the case of Punjabi language, politics entered in a serious way. Punjab was the only state in India, which was not reorganised on the linguistic basis after independence, as had been done in the case of other states. Consequently, the issue of Punjabi language emerged from the grave of Persian script in a way that the entire conflict led to the correspondence between language and religion. The religious communities started accusing each other on the issue. However, nobody mentioned Urdu and Persian script in the controversy. The way the Punjabi language was marginalised due to political factors tended to create communalism and construct the religion-language stereotypes. For example, it was usually said that if a person of a particular community speaks Hindi, it looks as if he is telling a lie. Still another discourse that emerged in Punjab, which included even the communists, was to blame a particular religious community for betraying Punjabi.

In the case of the DAV College, the militants acted according to the stereotyped construction of the Arya Samaj. It may however be added that the murderers of Lala Jagat Narain and his son Romesh Kumar, the editors of *Hind Samachar* group of newspapers, were associated with this perception. To what extent this perception was valid is an issue that requires a debate of a different kind, but the existence of this perception could be understood as a social fact.

We finally turn to the largest number of clarifications that originated from individuals. There could be many reasons for giving clarifications, but in terms of the nature and expression of the content, three were prominent that may be categorised as denial, submission, and seeking clarification. In the case of denial, we find two broad kinds of clarifications. The first was denying any affiliation to certain political parties, which were thought to be opposed to the militants and the second involved denying being police informer. In this respect, the communists were at the top of their list and the following clarification, appeared in the *Punjabi Tribune* on January 31, 1991 and is not the only one of its kind, makes it clear:

> I, Amarjit Singh (Village Barian, Block Nurpur Bedi, District Ropar) appeal to the militant Singhs that I am not a communist and I have nothing to do with communist party. Somebody personally opposed to me has misled the force about this.

It has been noticed in the last chapter that militants warned the police informers/touts. Obviously, some people who were accused of giving information to the police about the militants and their activities became the targets of militants' attack denied having done so. The clarification detailed below and published in the *Punjabi Tribune* on January 27, 1991, is of such a kind:

> I request my militant brothers that the accusation against me that I informed the police leading to the arrest of two militants from the village Jiwansinghwala is absolutely unfounded. I appeal to militant brothers that I have neither informed the police nor do I know about it. Militant brothers can talk to me anytime about this. If I am proved guilty, they can punish me even if it is death sentence.
>
> – Ruldu Ram, son of Shri Soni Ram, Jiwansinghwala.

It is clear from the above two denials that militants were obsessed with the police informers and kept on warning them. The political opponents automatically qualified as political informers. One of the major problems with regard to the police informers is that the underground movement, which is using terrorist methods, is largely incapable of securing information about them. To know who is a police informer or who informed the police, requires a network of voluntary and ideologically sympathetic informers. Some people would settle their scores with others by informing the militants who have no way of verifying such information. The result is killing the wrong man. Such occurrences lead to the decline of the movement. In the case of the Sikh militant movement, the people who were accused of being police informers, were either informed through warnings or by pasting the letter on the wall of their houses. This was however not enough, as in most of the cases such clarifications were not sought. Here, we find that giving clarification is an attempt to save one's life by informing of one's innocence.

The second kind of individual clarifications indicated the way the people submitted to the warnings of the militants. The following advertisement, published in the *Ajit* on December 11, 1991, shows how some people informed their total submission to the militants' order:

> We, Gurtej Singh Bambi and Binder Singh of village Tajoke, tehsil Barnala (Sangrur) and police station Tappa appeal to all that our father Jawala Singh and brother Bhola Singh have met with the punishment for their wrongdoings. The innocent family may be forgiven. We have become amritdhari and the fact may be investigated.

In most of the cases of submission, the individuals tried to inform the concerned militants/organisations that whatever was their command had been complied to. In this class of clarifications, a large variety of people were covered. It included those who were drinking alcohol but were associated with the Sikh religious practices, harassing their daughter-in-laws or wives, and occupying some land belonging to others. From the fact sheet of these clarifications, it seems that the militants tried to right the wrong at the grass-roots level. Unfortunately, this was too large a domain for any militant movement to make any impact. These issues could not be handled and resolved by using the threat of elimination. What would happen after the end of the movement? It never occurred to the people on both sides of the clarifications, namely, the sender and the addressee. If we assume that they knew, then it was a great game of pretension.

Finally, we may turn to those individuals who sought clarifications from the militants. Included in this were both women and men. For example, Amarjit Kaur of village Dugga, district Sangrur issued an appeal in the *Ajit* on April 12, 1992 seeking clarification from the militants whether the militants had kidnapped her husband. The following is another kind of clarification, also published in the *Ajit* on April 19, 1992, sought from the militants thus:

> I, Sohan Singh, son of Babu Singh of village Dhadiala near Tanda appeal to the brothers that some persons came to my farmhouse and demanded some money. Brothers are requested to kindly clarify the matter.

Apparently, Sohan Singh believed that the persons who came to his farm house pretended to be militants. He wanted to make it sure whether they were real or not. It also implies that in case he was convinced that the real militants were demanding money from him, he would have given it to them. Or was he bidding for some time to avoid paying the money. In this sense, Sohan Singh was a playing a game with the militants. Without facing any real threat to his life he wanted to avoid giving money to any body irrespective of whether the persons were militants or not. If it was so, then he was using the game that militants had been playing with the people. As we have seen in the seventh chapter, the militants frequently warned the looters/extortionists. It was thus obvious that the same logic could be applied to save the situation. There were many who followed Sohan Singh's game. It is in fact the previous clarification given by Gurtej Singh Bambi and Binder Singh in which we find the extreme state of submission. It also deconstructs valour of the Punjabis in general and the Sikhs in particular. There are arguments offered by social anthropologists, particularly Pettigrew (1978) in the case of Jat Sikhs of Punjab, that the tradition of revenge and sense of honour are ingrained in the Punjabi cultural tradition. The Sikh religion has reinforced and regulated it towards the collective good. All such arguments stand dismantled and deconstructed in the face of the kind of terror that militant movement had had on the people. More important was the fact that the militant movement progressively lost its legitimacy among the people. It is evident from the fact that the militants had to warn anti-social elements present in their ranks against objectionable behaviour. They had to clarify why they had killed some militants.

It also becomes clear that the militant movement became terrorist in practice as a result of which it created indiscriminate fear. It could not identify its enemy in the political sense of the term. Its inward orientation was evident from the fact that most of the warnings were issued to and clarifications came from Sikhs. It bordered on the ethnic cleansing in which the only construction of legitimate actions were created through the upholding of the tradition of martyrdom as if this was the key to Khalistan. The nation was dreamt and invented but it could not be defined for which a different set of ideological praxis was required. The relationship between the sender and the addressee was underlined by power owing to which the narrative changed into a complex process in comparison to the situation where both are of equal status. Each narrative was not a simple message of implicating whatever was said and comprehended as a linguistic expression. It contained hidden expressions that were not to be understood by the addressee, that is, the militants. In the case of warnings, the effort was to legitimise the actions of the militants, whereas the purpose behind clarifications was to save one's life but simultaneously hiding something that was under threat also. The classical illustration of such an effort was the clarification of the liquor contractors, who time and again told the militants that they agreed with their social reform programme, but the economic compulsions were such that they had to run the liquor shops till March 31. Interestingly that March 31 never came and they showed that they had nothing to do with the social reform programme. However, the effort at legitimising the movement through denotative messages by attributing martyrdom to the slain militants misfired when the inter-organisational conflicts led to the killings of many militants.

In the end, it may be stated that warnings and clarifications were related to each other in a way that the latter validated the former. Both constituted discursive elements in the project of nationhood directly and indirectly. Clarifications contributed to this project indirectly rarely betraying or manifesting the intention and the purpose. Since most of the clarifications indicated compliance, the militants' objective of creating a moral community as autonomous, united and having single identity seemed achieved. However, the complex social milieu from which the clarifications emerged remained more or less unchanged though a degree of adaptation certainly occurred. One obvious example of this adaptation is addressing the militants as 'brothers', and stating that their social reform programme was acceptable. It was a kind of waiting for the movement to end. Till then, the most important thing was to live.

Notes

1. The idea of the title of this chapter has come from Siegel (1986).
2. See Chapter 6, in which a detailed discussion on tributes covers the case of Toofan Singh Toofan.
3. Dulla Bhatti was a famous bandit and was contemporary of Emperor Akbar. A considerable number of folk songs are found in Punjab about his legend. What epitomises the top status of Dulla Bhatti is the well-known song of Lohri festival thus: "*Sunderye Munderye, Tera kaun Bichara, Dulla Bhatti wala*" (Oh Sundari! Only Dulla Bhatti can be your saviour). Sucha Surma belonged to the 20th century period and served in the British Indian Army, but came back to save the honour of his family. After killing his enemy in the village, he absconded and did help poor people. Finally, he was caught and hanged.
4. This issue has also been partly covered in Chapter 7.
5. Personal interview with Jagrup Singh Sekhon who collected extensive information regarding kidnapping and other such activities linked with the collection of money on the part of the militants.
6. Five militant organisations were, as pointed out earlier, comprised of the KCF (P), the KLF, the BKI, the AISSF (Bittu), and the BTFK (S). Had the warning been issued in the beginning of 1990, there would have been four militant organisations.

7. See Chapter 6.
8. In the collaborative study of the author (Puri, Judge and Sekhon 1999), it was found in village Ghasitpur in Gurdaspur district that a Mazbi woman was killed, because the militants were of the view that she was of loose morals. Such a fact they knew, because a Babbar Khalsa militant belonged to the village.
9. "*Bole So Nihal*" is said at the end of the prayer in Sikh congregation and it is followed by "*Sat Sri Akal*".

9

Concluding Remarks

Sociologically speaking, there is a fundamental distinction between religion and community. Culture is to community what blood is to body. The symbiotic relationship between the two reinforces and sustains each other. The distinction between religion and culture in the case of Islam and Christianity becomes quite obvious mainly because of the their geographical spread. For instance, the people of both Pakistan and Albania are predominantly Muslims, but they constitute different communities. Even within a nation-state, we can find and observe such a difference, the obvious example of which could be India. The major proportion of the people of India is Hindu by faith, but there are numerous communities with varieties of cultural practices and traditions. At the same time, India is also multi-religious. Religion and caste have become the basic indicators of analysing the Indian society, but the understanding of community in singular sense by using these two indicators would be an inappropriate way of understanding Indian society. The same religion and caste have tremendous variations across regions. In the case of Sikhism, however, such a complexity is not present largely due to its confinement to

Punjab. Even then, the Sikh tradition, as pointed out by Oberoi (1994), has composite character.

In the western tradition, society is generally understood as a moral community, which assumes that there is a degree of homogeneity to make a society. The western experience of the emergence of nation-states with underlying religious unity gave credence to the notion of moral homogeneity among the people. It also subsumed that to be a society there must be a degree of homogeneity, because one expected that there must be a force that holds all members together. This however did not prevent the communities from emerging with heterogeneity and a greater sense of togetherness within the society. Communities developed their own identities depending on various denominations like village, locality, region, etc. The assumption that all communities have to be homogeneous (Dumont 2002) was unacceptable even in the case of the West, as class distinctions had always existed. In India, the communities were largely heterogeneous owing to the caste divisions that existed and persisted with the power of religion behind them. Owing to the heterogeneous structure of communities that were characterised by cultural plurality, their durability and persistence were never threatened. As most of the empirical studies of various non-Hindu religious communities in India suggest, the caste system existed among them owing to which it seemed least probable that any religious community in India could be homogeneous even if we do not mention class distinctions. In other words, the Indian society never constituted a moral community in the western sense of the term. Religious communities co-existed and at the village levels they tended to form and exist as one social unit. It always depended on the particular religious groups that existed in the villages. It also implies that communities were fuzzy (Kaviraj 1992), but this should not imply that there were no demarcations (Chatterjee 1993). To make sense of what Kaviraj and Chatterjee are emphasising, let us compare with special reference to the Sikhs the constructions of communities in the pre-colonial, colonial and post-colonial Punjab.

The most important pre-colonial text that was written in 1762 is Waris Shah's (n. d.) famous love epic, *Heer*. From the 18th century onwards Punjab had three religious communities, namely, Hindus, Muslims and Sikhs. It is clear from the *Heer* that the Hindus and the Muslims interacted with each other as a unitary whole, particularly in the areas where the Jats were predominant. By identifying 32 castes in a village, Waris Shah depicted the unity and diversity in the village community. He made no distinctions between the Hindus and the Muslims in terms of either the existence or lack of castes. Each caste group, as Waris Shah informs, had its own deity to be worshipped. However, the diety of the Muslim carpenter was different from that of his Hindu counterpart. Waris Shah emphatically presents the already existing eclectic zone between Muslim and Hindu religious communities. Since the story of the love of Heer and Ranjha has remained unchanged with the exception of the ending, it therefore may be assumed that the eclectic space already existed. What is original about this space in Waris Shah is his recognition of its existence. He makes a distinction between the established clergy and the Sufi tradition. The interaction between the Hindu and the Muslim religions was mediated by the eclectic space created by not only the Sufi tradition but also the Jogi tradition. Ranjha, who is a Muslim and is blessed by the five *pirs*, finds no difficulty in becoming a Hindu Jogi after Heer is forcibly married to Saida Khaida. To reclaim Heer, Ranjha goes to Bal Nath – the head of a Jogi sect – and persuades him to bless him and make him a Jogi, which he does. Waris Shah also informs that at the celestial level all diverse religious practices converge and merge with God. The implications of Waris Shah's narrative are quite obvious. An eclectic space where the two religions were meeting, interacting and influencing each other marked the boundaries between Islam and Hinduism in Punjab.

When we move to the colonial period, the language of discourse undergoes a change, but it must be specified here that this change must be contextualised in terms of the impact of colonialism. Bhai Vir Singh's novel, *Sundari*, and Kahn Singh Nabha's polemical work, *Hum Hindu Nahin*, both published in 1898, mark the beginning of a new phase in the history of the Sikh community. It was no coincidence that both were published in the same year. These were the culmination of the way the Singh Sabha movement constructed the Sikh history. After *Heer* of Waris Shah, *Sundari* is the most read literary work in Punjabi but with one difference. Whereas the former was read by most of the Punjabis, the readership of the latter remained confined to the Sikhs only. Besides his construction of gender in response to the activities of the Christian missionaries in Punjab (Jakobsh 2003), what Bhai Vir Singh has done in his novel is that he created the society of the 18th century Punjab about which we have already found evidence of the presence of eclectic space. *Sundari* shows three religious communities interacting with each other not in a harmonious manner but in a contentious form. The Muslim is *a priori* oppressive and cruel, whereas the Hindu is depicted as coward and incapable of defending himself against the former. Everything good is said about the Sikhs, as they are portrayed as being valiant, possessing a great sense of honour, saviours and always prepared to sacrifice their lives. Notably, even the Hindu could oppress the Sikhs by joining the Muslim rulers. There is a presence of a small eclectic zone between the Sikhs and the Hindus, which operates only when a radical change occurs after a Hindu converts to Sikhism. After baptism and becoming Khalsa, a Hindu transforms from a jackal (coward) to a lion (brave).

The construction of communities in *Sundari* deprives them of any eclectic space. Valorisation of the Sikh tradition has been completed in the story of the novel. At both the theoretical and polemical levels, Kahn Singh Nabha complimented Bhai Vir Singh. Since both the works were published in 1898, it was clear that there was an objective and intention involved and this was the construction of a singular tradition in Sikhism. Nabha (1973) makes it clear that Hindus and Sikhs are distinct from each other on account of the nature of social structure and the personality traits. Hindus are shown to have caste system, whereas no such distinctions exist among the Sikhs. The Sikhs are the saviours of Hinduism, but the latter are seen as ungrateful. The sacrifices of the Sikhs have gone in vain. The Hindus are trying to convert the Sikhs into their faith – this observation might have been made by Nabha on the attempts of the Arya Samaj to reconvert the people even from Sikhism into the Hindu fold.

At the beginning of the 20th century, the efforts of the Singh Sabha leaders in creating a new identity paid rich dividends as the number of the Sikhs began to rise. One may also give some credit to the British government's recruitment policy according to which a Sikh was defined in a particular form, that is, as Khalsa. During the first two decades of the century, the real population of Punjab saw a decline due to epidemics like plague and influenza, but the number of the Sikhs showed an increase in their numbers (Singh 1997). The proselytising activities of the Singh Sabha complimented by the Arya Samaj contributed to the undermining and decentring of the eclectic space. This is evident from the fact that in the first census of 1881, a considerable number of Punjabis informed that they were the followers of Sakhi Sarvar. It also indicated that most of the people, particularly in the villages, lived and conducted their lives in the shadow of folk religion where different religious communities shared considerable eclectic space. In the popularisation of the singular Sikh tradition constructed and presented through the idiom of martyrdom, the *kaveeshars* and *dhadis* (bards) played an important role at the grassroots level. The Gurdwara Reform Movement was conducted along the Gandhian principle of *satyagraha*.

Subsequently, the demands of the Akalis were accepted, and the Sikh Gurdwara Act in 1925 was passed, which gave recognition to the newly formed Shiromani Gurdwara Prabhandak Committee (SGPC). The entire process transformed a composite tradition into a singular one. The Act clearly demarcated the Sikh and the Hindu shrines. The SGPC took control over the historical Gurdwaras and also the Sikh religious affairs. All these developments provided space not only for the redefinition of the community, but also the imagining of nationhood. This development did not take long to occur though the source was located somewhere else. The demand for Khalistan was first raised in 1940 and it happened immediately after the Muslim League had passed its Lahore Resolution.

Irrespective of religious affiliations, the people of Punjab had (and still have) a strong tradition of folk religious beliefs and practices in which they share the eclectic space. As the primary concern in this work is the Sikh community, it is worthwhile to elaborate the issue of folk religion in this context. Bhatti (2000) identifies two kinds of sects in Sikh religion that have existed for a long time. Peripheral sects, such as Udasis, Nirmalas, Namdharis, Radha Soamis, and there are sects that constitute the Sikh body, namely, Rarewale, Kaleranwale, etc. Besides these sects, the Sikhs have been indulging in various kinds of religious practices other than that of the established religion. Bhatti (ibid.: 41) observes that "sizeable sections of Sikh population visit shrines of *Kali Devi*, *Naina Devi*, *Mansa Devi* at the annual fair. Such fairs are also held at the shrines of *Gugga*, *Mata Rani* and *Sakhi Sarvar*". This observation reiterates and reinforces the simple fact that all attempts at purging the Sikh religion (or for that matter Hinduism) from composite traditions have fundamentally failed. The Sikhs continued to move to the eclectic space, which they shared with both the Muslims and the Hindus. In spite of the fact that most Muslims left the Indian Punjab in 1947 following large-scale riots, the worship of Muslim *pirs* has been going on unabated and unhindered. In many villages of Punjab, fairs are organised at the *mazaars* of the *pirs* once a year and on Thursdays the people come to the place to pay their obeisance to them.

The construction of the Sikh identity in the colonial period was a result of negotiation between the British and the leaders of the Singh Sabha movement (Pashaura Singh 204). Bhai Vir Singh's *Sundari* was the culmination, objectification and justification of that identity through the invention of tradition. For the British, the defined identity was the essential condition for the community to exist in the demarcated boundaries and its central feature was that it could be enumerated. The British saw and interpreted the Asian population in terms certain racial characteristics (Hirschman 1986). This led to the blurring or fuzziness that characterised the community identities, which by minimising the eclectic space paved the way for the construction of nationhood. Chatterjee (1993: 223) observes: "One of the fundamental elements in the colonial conceptualisation of India as a 'different' society was the fixed belief that the population was a melange of communities. ... If the colonial state was to seek legitimacy, it had to do so by picking out and bringing over to its side the 'natural leaders' of the various communities." In the case of the Sikhs, the latter part of this observation has remained largely valid even in the post-colonial period and facilitated the imagining of nationhood.

In the post-colonial period, the affirmation of the Sikh values continued with a purpose of dissuading the common Sikhs from worshipping graves, and other non-Sikh deities. However, as we know from the study of Bhatti (2000), such attempts remained largely unsuccessful. The formation of Pakistan was an assertion, realisation and reinforcement of religious nationalism, and lent credence and legitimacy to the claim of combining religion with politics. This trend did not remain confined to the Sikhs; rather it covered other religions too. It was in stark contrast to the ideal of secularism visualised by Indian nationalist leaders who maintained that India could be a nation. Once religion entered the political space, the trajectory of social contestations changed and godmen, saints, swamis, etc. began to transgress boundaries that were created by the nationalist and secular discourse. A new era of religious communities – competing, struggling and fighting in the political space – began subverting the communities. In a general sense, the process of subverting the community begins when the religious leaders begin to define the religion and the community in singular terms by inventing and constructing the exclusive traditions. In the process, every other culture and religion becomes the excluded self. Such a process occurs only when power operates. Power has the ability to create knowledge (Flyvbjerg 2001) and also to impose it coercively as well as manipulatively. However, it is possible to reduce or minimise the eclectic space, but it seems least probable that it would be made to disappear completely. The forcible movement from community to congregation tends to subvert the community. However, a congregation is a temporary collectivity and any attempt to make it permanent is also to intensify and deepen the collective perceptions, sentiments and emotions. In India, communal riots/conflicts in which social life becomes volatile highlight instances of this process where the eclectic space is temporarily minimised. In long terms, it is impossible to keep an entire community in a volatile or tumultuous stage.

In the case of the militant movement, motive, intention and objective of the narratives were to transform the Sikh community into a state of preparedness to fight and struggle for its legitimate rights. The legitimacy was derived from religion and the 'perceived crisis' to the *panth*. The militants did not innovate various elements of the narratives, but they coercively imposed the already available narratives on the Sikh masses. This availability had two sources, namely, the Akali-SGPC politics of power and religion, and the popularisation of invented religious tradition through various channels, such as *kirtani jathas*, preachers, *kaveeshars* and *dhadis*. In fact, *kaveeshers* and *dhadis* remained largely the popularisers of the tradition, whereas the invention of the tradition owes its origin to the preachers and *kirtani jathas* who depend upon the patronage of the SGPC for their survival.

Since the Akali Dal controls the SGPC, the issue of Sikh identity is invariably kept alive to suit the political interest. It has emerged as a trap that has no simple solution and it also has not undergone any substantial change during the last fifty years. The struggle for Punjabi Suba was largely a fight for a Sikh majority state, which the Akali Dal got in 1966. Since then, the politics of power has constantly shaped and influenced the political orientation and actions of the Akali Dal. During the period of the Congress rule in Punjab, the Akalis came out with the Anandpur Sahib Resolution, which was a proposal and programme marking the struggle for change and reform in centre-state relations. It was, however, read and interpreted as a document professing and propagating Sikh separatism. In fact, it was a boldly framed document, as at that time the Akalis were out of power. From thereon began the journey of a conscious attempt at subverting the Sikh community into a congregation when the Anandpur Sahib Resolution became the core issue for Bhindranwala. There were many other conditions that had influenced and facilitated the emergence of the militant discourse.

Koehn (1991) attributes the emergence of Sikh militancy to the modernisation process in which the relationship between different communities changed as a result of economic development. This observation is quite close to Huntington's (1968) views on the relationship between economic development and political order in developing societies. The context of the

Green Revolution in Punjab acquires centre stage in the understanding of militancy. Not much attention, however, is paid to the political conditions in the 1970s. It should be noted that in 1975 the imposition of emergency by Mrs. Indira Gandhi, the then Prime Minister, marked the opening of a new chapter in the history of post-independent India. It was a gross misuse of the two-third majority, which the Congress enjoyed in the Lok Sabha. During emergency, when most of the political leaders were put behind the bars or went underground, one of the few islands of struggle against its oppression was the Akali Dal under the leadership of Sant Harchand Singh Longowal. More importantly, Sant Kartar Singh Bhindranwala, through his organisation of *jathas*, emerged as one of the major figure to pose a challenge to the authority of Indira Gandhi and the Congress Party. In the elections of 1977, when the Janata Party came to power, the Akali Dal was one of the partners in the government. Within a year the clash took place between the Nirankaris and the *jatha* led by Jarnail Singh Bhindranwala. The emergency period had already created stress in the social and political life of the country. Owing to the constant struggle that the Akalis waged against the emergency, the life in Punjab got more intensified and volatile than other areas. During the emergency, Giani Zail Singh, the then Chief Minister of Punjab, had competed with Akalis by using their idiom of the Sikh *panth*. He tried to intervene in the SGPC elections by promoting Jarnail Singh Bhindranwala, who was believed to be close to him. In the process, the religious affairs and politics got so enmeshed and entwined that the Sikh community remained in a state of heightened intensity and volatility, which constantly minimised the eclectic space. The Akalis always maintained that religion and politics could not be separated. It was a good tactic to legitimise their control over religious and political institutions, but they never anticipated that the same legitimising narrative could be used to marginalise them.

Bhindranwala emerged as a protagonist for his ability to state clearly and unequivocally the issues where the Akalis were ambivalent, uncertain and fuzzy. He defined the Sikh and excluded the others and evoked the militant tradition of Sikhism. Most of his speeches were given to the congregations/gatherings at the Golden Temple. The Sikh community and congregation overlapped in his speeches. He told the gatherings to hate others, to prepare for 'war', to save the honour of the Sikhs in India and this could only be done through militant struggle. He wanted the Sikhs to get baptised and become the true sons of the tenth guru. His rhetorical speeches, with rustic colloquial expression, were easily understood by the gatherings. His efforts at transforming the community into congregation were persuasive yet they remained incomplete. But he certainly succeeded in reducing the eclectic space. A spate of murders in Punjab further communalised the situation. Bhindranwala made it quite clear to his followers that if there were an attack on the Golden Temple, then no person without a turban should be seen in Punjab. Obviously, all the people in Punjab who claimed to be Sikhs were not turbaned. It was thus an attempt to subvert the community to turn it into the collectivity of puritan Sikhs strictly observing the *rahat maryada*. The volatility of the Sikh community reached its peak when in the first week of June 1984 the Indian Army attacked the Golden Temple. Indira Gandhi's assassination and subsequent riots against the Sikhs, particularly in Delhi, sustained the intensification of community life. Thus, when the militants reorganised themselves and started their activities in 1985, they had a volatile Sikh community allegedly alienated from the Indian state. Readily available support to the militants from the Sikh masses accelerated the militant movement and it was made clear that the.objective of the movement was to achieve the sovereign state – Khalistan. Bhindranwala never spelled out clearly that the goal of his movement was the attainment of Khalistan, but in less than two years of his death, the trajectory of the movement changed to theocratic politics.

The militants in 1987 launched the social reform movement to purge the Sikh community from all ill influences and practices and then began the process of warning others to mend their behaviour. In an interview with Juergensmeyer (2001), Sohan Singh explained the logic of such warnings. Juergensmeyer (ibid.: 99) writes: "Sohan Singh claimed that killings undertaken by militants were always done for a purpose; they were not 'killing for killing sake'. Moreover, Sohan Singh said that warnings were given and punishment was meted out only if offenders persisted in the conduct that the militants regarded as offensive." From the magnitude of killings and the responsibilities claimed for the same by the militants, one may come to the conclusion that there were too many offenders and most of them persisted in their conduct. The clarifications offered by individuals, villages and other people from different walks of life could be understood as efforts on the part of the warned or threatened to save their lives. Despite all this, the social life remained the same in many ways. The effort to create a community that corresponded with the congregation failed miserably.

In the post-militancy phase, the social reform programme was put in the garbage by the youth by reverting back to the fashion and trimming beards. People began to increase the size of marriage parties, accept and give dowry, and there was also much increase in liquor consumption. However, the efforts of the Sikh clerical and political leadership at creating a Sikh community, distinct and insulated from all other influences, have not come to an end. This time the SGPC duly supported by the Akali Dal adopted the "Nanakshahi Calendar" with effect from 2003. According to this calendar, the reference point begins from the birth of Guru Nanak Dev. There is nothing wrong in this, as most calendars associate with the similar events relating to the founder of the religion. Thapar (2000: xii) rightly points out that these "can be ideologically charged to commemorate various events". In the coming years, there is likelihood that Sikhs and Hindus will have separate dates for the celebration of Diwali. It is going to be a testing time for the traditions of the two communities. The same is the case with the two important festivals, namely, Lohri and Baisakhi. From the experience of Lohri it may be stated that the people will remain confused for some time. However, adherence to new or old calendar may not transform the community into congregation, but it may create clear-cut demarcation between the two religious communities over the celebration of some festivals, particularly Lohri, Baisakhi and Diwali.

The Akali Dal and the Sikh militant movement were caught in the narratives of religion and politics within the discursive space of the post-colonial Indian state at the end of which the politics dominated. The militant movement, however, used violence as discourse of creating a moral community, whereas the Akali Dal, both as a political body and the controller of the SGPC, had been doing it with the threat of ex-communication and imposition of penance in certain cases of violations and digressions. Simultaneously, the narratives of the Sikh militant movement were logical culmination of the Singh Sabha-Akali Dal efforts at and objective of bringing politics into the centre by decentring the composite Sikh tradition through the construction of distinct identity followed by distinct nationhood. It is obvious that the bone of contention was not religion; rather it was all politics of power for which the community was subverted.

Indian nationalism began with the arrival of print capitalism (Anderson 1991) and emergence of an educated class (Gellner 1983). The construction of Sikh nationhood followed the same pattern and conditions. The specificity of Indian nationalism also reflected in the case of the Sikh resurgence. Chatterjee (1993) traces the emergence of nationalism in Bengal and points out how the educated middle class articulated nationhood in religious idiom. Obviously, the case of the Sikhs was not much different from the dominant trend, but the notable feature of the Sikh community was its small number. The Sikh leaders showed ambivalence to the national movement in the sense that on the one hand, they tried to create their distinct religious identity, but, on the other hand, they joined the Gandhi-led *satyagraha*. The seeds thus sown when resulted into the partition of the country, the idea of distinct identity of the Sikhs turned into the construction of nationhood in the fundamentalist discourse. The Sikh militant movement was a logical culmination of the way the Indian nation was imagined in the colonial period.

Bibliography

Primary Sources

Audio-cassettes of the recorded speeches of Jarnail Singh Bhindranwala. He delivered these speeches between 1982 and 1984 to the Sikhs who had visited the Golden Temple either as pilgrims or as activists. There are fourteen audio-cassettes of his speeches. The author transcribed all his speeches.

The Punjabi newspaper, the *Ajit,* was consulted and the information was collected between 1986 and 1993. In addition, the *Punjabi Tribune* was also consulted.

Punjabi Sources

Damdami Taksal. 1994. *Itihas Damdami Taksal*. Amritsar: Damdami Taksal Jatha Bhindran (Mehta).

Judge, Paramjit S. 2000. *Parvas: Sabhiacharak Sankat*. Jalandhar: NRI Sabha.

Nabha, Kahn Singh. 1973. *Hum Hindu Nahin*. Amritsar: Singh Sabha Shatabadi Committee (first published in 1898).

Shiromani Gurdwara Parbandhak Committee. 2003. Nanakshahi Calendar. Amritsar: SGPC.

— 1973. *Sikh Rahat Maryada*. Amritsar: Dharam Parchar Committee, SGPC.

Singh, Bhai Vir. 2003. *Sundri*. New Delhi: Bhai Vir Singh Sahit Sadan (first published in 1898).

Singh, Dalbir. 2000. *Nairhion Dithe Sant Jarnail Singh Bhindranwale*. Jalandhar: Panth Khalsa Parkashan.

Singh, Gurtej and Swaran Singh (eds.). 2001. *Shahid-Bilas Sant Jarnail Singh*. Chandigarh: Satsandhi Parkashan.

Singh, Nahar. 1999. '*Punjab da Virsa: Lokdharai Paripekh*', paper presented in the Third Annual Convention of NRI Sabha, Jalandhar.

Singh, Naraien (ed.). 2003. *Singh Garj: Speeches and Interviews of Sant Jarnail Singh*. Amritsar: Gurmat Pustak Bhandar.

Singh, Puran. 1964. 'Jawan Punjab', in M. S. Randhawa (ed.), *Puran Singh da Jeevan te Rachna*. Delhi: Sahit Academy.

Singh, Talwinder. 1998. *Yodhe*. Jalandhar: Chetna Parkashan.

Singh, Tejshadeep. 2004. 'Ao Ikmuth ho ke Turye', *Sikh Shahadat*, June, p. 23.

Sources in English

Anderson, Benedict. 1991. *Imagined Communities: Reflections on the Origin and Spread of Nationalism*. London: Verso (Revised Edition).

AIFODR (All India Federation of Organisations for Democratic Rights). 1987. *People Fight Back: A Report to the Nation*. Bombay: AIFODR.

Bal, Gurpreet. 1995. *Development and Change in Punjab*. New Delhi: National Book Organisation.

— 2003. 'A 19th-Century Woman Poet of Punjab: Peero', *Indian Journal of Gender Studies*, 10 (2), pp. 183-200.

— and Paramjit S. Judge. 2001. 'Terrorism and Rural Entrepreneurship in Punjab', *Journal of Entrepreneurship*, 10 (2), pp. 191-208.

Ballantyne, Tony. 2004. 'Maharaja Dalip Singh, History, and the Negotiation of Sikh Identity', in Pashaura Singh and N. Gerald Barrier (eds.), *Sikhism and History*. New Delhi: Oxford University Press, pp. 151-175.

Banerjee, Indubhushan. 1962. *Evolution of the Khalsa*, Vol. 2. Calcutta: A. Mukherjee & Co.

Barrier, Norman G. 1979. 'The Formulation and Enactment of the Punjab Land Alienation of Land Bill', *The Punjab: Past and Present*, XIII-I (25), April, pp. 193-215.

— 2004. 'Authority, Politics, and Contemporary Sikhism: The Akal Takhat, the SGPC, *Rahit Maryada*, and the Law', in Pashaura Singh and N.G. Barrier (eds.), *Sikhism and History*. New Delhi: Oxford University Press, pp. 194-229.

Basran, Gurcharan S. and Bolaria, B. Singh. 2003. *The Sikhs in Canada: Migration, Race, Class and Gender*. New Delhi: Oxford University Press.

Bhatti, H. S. 2000. *Folk Religion: Change and Continuity*. Jaipur: Rawat.

Bingley, A. H. 1985. *The Sikhs*. Delhi: National Book Shop.

Blumer, Herbert. 1957. 'Collective Behavior', in J. B. Gittler (ed.), *Review of Sociology: Analysis of a Decade*. New York: John Wiley & Sons.

Bourdieu, Pierre. 1979. *Algeria 1960*. Cambridge: Cambridge University Press.

Brar, K. S. Lt. Gen. 1993. *Operation Blue Star: The True Story*. New Delhi: UBS Publishers.

Cameron, Wm. Bruce. 1967. *Modern Social Movements: A Sociological Outline*. New York: Random House.

Cervantes, Miguel De. 1981 *Don Quixote*. Edited by Joseph R. Jones and Kenneth Douglas. New York: W.W. Norton & Company.

Chadda, Maya. 1997. *Ethnicity, Security and Separatism in India*. Delhi: Oxford University Press.

Chatterjee, Partha. 1993. *The Nation and its Fragments: Colonial and Postcolonial Histories*. New Delhi: Oxford University Press.

Chohan, Sandeep and Ron A. Geaves. 2001. 'The Religious Dimension in the Struggle for Khalistan and its Roots in Sikh History', *International Journal of Punjab Studies*, 8 (1), pp. 79-96.

Cohn, Bernard S. 1987. *An Anthropologist among Historians and Other Essays*. New Delhi: Oxford University Press.

Das, Veena.1995. *Critical Events: An Anthropological Perspective on Contemporary India*. New Delhi: Oxford University Press.

— and Bajwa, R. S. 1993. 'Community and Violence in Contemporary Punjab, in D. Vidal, G. Tarabout and E. Mayer (eds.), *Violences and Non-Violences in India. Purusartha* 16. pp. 245-259.

Dhami, M. S. 1977. 'Political Parties and State Autonomy Issue: A Case Study of Akali Party' in K.R. Bombwall (ed.), *National Power and State Autonomy*. Meerut: Meenakshi Prakashan, pp. 144-161.

— 1981. 'Caste, Class and Politics in the Rural Punjab: A Study of two Villages in Sangrur District', in Paul Wallace and Surendra Chopra (eds.), *Political Dynamics of Punjab*. Amritsar: Guru Nanak Dev University, pp. 292-317.

— 1989. 'Religio-Political Mobilisation and Shifts in the Party Support Base in 1985 Assembly Elections', in Moin Shakir (ed.), *Religion, State and Politics in India.* New Delhi: Ajanta Publications. pp. 351-372.

Domin, Dolores. 1974. 'Some Aspects of British Land Policy in Punjab after its Annexation in 1849', *The Punjab: Past and Present*, Vol. VIII-I (15), pp. 12-31.

Dumont, Louis. 2002. 'The 'Village Community' from Munro to Maine', in Vandana Madan (ed.), *The Village in India.* New Delhi: Oxford University Press, pp. 31-50.

Durant, Will and Ariel Durant. 1961. *The Story of Civilization. Part VII: The Age of Reason Begins.* New York: Simon & Schuster.

Durkheim, Emile. 1976. *The Elementary Forms of the Religious Life.* London: George Allen & Unwin Ltd. (First Edition 1915).

El-Dareer, A. 1982. Women, *Why Do You Weep? Circumcision and its Consequences.* London: Zed Books.

Fenech, Louis E. 2000. *Martyrdom in the Sikh Tradition: Playing the 'Game of Love'.* New Delhi: Oxford University Press.

Flyvbjerg, Bent. 2001. *Making Social Science Matter: Why Social Inquiry Fails and How it can Succeed Again.* Cambridge: Cambridge University Press.

Fox, Richard G. 1987. *Lions of the Punjab: Culture in the Making.* New Delhi: Archives Publishers.

Geertz, Clifford. 1971. 'The Integrative Revolution: Primordial Sentiments and Civil Politics in the New States' in Clifford Geertz (ed.), *Old Societies and New States: The Quest For Modernity in Asia and Africa.* New Delhi: Amerind, pp. 105-153.

— 1973. *The Interpretation of Cultures.* New York: Basic Books.

Gellner, Ernest. 1983. *Nations and Nationalism.* Oxford: Blackwell.

Ghurye, G.S. 1969. *Caste and Race in India.* Bombay: Popular Prakashan.

Gill, K.P.S. 1997. *Punjab: The Knights of Falsehood.* New Delhi: Har-Anand.

Gill, Sucha Singh.1994. 'Socio-economic Contradictions Underlying Punjab Crisis', in Gopal Singh (ed.), *Punjab: Past, Present and Future.* New Delhi: Ajanta Publications, pp. 289-302.

— and Singhal, K.C. 1985. 'Genesis of Punjab Problem', in Samiuddin, Abida (ed.), *The Punjab Crisis: Challenge and Response.* Delhi: Mittal Publications, pp. 37-51.

Grewal, Jagtar. 1996. 'Punjabi Identity: A Historical Perspective', in Pritam Singh and Shinder Thandi (eds.), *Globalisation and the Region: Explorations in Punjabi Identity*. Coventry: Association for Punjab Studies, pp. 41-54.

Guha, Ranjit. 1983. 'The Prose of Counter-Insurgency', in Ranjit Guha (ed.), *Subaltern Studies II: Writings on South Asian History*. Delhi: Oxford University Press, pp. 1-42.

Gupta, Dipankar. 1997. *The Context of Ethnicity*. New Delhi: Oxford University Press.

Gurr, Ted R. 1970. *Why Men Rebel*. Princeton: Princeton University Press.

Habib, Irfan. 1976. 'Jats of Punjab and Sind' in Harbans Singh and N.G. Barrier (eds.) *Punjab: Past and Present: Essays in Honour of Dr. Ganda Singh*. Patiala: Punjabi University, pp. 92-103.

Hans, Raj Kumar. 2002. "Gurdwaras as a Cultural Site of Punjabi Community in British Columbia, 1905-1970". Paper presented at International Workshop on the *Indian Diaspora in Canada*, Department of Sociology, University of Pune, Pune, 23-23 February.

Heberle, Rudolf. 1968. 'Social Movements: I-Types and Functions of Social Movements', in David L. Shills (ed.), *International Encyclopaedia of Social Sciences,* Vol. XIV. New York: Macmillan, pp. 438-444.

Helweg, Arthur W. 1986. 'The Indian Diaspora: Influence on International Politics', in Gabriel Sheffer (ed.), *Modern Diasporas in International Politics*. London: Croom Helm, pp. 103-129.

— 1990. 'The Gurdwara and the Sikh Diaspora', *The Sikh Courier*, 30 (70), pp. 44-52.

Hirschman, Charles. 1986. 'The making of Race in Colonial Malaya: Political Economy and Racial Ideology', *Sociological Forum*, 1 (2), Spring, pp. 330-361.

Hundal, Manjit. 2003. "Terrorism and Women", in Paramjit S. Judge, S. L. Sharma, S.K. Sharma and Gurpreet Bal (eds.), *Development, Gender, and Diaspora: Context of Globalisation*. Jaipur: Rawat, pp. 187-206.

Huntington, P. Samuel. 1968. *Political Order in Changing Societies*. New York: Feffer and Simons, Inc.

Hutchinson, John and Anthony D. Smith. 1994. 'Introduction', in Johan Hutchinson and Antony D. Smith (eds.), *Nationalism*. Oxford: Oxford University Press.

Ignatieff, Michael. 1994. *Blood and Belonging: Journeys into the New Nationalisms*. Penguin Books.

Jafar, Ghani. 1988. *The Sikh Volcano*. New Delhi: Atlantic Publishers.

Jain, Sharda. 1995. *Politics of Terrorism: The Case of Punjab*. New Delhi: Deep & Deep Publication.

Jakobsh, Doris R. 2003. *Relocating Gender in Sikh History: Transformation, Meaning and Identity*. New Delhi: Oxford University Press.

Jeffrey, Robin. 1986. *What's Happening to India? Punjab, Ethnic Conflict, Mrs. Gandhi's Death and the Test for Federalism*. New Delhi: Macmillan.

Judge, Paramjit S. 1992. *Insurrection to Agitation: The Naxalite Movement in Punjab*. Bombay: Popular Prakashan.

— 2002. 'Religion, Caste and Communalism in Punjab', *Sociological Bulletin*, 51 (2), pp. 175-194.

— 2002a. 'Globalisation and Punjabi Society' in Parkash Singh Jammu (ed.), *Globalisation and Punjab: Impact on Economy, Polity and Culture*. Jalandhar: Punjab Academy of Social Sciences, Literature and Culture & Punjabi Bhasha Akademi.

— and Gurpreet Bal. 1996. *Strategies of Social Change in India*. New Delhi: MD Publications.

Juergensmeyer, Mark. 1988. 'The Logic of Religious Violence: The Case of Punjab'. *Contributions to Indian Sociology*, 22(1), pp. 65-68.

— 2001. *Terror in the Mind of God: The Global Rise of Religious Violence*. New Delhi: Oxford University Press.

Jyoti, Surinder K. 1983. *Marriage Practices of the Sikhs*. New Delhi: Deep & Deep Publications.

Kakar, Sudhir. 1996. *The Colours of Violence*. New Delhi: Penguin Books India.

Kaur, Amarjit et.al. 1984. *The Punjab Story*, New Delhi: Roli Books International.

Kaur, Harminder. 1990. *Blue Star over Amritsar*. New Delhi: Ajanta.

Kaur, Madanjit. 1995. 'Dhir Mall', in Harbans Singh (ed.), op. cit. Vol. I, pp. 559-580.

Kaur, Ravinder. 1986. 'Jat Sikhs: A Question of Identity', *Contributions to Indian Sociology*, 20 (2), pp.221-240.

Kaur Singh, Nikky-Gurinder. 2004. 'Mythic Inheritance and the Historic Drink of the Khalsa, in Pashaura Singh and N. Gerald

Barrier (eds.), *Sikhism and History*. New Delhi: Oxford University Press, pp. 51-76.

Kaviraj, Sudipta. 1992. 'The Imaginary Institution of India' in Parytha Chatterjee and Gyanendra Pandey (eds.), *Subaltren Studies VII*. New Delhi: Oxford University Press, pp. 1-39.

Klausner, Samuel Z. 1987. 'Martyrdom', in Mircea Elaide (editor-in-chief) *The Encyclopaedia of Religion*, Vol. 9. New York: Macmillan, pp. 230-238.

— 1987. 'Violence', in Mircea Elaide (editor-in-chief), *The Encyclopaedia of Religion*, Vol. 15. New York: Macmillan. pp. 268-272.

Koehn, Sharon D. 1991. 'Ethnic Emergence and Modernization: The Sikh Case', *Canadian Ethnic Studies*, XXXIII (2), pp. 95-116.

Korpal, Harkanwal. 2001. *Genesis of Damdami Taksal*. Amritsar: Bhai Gurdas Foundation.

Kundera, Milan. 1983. *The Joke*. Harmondsworth: Penguin Books.

Lyotard, Jean-Francois. 1986. *The Postmodern Condition: A Report on Knowledge*. Mancheser: Manchester University Press.

Lukacs, Georg. 1971. *History and Class Consciousness*. Cambridge: The MIT Press.

Marenco, Ethene K.1976. *The Transformation of Sikh Society*. New Delhi: Heritage Publishers.

Magee, Bryan. 1973. *Popper*. Glasgow: Fontana/Collins.

Mahmood, Cynthia Keppley. 1996. *Fighting for Faith and Nation: Dialogues with Sikh Militants*. Philadelphia: University of Pennsylvania Press.

Marx, Karl. 1973. *Surveys from Exile*. Harmondsworth: Penguin.

Marx, Karl and Frederick Engels. 1975. *Collected Works*, Vol. 3. Moscow: Progress Publishers.

McLeod, W.H. 1975. *The Evolution of the Sikh Community: Five Essays*. Delhi: Oxford University Press.

— 1989. *Who is a Sikh? The Problem of Sikh Identity*. Oxford: Clarendon Press.

— 1989a. 'The First Forty Years of Sikh Migration: Problems and Some Possible Solutions', in N. Gerald Barrier and Verne A. Dusenberry (eds.), *The Sikh Diaspora: Migration and the Experience Beyond Punjab*. New Delhi: Chanakya Publications, pp. 29-48.

— 1995. *Historical Dictionary of Sikhism*. New Delhi: Oxford University Press.

Melucci, Alberto. 1985. 'The Symbolic Challenge of Contemporary Movements', *Social Research*, 52 (4), pp. 789-816.

Monroe, Kristen. 2003. 'How Identity and Perspective Constrain Moral Choice', *International Political Science Review*, 24 (4), pp. 405-425.

Nadel, S.F. 1957. *The Theory of Social Structure*. London: Cohen & West Ltd.

Narang, A.S. 2000. 'The Punjabi Suba Movement', Harish K. Puri and Paramjit S. Judge (eds.), *Social and Political Movements*. Jaipur: Rawat.

Nayar, Baldev Raj. 1966. *Minority Politics in the Punjab*. New Jersey: Princeton University Press.

Narayanan, V.N. 1996. *Tryst with Terror: Punjab's Turbulent Decade*. New Delhi: Ajanta.

Oberoi, Harjot. 1994. *The Construction of Religious Boundaries: Identity and Diversity in the Sikh Tradition*. New Delhi: Oxford University Press.

Pandey, Gyanendra. 2002. *Remembering Partition: Violence, Nationalism and History in India*. New Delhi: Cambridge University Press (Foundation Books), First South Asian Edition.

Pettigrew, Joyce.1978. *Robber Noblemen: A Study of Political System of the Sikh Jats*. New Delhi: Ambika Publications.

— 1995. *The Sikhs of the Punjab: Unheard Voices of State and Guerrilla Violence*. London: Zed Books Ltd.

Puniyani, Ram. 2003. *Communal Politics: Facts Versus Myths*. New Delhi: Sage.

Purewal, Shinder. 2000. *Sikh Ethnonationalism and the Political Economy of Punjab*. New Delhi: Oxford University Press.

Puri, Harish K. 2003. 'Scheduled Castes in the Sikh Community: A Historical Perspective', *Economic and Political Weekly*, 38 (36), pp. 2693-2701.

— Paramjit S. Judge and Jagrup S. Sekhon. 1999. *Terrorism in Punjab: Understanding Grassroots' Reality*. New Delhi: Har-Anand.

— 1989. 'Religion and Politics in Punjab', in Shakir, Moin, op. cit. pp. 307-350.

— 1983. 'The Akali Agitation: An Analysis of Socio-Economic Bases of Protest', *Economic and Political Weekly*, XVIII (4), January 22, pp. 113-118.

Rao, M.S.A. 1978. 'Conceptual Problems in the Study of Social Movements', in M.S.A. Rao (ed.) *Social Movements in India*, Vol. 1. New Delhi: Manohar, pp. 1-15.

Riar, Sukhmani. 1996. 'Khalistan: The Origin of the Demand and its Pursuit Prior to Independence' in Pritam Singh and Shinder S. Thandi (eds.), *Globalisation and the Region: Explorations in Punjabi Identity*. Coventry: Association For Punjab Studies (UK), pp. 233-244.

Saberwal, Satish. 1990. *Mobile Men: Limits to Social Change in Urban Punjab* (Revised Edition). Shimla: Indian Institute of Advanced Study in association with Manohar, New Delhi.

Sekhon, Jagrup S. 2002. 'Portrait of a Kidnapped Person During Terrorism in Punjab', *Punjab Journal of Politics*, XXVI (1), pp. 93-105.

Shah, Waris. n. d. *Heer*. Amritsar: Bhai Chattar Singh Jiwan Singh.

Sheffer, Gabriel. 1986. 'A New Field of Study: Modern Diasporas in International Politics', in Gabriel Sheffer (ed.), *Modern Diasporas in International Politics*. London: Croom Helm, pp. 1-15.

Shergill, H.S. and Gurmail Singh. 1995. 'Poverty in Rural Punjab: Trends over Green Revolution Decades', *Economic and Political Weekly*, 30 (25), June 24, pp. A80-A83.

Shiva, Vandana. 1989. *The Violence of Green Revolution: Ecological Degradation and Political Conflict*. Penang: Third World Network.

Siegel, Paul N. 1986. *The Meek and the Militant: Religion and Power Across the World.* Delhi: Oxford University Press.

Sims, H. 1988. *Political Regimes, Public Policy and Economic Development: Agricultural Performance and Rural Change in two Punjabs.* New Delhi: Sage.

Singh, Birinder Pal. 2002. *Violence as Political Discourse: Sikh Militancy Confronts the Indian State.* Shimla: Indian Institute of Advanced Study.

Singh, Fauja. 1996. 'Guru Hargobind' in Harbans Singh (ed.), *The Encyclopaedia of Sikhism,* Volume II. Patiala: Punjabi University. pp. 232-235.

Singh, Ganda. 1996. 'Khalsa', in Harbans Singh (ed.) *The Encyclopaedia of Sikhism,* Volume II. Patiala: Punjabi University. pp. 473-474.

— 1996. 'Hukamnama', ibid., pp. 289-291.

Singh, Gopal. 1985. 'Socio-Economic Bases of the Punjab Crisis', in Abida Samiuddin (ed.) *The Punjab Crisis: Challenge and Response.* Delhi: Mittal Publications, pp. 75-89.

Singh, Gurharpal. 2000. *Ethnic Conflict in India: A Case-Study of Punjab.* Houndsmills: Macmillan Press.

Singh, Jagjit. 1985. *Perspectives on Sikh Studies*. New Delhi: Guru Nanak Foundation.

Singh, Joginder. 1997. *Sikh Resurgence*. New Delhi: National Book Organisation.

Singh, Khushwant. 2002. *Truth, Love and Little Malice: An Autobiography*. New Delhi: Ravi Dayal and Viking.

Singh, Parkash. 1997. 'Nishan Sahib' in Harbans Singh (ed.), *The Encyclopaedia of Sikhism,* Vol. III. Patiala: Punjabi University, pp. 239-240.

Singh, Pashaura. 2004. 'Sikh Identity in the Light of History: A Dynamic Perspective, in Pashaura Singh and N. Gerald Barrier (eds.), *Sikhism and History*. New Delhi: Oxford University Press.

Singh, Sarab Jit. 2002. *Operation Black Thunder: An Eyewitness Account of Terrorism in Punjab*. New Delhi: Sage.

Smelser, Neil J. 1962. *Theory of Collective Behavior*. London: Routledge & Kegan Paul.

Smith, Anthony D. 1976. 'Introduction: The Formation of Nationalist Movements', in Anthony D., Smith (ed.), *Nationalist Movements*. London: Macmillan Press, pp. 1-30.

Smith, Mark J. 2002. *Culture: Reinventing the Social Sciences*. New Delhi: Viva Books.

Srinivas, M.N. 1966. *Social Change in Modern India*. Bombay: Allied Publishers.

— 1987. *The Dominant Caste and Other Essays*. New Delhi: Oxford University Press.

Talib, G.S. 1997. 'Martyrdom' in Harbans Singh (ed.), *The Encyclopaedia of Sikhism* Volume III. Patiala: Punjabi University, pp. 55-61.

Tandon, Parkash. 1963. *Punjabi Century 1857-1947*. London: Chatto & Windus.

Thapar, K.S. 1996. 'Gurmata', in Harbans Singh (ed.), *The Encyclopaedia of Sikhism* Vol. II. Patiala: Punjabi University, pp. 152-155.

Thapar, Romilla. 2000. 'Will a Millennium be Coming Our Way?' in Romilla Thapar (ed.), *India: Another Millennium?* New Delhi: Viking, pp. ix-xxxi.

Touraine, Alan. 1985. 'An Introduction to the Study of Social Movements', *Social Research*, 52 (4), Winter, pp. 749-788.

— 1988. *Return of the Actor*. Minneapolis: University of Minnesota Press.

Tully, Mark and Satish Jacob. 1985. *Amritsar: Mrs. Gandhi's Last Battle*. New Delhi: Rupa & Co.

Uberoi, J.P.S. 1996. *Religion, Civil Society and the State: A Study of Sikhism*. Delhi: Oxford University Press.

— 1999. 'Martyrdom', *Seminar*, 476, April, pp. 50-58.

van der Veer, Peter. 1998. *Religious Nationalism: Hindus and Muslims in India*. New Delhi: Oxford University Press.

Walia, Varinder. 2003. 'Kala Afghana Excommunicated', *The Tribune*, July 11, Friday.

Weber, Max. 1948. *From Max Weber: Essays in Sociology*, (Tr. and ed. by H.H. Gerth and C. Wright Mills). London: Routledge and Kegan Paul.

— 1976. *The Protestant Ethic and the Spirit of Capitalism*. London: George Allen & Unwin Ltd. (first published in 1930).

Wittgenstein, Ludwig. 1961. *Tractatus Logico-Philosophicus*. London: Routledge and Kegan Paul.

Index